Woman between Two Worlds

Judith Olmstead

Woman between Two Worlds
~

Portrait of an Ethiopian Rural Leader

University of Illinois Press
Urbana and Chicago

Library of Congress Cataloging-in-Publication Data
Olmstead, Judith V.
    Woman between two worlds : portrait of an Ethiopian rural leader /
Judith Olmstead.
        p.   cm.
    Includes bibliographical references (p.   ) and index.
    ISBN 0-252-02283-1 (cloth : acid-free paper). —
ISBN 0-252-06587-5 (pbk. : acid-free paper)
    1. Women, Gamo—Biography. 2. Gamo (African people)—Politics and
government. I. Title.
DT380.4.G19055   1997
963'.06'092—dc20
    [B]   96-10068
                                                            CIP

To my mother
Ruth Yates Olmstead
1914–90

Contents

Acknowledgments

Chimate Chumbalo, the subject of this book, fed, housed, protected, and cast around me the glow of an extraordinary intelligence and vehemence for politics. She allowed our periods of conflict to mature rather than destroy our friendship. To her my deepest thanks and love.

Gida Gaiza, my assistant, gave fully of his time and attention, becoming a true partner in the work. He, too, has my special thanks, as do the many Gamo Highland people who welcomed me warmly into their homes, bore patiently with my mistakes, and enriched my life with their friendship. Ethiopians I encountered outside the Gamo Highland showed a lively interest in my work and went out of their way to help and befriend me. I hope that by adding another piece to the mosaic of Ethiopian history, I will begin to repay my debt to all these people.

During my graduate work at Columbia University, Alexander Alland Jr. provided me with the initial support so necessary to conceive and carry through a fieldwork project. Allan and Susan Hoben eased my introduction to Ethiopia. Dan Sperber was my intellectual companion and fellow field-worker. During subsequent years, his careful and critical reading of my work and above all his friendship as expressed in many ways have been invaluable to me. Work by Jacques Bureau on the division between the titles of king and balabat provided a theoretical nucleus for my discussion of the use of women as political intermediaries. During the writing of the first draft, Thomas Sykes offered not only moral support but help in typing and editing. Leila Charbonneau gave the second out of four drafts a thorough professional editing and took a personal interest in the project as well. Alexa Silver assisted me with the index. All these people have my warmest gratitude.

A long list of friends and colleagues read and commented upon drafts of the manuscript over the years. I particularly want to mention Donald Crummey, Donald Donham, Keith Eisner, Rosana Hart, Peta Henderson,

Dan Rubin, and Margaret Strobel. I thank all these people for their help and take full responsibility for the deficiencies that remain.

I am grateful for institutional support at various stages of work from Columbia University, the Institute of Ethiopian Studies in Addis Abeba, the University of Massachusetts at Boston, Boston University, and the Evergreen State College. Last but certainly not least I thank the National Institute for Mental Health for the initial fieldwork grant (MH-11576-01), the National Geographic Society for a month's return trip to Ethiopia in September 1971, the University of Massachusetts for a travel grant in summer 1973, and the National Endowment for the Humanities for a year's fellowship during which I wrote the initial draft of this book and made a brief return trip to Ethiopia.

During the arduous final stages of preparing the manuscript, my husband Rich Tyler shared his love and support. My thanks to him for his belief in me and the project.

Introduction

I have written this book to chronicle and to honor another woman's life. I will call her Chimate Chumbalo here—a woman I found alluring, dynamic, infuriating, formidable, but above all, deeply intelligent and creative. I was in my mid-twenties when I met Chimate Chumbalo, she in her early sixties. I was a young anthropologist, still in graduate school, she the leader of a rural community called Dita located in the Gamo Highland of southwestern Ethiopia.

At this distance of over twenty years I am tempted to romanticize Chimate. I find two photographs taken the day after I met her in January 1970. One picture shows the hem of Chimate's long dress, the iron tip of her walking staff, and a young woman kneeling, her white homespun garment wrapped around her, two gourds set on the ground beside her. She is kissing Chimate's shoes.

In the next photograph, the young woman stands, her chin cradled in Chimate's right hand, her head tilted back to one side. The young woman is bareheaded and radiantly beautiful, her softly rounded face glowing with her smile. Steadying herself on the walking staff, Chimate bends forward to kiss her on both cheeks. Chimate wears a homespun cotton cape over her dress and a black scarf wrapped around her head. Her profile shows a strong jaw and sharply pointed nose. Pursing her lips for the second kiss, her eyes almost closed, she is gently turning the young woman's face to reach her left cheek.

I cherished these two photographs of a traditional Ethiopian kiss of greeting in my first rush of attraction to Chimate. They were talismans of ease, justice, a possible haven by the side of a woman leader. I was a perpetual stranger and enigma in the eyes of the Gamo Highlanders. I behaved oddly for a young woman, traveling alone, unmarried, very far from my family and home. At times I felt very lonely among people who had few reference points to understand my life.

I identified with Chimate even as I also looked up to her. Chimate, too, was an anomaly, someone who did not easily fit Gamo Highland conceptions. She lived in an area where no woman could sit with the assembly of elders at the marketplace and was required to stand off to one side and shout when she addressed them. Yet Chimate, the widow of a local leader, had worked as the government-appointed *balabat* or leader of the Dita community for thirty years, serving as regent for the official holders of the balabat title, her son and then her grandson.

A third photograph taken a year later stops my romanticizing short. Again Chimate is in the marketplace. It is a cold day, and over her dress Chimate wears a long-sleeved sweater I knit for her and a light cape. Again in profile, she gestures vehemently with her right arm. She is arguing a point, her eyes fierce, brow creased. In the distance, seen over her left shoulder, sits the assembly of elders.

As I pause and gaze at this photograph, I shiver. I am not entirely comfortable with that much determination and personal power. I find myself remembering the conflicts that emerged between us. She saw in me a potential follower as well as companion; young though I was, I sometimes thought of her as a peer. For example, she expected me to give any gifts to her—even a tiny, empty cardboard box that had held batteries. She could use the box to reward the shepherd boy who worked for her. When I expected to give gifts as I pleased, to another child if I wished, I set myself up as a benefactor and rival. Expectations like these brought us into conflict, and it took time to reestablish our friendship.

I visited Ethiopia four times between 1969 and 1977, living both in the Gamo Highland and in the Ethiopian capitol, Addis Abeba, where men from the highland worked as weavers. From May 1969 to March 1971, I worked as a graduate student of anthropology gathering data for a doctoral dissertation. During these two years I lived primarily in a weaving community but also spent three months in Chimate's farming community. My dissertation, accepted by Columbia University in 1974, compared the weaving and farming communities, discussing the interrelationship of economic, social, and demographic factors as they affected female fertility in the Gamo Highland.

During the initial two years of fieldwork, I also collected a portion of Chimate Chumbalo's life history and got a sense of her day-to-day activities by living with her from January to March 1971. I returned to Ethiopia briefly during the fall of 1971, meeting with Chimate for a few days.

I made my work with Chimate the primary focus of my last two trips. I spent the summer of 1973 interviewing her. Her life in the highland was so busy that I persuaded her to travel north to Addis Abeba for the interviews. She consented to our writing a book about her life. My assistant Gida Gaiza helped me with the interviews, which were tape-recorded, and their transcription and translation. Finally, in the spring of 1977 I stayed for ten days in Ethiopia, seeing how the revolution of 1974 had affected Chimate. That was the last time I saw her; she died eight or nine years later. It is a commentary on my Ethiopian correspondents' lack of information about Dita that I cannot be sure of the date of her death.

The questions that came to mind when I first encountered Chimate have guided the writing of this book. I was astonished and pleased to meet a woman political leader. None of my experiences as an anthropologist doing fieldwork in Ethiopia had led me to expect this. It was men I had seen holding office in the central, provincial, and local levels of government.

Within Dita, Chimate was an important leader in her own right—an experienced mediator of conflicts and an eloquent guardian of local oral history. She also worked as the balabat, the intermediary between her people and the Ethiopian Empire. She supervised the yearly tax collection, conferred with other government officials, mediated cases sent to her by the government, referred difficult disputes to the courts, and organized the corvée (unpaid labor) demanded for tasks like repairing the police station in a nearby village.

Yet Chimate was illiterate and did not speak the national language, Amharic. I was curious to know how and why Chimate had become Dita's balabat. I wondered what her daily life was like and what ways being a woman helped or hindered her in her work. These questions underlie the main text of this book. Chapter 1 introduces Chimate by letting her share one of her favorite stories. Chapters 2–7 present Chimate and her life story up to 1970, when I first met her. These chapters show how a Gamo Highland woman came into a position of political prominence. Chapters 8–22 describe Chimate in action during my visits in 1971, 1973, and 1977, both before and after the 1974 Ethiopian revolution.

Throughout the book, I use pseudonymns for individuals in order to protect their identities.* Appendix 1 gives a short pronunciation guide to Gamo

---

*Many of the people mentioned in this book are still alive. Without their express permission, I do not feel free to use their names.

Highland words, lists and describes the main characters and communities mentioned in the book, and provides a note on military titles. A glossary of Gamo and Amharic words used in the text follows the appendixes.

Over the years I began to wonder if we could use Chimate's life as an example of other women's lives—other leaders like her, hidden from written history. Although surprised by my intial encounter with Chimate, I later discovered that two other women also worked as balabats of their communities in the Gamo Highland.* My hypothesis is that Chimate's case exemplifies processes of local factional politics through which women may acquire power as local-level administrators in an empire. I discuss this hypothesis in detail in Appendix 2. Appendix 3 provides suggestions for further reading on topics related to this book. These topics include Ethiopian history, Gamo Highland ethnography, life histories of African women, spirit possession, and politics.

In the years following my interviews with Chimate, I first taught anthropology at the University of Massachusetts at Boston and then spent many years as an applied anthropologist working in Washington State. In 1990 I became involved in alternative dispute resolution, first as a founding trustee of the Thurston County Dispute Resolution Center in my community, then as a mediator for the center, and finally as a mediator in private practice. My strong attraction to mediation came in part from my years in the Gamo Highland and the inspiration I drew from Chimate. In the highland, even small children learned the role of *chima* or mediator. Everyone, children and adults alike, sometimes took the role of chima—a Gamo word whose primary meaning is "old," thus implying "elder"—to help their peers settle conflicts.

In translating Gamo Highland social roles into English, I have chosen to use the word "mediator" for the role of chima. Although a chima, even a young child, might be more directive in telling disputants what to do than I would be as a mediator in my community, the face-to-face negotiations and the underlying goal of restoring social harmony are the same. I continue to use "mediator" to refer to the more judge-like role that Chimate was asked to take when cases were sent to her by the Ethiopian government's local officials because Chimate followed local practices: she relied prima-

---

*The French anthropologist Jacques Bureau discusses this in detail in "Étude Diachronique de Deux Titres Gamo."

rily on the skills and cultural ideals any chima would use, she could not force anyone to come to agreement, and she expected people who could not reach agreement to take their dispute to the local assembly of elders rather than to the district court.

As I got to know Chimate, I came to understand how difficult her position of intermediary could be. Unlike a modern nation-state, the Ethiopian Empire had not established routine surveillance of its citizens' daily lives. In peripheral areas like the Gamo Highland, local ethnic groups spoke their own languages, managed most of their own affairs, and often saw the empire as an unwelcome intruder. Neither the local people nor the local government officials fully trusted the local person who bridged the gap between them. The Gamo Highland's kings were the people initially appointed as balabats. Over time, Gamo Highland communities worked to dilute the power of the balabat position, giving the title of king to someone who was not the balabat and using regents like Chimate to do the work of the titled balabat.

Despite the difficulties of her role, Chimate was glad for the opportunity to serve as Dita's balabat. She told me emphatically, "Most women like to sit in their husband's homes. But I won't marry again. I'll do my work, I'll work on behalf of my children. Why should I lie down and do nothing? If I married, someone else would do my balabat work. I would be gone.

"I like this kind of work. Even when my husband was alive, I would go out and supervise the men tilling the fields or planting ensete. I never did sit at home like most women. Oh, when night came, I would spin cotton.

"If I were married now, I couldn't keep my own house any longer. Married, staying in my husband's house, I'd lose my own house and my own work. Why just sit around?"

Part One

The Woman and the Title

1   Sola's Story

*His blood was spurting to the roof in a line as straight
as water poured from a teapot.*

∼

I visited Chimate Chumbalo for the second time in June 1970. We sat together one night in the chilly bamboo house, warming ourselves by a small
fire of bamboo splints. A woman in her sixties with graying hair, Chimate
hugged her heavy cotton cape around her and complained of the cold, of
sinus headaches, of how her joints hurt.

"I'll knit you a sweater and send it to you," I said.

"And I'll build you a house here," she replied.

That was how we decided to live together. Six months later, I moved to
Dita. What might I contribute to the community, I wondered. Chimate suggested I buy something for the Ethiopian Orthodox Christian Church they
were building of eucalyptus poles plastered with mud and straw mortar. We
went together to look at it. One man, with a stark and sunken face, seemed
especially involved in the work.

"Judy wants to help us build our church," Chimate told him. "What
would be useful?"

"Can she buy wood for the doors?" the man asked.

I agreed to buy the wood. The man, pleased, confided, "I work on this
church as often as I can. When I was in jail I vowed to the Angel Gabriel
that if he set me free, I would make a church for him."

The man's name, Chimate told me as we walked back to her compound,
was Sola Kata. "Why was he in jail?" I asked.

"I'll tell you later," she said. Reminded of her promise that evening, she
called to the servant woman, who brought her a small basket. Chimate lifted
out a spindle and attached a tuft of cotton to its tip. She shook her right
hand, wrist relaxed, and the spindle began to whirl between her fingers. Over

the buzzing sound of the spindle she began to speak, her left hand and arm rising smoothly upward like a bird rising in flight as she drew the cotton into a fine white thread.

∾

Sola Kata, two of his brothers, and one of his sons have all killed other men. It is Sola's story that I often tell people. He had a violent nature, as is shown by the way he treated his first wife. She quarreled with him and went to her father's house.

At that time, although she was about to have a baby, she went with me and my son, Amano, to a funeral in Dokama. Sola also went. While she was kneeling to mourn, Sola took his big knife and cut her upper arm to the bone. He meant to cut it off. After he made the first cut, Amano caught him and had him imprisoned. Sola's wife was very sick, but two weeks later she gave birth to a son. While she was resting, Sola heard of the birth and wanted to go and bless her, but they refused to let him go.

"If you forbid me, I won't go," he said. But later he escaped over the prison fence; it was easy because at that time they tied a person up with his own clothing.

"I'll feed her," he said, and lived with his wife and baby. But the baby died when it was a month old, and he divorced his first wife.

In the past, it was common in this area for a man to take a knife and cut his wife if she insulted or refused him. The man might cut off her nose or cut the tendons behind her knees so that she could not walk. He would not be punished for his action. It was his right as a husband. During the Italian occupation of Ethiopia, one woman left her husband after bearing him a daughter, saying, "I don't like you and I don't want to live with you anymore."

One day when the husband was walking in the middle of the forest, he met her coming from a different direction.

"Aha! My wife who hates me, where are you coming from?" he asked.

She turned and took another path.

"I won't let you pass," he said, and caught her.

He cut her nose, trying to cut all of it off. But it was summer, and the roads were covered with dust. She took some dust from the road in her hand and threw it into his eyes. She escaped, although her nose was almost cut off. She ran away while he was cleaning the dust from his eyes.

Her sister ran to meet her and untied her sash, using it to tie the nose to her face. Then the woman told her sister to shout for help and for people to witness what had happened. The sister went to a lookout point and shouted. Soon the people came and took the woman to the Italian hospital. There she was treated.

The man was taken to prison. In court they asked him at his trial, "What did you do?"

"I tried to cut off my wife's nose. She insulted me by leaving me and trying to marry another man."

"Bono, bono," said the Italian judge, and set the man free. They sing a song about this:

> Bombe Bilboi cut the nose
> Elcho Balota called the witnesses
> Major Patria sewed the nose back on
> Elcho Elezei fed her while she was in the hospital.

So you see that Sola was following local custom when he cut his wife. After divorcing her, Sola married another woman, named Boye. This woman, like him, was divorced. For her first husband she had borne two daughters and two sons, but she disliked him and left him. Her husband wept when she left.

"My wife, my first wife, has refused to live with me. She will bear another man's children," he said as he cried.

Boye bore Sola two sons. While he was living with her, Sola quarreled with Goncho Gogula, the balabat of a neighboring community called Dokama, one market day. They were drinking in someone's house. Goncho, frightened by Sola's behavior, got up and left. Sola went to a distant community to sell a horse, but Goncho went to the town of Gulta, where the district capital was in those days.

Goncho said to the police, "Sola will kill me. I want to press charges against Sola for threatening me. Please give me some policemen to bring him here."

The chief of police gave him men. At night Goncho headed for Sola's house. For a while he was lost, but he finally found the house. He knocked on the door and a woman's voice answered.

"Who is it?"

"It's Goncho Gogula. I have business with Sola."

"Sola has gone to Bonke to sell a horse."

"Then I'll take you with me. Get up from your bed."

"Why should I get up when my husband isn't here?"

"Get up! We have come to take you."

"If you have a quarrel with my husband, take him. Why take me?"

"Get up!" he said, and the police ordered her to do so.

She cried out, "Don't take me along with you naked!" for she was wearing only a rag underneath, wrapped below her breasts and hanging to her knees. "Don't strip me! Why do you strip me? Neither my husband nor my father has ever pulled the clothes off my body!" she kept crying, and begged the policeman, "Don't let him take my clothes off!"

But Goncho left her with only the rag tied around her body and sent her fine *buluko* cloth to his own home. She walked along in front of the men until they reached Gulta, where they allowed her to sit down beneath the flag in front of the courthouse.

～

While Sola was returning from selling a horse that morning, someone stopped him on the road and said, "The police took your wife to Gulta." He prodded his horse into a gallop. This horse was named Shashonto and was so famous for its strength that Sola was known as the "Master of Shashonto." By noon Sola had reached Gulta.

We were there, three Dita officials and I, sitting in front of the treasury when he arrived, galloping. He saw his wife, naked to the waist, sitting under the flag. "Boye!" he called.

"Yes!"

"Who took off your clothes?"

"Goncho. Goncho stripped me."

"Goncho took off my wife's clothes?" he said, taking off the *natsala* cloth wrapped around his shoulders and giving it to her to wear. He sat down by the fence, sighing with fatigue. While we watched him, a voice summoned him from the courthouse, "Sola! Sola! Sola!"

For a long time he didn't answer; he sat and said nothing. Finally he replied, "Yes, sir," and went into the courthouse.

"Sign!" said the clerk.

"Why should I sign?"

"Sign!"

"Why?"

"Why have you quarreled with Goncho Gogula? Come and sign a statement that you won't touch him."

"Do I sign with one finger or with ten?"

"One is sufficient."

"Okay, show me," he said. The clerk inked Sola's thumb, and pressed it to the paper. Then Sola left and sat down with us. Goncho, wanting to be even safer from Sola, had gotten an order from the courthouse judge to have Sola imprisoned. He was carrying it to the police, peeping at it and trying to read it because he had had a little schooling. As Goncho walked haltingly by, Sola suddenly stood up and pulled out the pistol he always carried with him. He stepped up very quickly behind Goncho, who didn't see him because he was busy reading the paper. He caught up with Goncho as he was entering the police station. A policeman was sitting on the table and the chief of police was writing. Goncho was respectfully bowing; the chief of police continued to write. As Goncho looked up, Sola entered.

"I've got you!" shouted Sola, and with his left hand he caught up Goncho's natsala cloth, twisted it around his neck, and held him firmly in place. The bullet cut the tongue from its base so cleanly that it flew out, falling to the floor. The bullet continued down through the neck to come out through Goncho's left ribs and strike the left wrist of the chief of police, lodging in his arm near the elbow.

"My God!" shouted the chief of police, catching up his pen and running from the police station. The policeman followed him, stopping in front of the courthouse to yell, "Guns! Guns! Guns!"

Sola just stood there while everyone milled around outside. He simply stood and looked at Goncho, who was breathing in harsh gasps. His blood was spurting to the roof in a line as straight as water poured from a teapot.

I came to the courthouse from behind while the police were walking up and down outside, clicking their guns, "Ka-ka-ka-ka-ka." I came with two men, and called, "Sola!"

"Yes!" he replied. He looked as if he were laughing.

"Let disease devour you! What are you waiting for?"

A policeman came and slapped my hand down. I felt afraid and moved back. Sola shouted to the crowd, "I am Kata's son, and I don't know how to run away. I will surrender and throw my pistol to the police."

He came out, and everyone ran away in different directions. Five Dita men, who didn't want to see Sola killed because he had surrendered, caught him after he threw away his pistol. Lifting him shoulder-high, they carried him into a fence-surrounded house and locked the door on him.

Many of Goncho Gogula's people gathered around the fence. The Dita men were afraid. "You want to kill us," they said, and stayed inside the fence. "Go and call the elders."

The police warned the men not to come out. "Dita men, stay inside the compound. A fight was begun, and if you come out you will be killed!" they called.

Goncho's men were gathering on the hill above the police station. Since they didn't know who I was, I ran from house to house, gathering weapons. I slipped them through the fence. To one of the Dita men I gave an axe, to another a big harvesting knife, "Use this to protect yourself."

Finally, Goncho was buried in the Gulta churchyard, and Sola was put in prison. For six years he awaited judgment in Chencha, the subprovincial capital, but still without a verdict he was sent to the provincial capital of Gidole. There he received a death sentence. He appealed it. The brother of Goncho decided to make sure that Sola was condemned. "I can't let this matter rest. He killed my brother," he said, and went to Addis Abeba. At the same time, a large number of armed policemen accompanied Sola to Addis.

The high court's verdict was also death. Sola made a final appeal to the Emperor Haile Selassie. He said, "I killed on account of my wife," and produced witnesses.

The emperor commuted the death sentence, saying, "He killed because of his wife. His blood boiled, and he killed. He shall not die."

The sentence was set for twenty years, to include the six years he spent in Chencha and the six he spent in Gidole.

As for Sola's wife, Boye, when he first killed Goncho, she ran and hid away. Then she came to Chencha and stayed near Sola during his six years there and also spent four years in Gidole, bringing him food in prison. But one day she was walking on the road and a policeman caught her and slept with her. When she knew she was pregnant, she ran away, fearing that Sola would kill her. She did not go to Dita. In the past, if a woman became pregnant by a man other than her husband, she wouldn't come home.

At the same time, Boye's eldest daughter, child of Boye's first marriage, became pregnant. She persuaded her mother to come and live with her in

Gulta, and there they both gave birth to sons. Soon Boye's daughter and the daughter's baby became ill and died.

Boye said, "Since my daughter died, I don't want to live." She took the sash from her waist and, lying down on her bed, strangled herself.

After she died, I was the first to reach her house. I had walked all night to Gulta to mourn with her over her daughter's death. I began to give cries of commiseration as I approached her house. But I heard no answering cries.

"Boye, Boye!" I called.

The house was silent. Only the birds sang with the dawn. I looked in the window and saw Boye lying in her bed.

"I'm not going in," I said to myself, and went to the police station. I told them, "A woman whom I came to visit didn't move or speak when I called her. I looked; she is lying dead. She strangled herself. Come, see for yourselves."

The police came, looked, blew their whistles to collect more policemen, and untied the sash from her throat. They took it to the police station and hung it up. "Just why did you come here?" they asked, interrogating me.

"Her daughter died, so I came to mourn," I answered. They thanked me for contacting them so promptly and let me go.

Sola was still in prison, so Boye's first husband came and buried her. I myself brought with me a new buluko cloth worth twenty-three Maria Theresa thalers which the Dita people contributed.* We buried her in Gulta, because a person who commits suicide is refused burial in our traditional burial grounds in Dita. Later the policeman came and took his illegitimate baby boy, but the baby soon died.

Four people died from one house. Four people—mother, daughter, and two baby boys. They all died because of *gome*, a taboo which fell on them because Boye's first husband cried when she left him. The eldest girl also left with her mother. They left, and many years later, the taboo caught up with them and sent them to a hole in the ground.

I have seen other people commit suicide as Boye did. Since my marriage when I first came to Dita, fifteen people have drowned in the Aba pond alone. If a man's brother dies, if his child dies, if he gets angry, if he fights

---

*These silver coins from Austria bore the image of the Empress Maria Theresa. They were a popular coinage throughout East Africa during the nineteenth century and were still used as a unit of account in reckoning money obligations in 1973 when I worked with Chimate on her life story.

with someone, he runs and jumps into the pond. In one minute he will sink. After he dies, though, the water returns him; he floats to the top. One Amhara died there, too; he came from Ele and died. Another man came from Anduro and died, and just this year a woman from Marzo jumped in. Just in the Aba, fifteen have died. The Amhara had lost his father's gun, and the father said, just like a local Gamo man, "Why don't you jump in the Aba?" The son jumped, and died. "My son! My son!" the man cried out, but there was no reply.

The Aba didn't kill one woman. The people quickly cut bamboo poles after the woman jumped in and got her out. "Don't go there any more," they said, and she agreed not to go. She lived alone, and one night she put grass on the floor of her house and smeared butter over the door. She put on her best dress and, setting fire to the house, she entered it and died. People came and kicked the door, but the strong flames drove them back. The woman died in the fire, and when the people dug her body out, it had shrunk to a very small size. They took the corpse and threw it away in the forest. They won't bury anyone who burns himself to death.

～

Sola finally was released from prison three years ago. While in prison he made a vow to the Angel Gabriel to build a church in Dita if he got out after twenty years. That's what he tells us; we have no way of knowing.

"If I make a church for Gabriel, I will be famous," he says. He wants to take all the credit for the church which we are now building, but the Dita people were thinking of building a church before he came. That's why it was so easy for him to organize the work. But I must admit that he has helped a lot. He built a wall of woven bamboo himself.

There is a lot of violence in his family. One of his brothers, Wata, heard another brother singing the song the people made up about Sola: "Isn't Kata's son Sola? / He killed a man right in front of the policemen!"

Wata became very angry at his brother for singing this and shouted, "Isn't it true that he killed the shepherd Goncho? Aren't you singing that he killed the slave Goncho? Am I not also Kata's child, Wata? I kill everywhere!"

So shouting, Wata picked up his iron-tipped walking stick and threw it at his brother. Only God kept the stick from killing the boy. Then Wata caught him by the neck and his brother fainted.

Later, Wata killed a tanner. Still another brother killed a man and was put in prison. And Sola's son hit a boy on the forehead with a stick and killed him. The father of the boy came and said to me, "A man hit my son and blood came out. Come and see, come be a witness!"

I went and looked; the son was bleeding from his forehead. After washing and cauterizing his wound, we laid him down. "Sola's son, Dafare, killed me," the boy said before he died. We wrote a paper and signed it and sent it to the police station. Although Dafare was imprisoned for two years, he was set free because of lack of evidence. Only one of that family is still in prison, although they killed four men.

~

Gida and I were still learning the Dita dialect and followed all the details of this story only after hearing it repeated several times. Chimate's Dita audience—a servant woman and one of Chimate's granddaughters—listened in silence, responding with all the unthought movements and quiet murmurs that knit storyteller and listeners into one unit. Let Chimate's audience of readers create a world they do not know, a world without books or radios or television sets or cinemas, and the impact of a spinner of words such as Chimate may be imagined.

Just who was this woman who was willing to smuggle weapons to the Dita men as they guarded Sola? She seems to have stepped forward without hesitation, seeing a task to be done and doing it. Her woman's clothing, full skirt and enveloping cape, gave her means to hide the weapons. Would the policemen have allowed a man to approach the fence so closely? By what combination of initiative and luck, exploitation of her female identity and suppression of it, had Chimate carved out a political role for herself?

2 First Encounter with Chimate

Let's not use that letter to the Dita balabat. Let's just tell her that we have a picture of her dead son in a book.

Her son? The balabat is a woman? Which picture?

Dita is found in a mountainous corner of Africa. Even the plains below, with their lions, crocodiles, and herds of humpbacked cattle, lie three thousand feet above sea level. The Gamo Highland stands from five to eight thousand feet higher. Altitude gives to the highland sunlight a distinctive quality. Like juice squeezed from a lemon, it is thin, pale, clear, and astringent. It falls upon a landscape dominated by just three colors. The browns are paths, roads, floors of living compounds, market areas, threshing grounds, and newly cultivated fields. Once a year the barley fields flare into a spectrum of yellows as the crops ripen. The rest is green—the green of potato fields and growing grain, of eucalyptus trees and bamboo groves, of thirty-foot-tall false banana plants, and of ancient trees hung with moss, guardians of the churches and sentinels above the graves of the dead.

I reached the Gamo Highland in May 1969, a graduate student of anthropology planning to do dissertation research among the Dorze weavers and traders. By the following year I was eager to visit other highland communities and to compare them with Dorze. As market days ended, I watched itinerant merchants leave on foot or on muleback for other markets in other communities. I looked at sketch maps of the highland and read the names of these communities—Doko, Zad'a, Shame, Ezo, Shara, Anduro, Zaba, Wobara, Zute, Dita, Bonke.

On January 7, 1970, I left Dorze on a walking tour of the Gamo Highland. Two young men, one my assistant and one a day laborer hired to carry our baggage, went with me. What surprises me today is my simple con-

fidence as I planned that journey and my lack of awareness of the antagonism people would feel for the police and for the government. I expected
to find lodging among strangers as I walked west across the highland. I
didn't doubt that someone would take us in, although rented rooms were
found only around the Dorze marketplace and in Chencha, the village administering the subprovince, located an hour's walk from Dorze.

I even had official letters written by hand in Chencha, stamped with the
lion of Ethiopia, and elaborately signed. These letters were addressed to the
few police stations in the highland and to the local balabats, who acted as
intermediaries between their communities and the government. I assumed
that I could arrive at a balabat's home, produce a letter, ask to spend the
night, and contribute to the household by buying a sheep for us all to eat.
In fact, during my six days' absence, nothing worked quite that way.

By eight A.M. the first day we had breakfasted on barley porridge and had
stepped across the doorsill of my house. We went west across the meadow,
walking on our own shadows, and soon reached one of the two major east-
west paths crossing the highland. It lay along the southern edge and over-
looked the recently built provincial capital, Arbaminch, with its commercial farms planted in cotton and maize. By noon we had followed the path
to the village of Gulta and its police station. From among the sheaf of letters I carried I found the one addressed to these policemen. They tried to
assign me an escort for the whole trip. I refused but foolishly asked, "How
do you get to Zute from here?"

"I'll show you the way," insisted a young policeman, and began to walk
with us.

On that day sunlight almost overflowed the landscape. The tall false
banana plants showed their translucent greens and barley fields glowed with
all the colors of ripening and ripeness—green, orange, gold, yellow, pale
yellow, white. By mid-afternoon we had reached the compound of the Zute
balabat. As the policeman left, we called past the closed door in the bamboo fence. We called again.

"Yay!" a woman's voice responded.

"We came to see the balabat. We have a letter for him."

"He's not home."

"Can we speak to you?"

The sliding panel in the fence moved sideways, and we entered the compound. The old woman regarded us sourly. We asked again after her son,

showing her the letter, which she could not read. We asked for a place to sleep overnight. No, without her son, she would not allow us to enter. We later learned that she sent him a message that evening, "A foreigner is here asking for you. Don't return home."

Wondering what to do, we walked along a path edged on both sides by short, loosely woven bamboo fences. A group of people stood in a field, pulling up barley by the roots and gathering it into sheaves. We called out a blessing on the harvest, "May you prosper!"

"May you prosper in turn! Where have you come from?" asked the oldest man, the barley he held in one hand dripping soil from it roots.

"From Dorze. I have a house there." The man invited us to visit his house, indicating a large compound to the left of the field. A bamboo fence circled ten houses of various sizes and shapes—houses bespeaking prosperity and fertility of people and flocks. Soon we were seated with him in the largest house, drinking thick, sour barley beer from gourds and talking.

A man entered, our host's eldest son. A weaver, he worked in Addis Abeba much of the time. He had seen my house in Dorze. On the hill overlooking the marketplace it stood alone, a huge bamboo basket built in traditional Dorze fashion, its new thatch a pale yellow against the green meadow. In the days to come, we found that others who had visited the Dorze marketplace were willing to accept me. Curiosity that I was, I had chosen to live like local people. It amused and embarrassed and pleased the highlanders. Had I built a "modern" wattle-and-daub square house with a tin roof, I would have been less peculiar and less endearing.

The family invited us to stay with them; the son's knowledge of me clinched the matter. We spent two nights in Zute, but in the absence of the balabat no one would answer the list of questions I had prepared. Walking back toward Dorze, I spent part of a day talking with people in another community who had heard of me and were willing to respond to my survey. In those communities bordering on the Dorze weaving community, it seemed, many of the men were weavers and were used to traveling north to Addis Abeba with its mixture of ethnic groups and nationalities. The farther the distance from Dorze, the fewer the weavers in proportion to farmers and the greater the suspicion of me and my work.

I next walked farther west of Zute to Wobara, where I wanted to prepare the balabat for my visit. He was not at home but people assured me that he would be there the next day. On the third day after a long wait, we saw the balabat. He discovered that we had letters to others but none addressed to him. "I can't let you stay here or answer your questions," he told us, "unless you bring me a letter."

I felt tired and discouraged. Both villages where I could get such a letter were a hard day's journey away. I asked my assistant, "What is the closest community for which we do have a letter?"

He found one for Dita, directly west of Wobara. My carrier picked up his pack, and we started out again. By this time the two young men had worked up a litany on the ignorance of the local people, contrasting them with their own people, the Dorze. "In Dorze, people aren't so cowed by a foreign face as to refuse help when we ask! Here people won't tell us how to get to the balabat's house!" one would complain.

"When you finally find someone willing to talk to you, someone else comes up and says, 'Don't tell them anything!'" responded the other.

"People here are rude and ignorant. Now back home in Dorze . . ." On and on they went.

The first half of our trip from Wobara to Dita was easy. We followed an Italian-made road, cut into the very margin of the highland. Below us to the left we could see Arbaminch, surrounded by squares of tractor-culti-vated fields and beyond the town two of the Rift Valley lakes. A barefoot man trotted toward us along the wide, stony ledge. A cotton cape that looped around his shoulders billowed down to his knees and swayed back and forth. He grinned as he passed us.

The air was cool. We walked in silence. No one was out farming, and no market day drew people along the road. A few children sent out to guard sheep clustered together on a ridge. Each wore a whole sheepskin as a cloak.

A man came up behind us, dressed in conventional Gamo Highland fash-ion except for the many silver rings on his fingers. When he turned right and took a path uphill to a large tin-roofed house, my assistant fell into step beside me, saying, "He's a famous curer, a tanner who can suck illness from people's bodies." He paused, then continued thoughtfully, "Let's not use that letter to the Dita balabat. Let's just tell her that we have a picture of her dead son in a book."

"*Her* son? The balabat is a woman? Which picture?" I blurted out, sur-prised.

"I haven't met her," he replied, "but her daughter is married to a Dorze man and lives near my parents. When that German man who came to Dorze went on to Dita, he stayed with her son and took his picture."

In my Dorze house I kept Helmut Straube's *Westkuschitische völker Süd-*

Äthiopiens, the only book that had been written about the highland. The author had visited Dita in the 1950s. Among the portraits at the end of the volume is one of a bearded man with a broad forehead and narrow jaw. He holds his eyes and eyebrows tightly contracted, his lips pulled slightly back. One is uncertain just what that sharply drawn curtain masks. Perhaps sadness, passion, the impulse to laugh, shyness. He stares firmly away to the right, avoiding the camera's gaze.

I met his mother in the late afternoon. Turning right into the Dita valley, we began a two-hour climb to her home. We waded a river that almost reached our knees. We followed narrow dirt paths worn into gullies and clambered from terrace to terrace at the edge of fields. Finally, the local man guiding us ran on ahead to warn Chimate's household and beckoned to us from the opening in a tall bamboo fence. Stepping over a spring oozing forth by the door, we entered a busy work space.

Two men were building a typical Dita house. They had finished the cylindrical bamboo wall and were making the roof. This was a flattened cone of bamboo splints that would later be thatched with straw.

We stood in a narrow corridor, a bamboo fence on either side, the red earth underfoot tamped down and swept clean. Making our way to the reception house was like finding a goal at the end of a labyrinth. We advanced down the corridor, passed a cluster of houses, turned left, and followed another corridor. A woman wearing a twist of copper on a red cord around her neck told us to enter the last house. "The balabat is visiting a sick neighbor. She'll return soon," the woman said. Leaving us, she went to the house next door, where we could hear her grinding grain.

My assistant and I sat down on rawhide chairs at the back of the room, facing the door, and our carrier lay down on a woven bamboo bench built into one-third of the wall. As we waited I looked around the single room. It was about twenty feet across. In addition to the bench, along the wall stood two wood and rawhide beds, a table, a locked wooden trunk, and a pile of cushions fashioned by binding straw into a doughnut shape and wrapping the straw with dried leaves of the false banana plant. In the center of the room was the fire pit, a cup dug into the earth. Bamboo poles embedded in the floor several feet from this cup formed a protective square; the floor outside the square was strewn with wiry grass.

An hour after our arrival, the two young men suddenly stood up. A woman was entering the room, bending to pass through the short door frame and gathering up her skirt. I jumped to my feet, calling, "*A'he*—welcome!" Several men were entering behind the woman, one carrying a plastic attaché case as a sign he was a scribe. A young man brought in two saddle pads, their red cloth and colored embroidery dusty, and laid them on a bed.

"*Al'ite*—prosper," the woman replied in a low and slightly husky voice that carried clearly. She was of normal height but seemed tall because of a certain alertness in her stance. She chose a cushion by the door where the light spread fan-wise into the room and sat down. Her slender neck, arms, and hands contrasted with a solid body. A long-sleeved gray dress reached her shoes, and around her shoulders she wore a white cotton cape with inch-wide colored borders at each end. Graying hair had come loose from the black scarf knotted up over her head, and it fringed her face.

Chimate's face impressed me not for its features—oval shape, firm jaw, narrow lips, long nose—but for the energy it possessed. Most people inhabit their faces intermittently. But she was entirely present, feeling something and expressing it. Just as a magnifying glass can catch and concentrate a beam of light, so did her face—particularly her eyes—catch and concentrate emotion. There was nothing spontaneous about this. It was a dramatic act that gave her a reservoir of privacy.

Now she looked at us with a slanting upward glance, head level and eyebrows raised. My assistant answered that implied question with a speech he had given before about me, my work learning the local language and traditions, and how my parents and relatives in America were concerned about me and hoped that people here would help me and make me at home. He told her about her son's picture in the book. Yes, she said, she remembered that a foreigner had lived with her son. She had never seen the man; she had been in the village of Gulta at the time.

Chimate turned from us and began to organize the household for a meal. The servant woman whom we had met earlier lit a fire and poured us glasses of barley beer from a small olive oil tin that she filled from a clay pot under the table. The beer was almost sweet, like a thick cream. The servant roasted chickpeas on a thin iron griddle. We heard a clicking sound as sheep came through a door in the fence at the end of the compound. Chimate watched them enter, frowned, and left the house, disappearing into the false banana grove beyond the fence. Soon I could see her climbing the hill. The twilight flattened her figure into a silhouette.

"Kafe! Where are my sheep?" Her shout reached us clearly.

"Gone, My Mother," answered a boy's voice.

"Let disease eat you! Three sheep are missing! Don't just stand there, go and find them!"

"Yes, My Mother," he said, speaking softly.

Chimate joined us again only long enough to eat the hot chickpeas and fresh barley—still in the milky stage and sweet when eaten raw—served to us. Then she and the scribe left, each to sleep in other parts of the compound. Three young men, the eldest of her grandsons, came into the house and looked us over as they ate. Soon Wombara, heir to the title of balabat, brought out a five-stringed lyre and began to strum dancing rhythms. The young men with me danced with the other grandsons, each choosing a bamboo splint from the stack used to feed the fire—pretending to have spears. Facing one another in pairs, they advanced and retreated in mock battle, vibrating the sticks in the air, drumming out rhythms with their feet, crossing paths and turning to face one another again, panting loudly and making little yelps in their excitement.

One grandson stayed the night with us in the reception house; we barred the door after the other two left. The next morning began with the making of coffee in the reception house. Chimate's twelve-year-old granddaughter Nigatu brought firewood and tinder into the room. As she lit a fire with a live coal brought from the cookhouse, a man with a baby in his arms entered. He held the baby as if it were a live coal, one he would prefer to drop. Come to petition Chimate, he chose a seat right by the door and sat staring at the ground outside.

Chimate entered with her scribe and several women. From another house came the sound of the grandsons joking together. Chimate sat on a cushion by the fire, opposite the man with the baby. One heavy-bodied woman seemed to want to hide in the shadows behind Chimate. Chin on her chest, she averted her face from our gaze.

Nigatu brought Chimate a white enamel dish with coffee beans in it. Chimate shook the dish from side to side, looking carefully at the beans and discarding a few. A desultory conversation began as people waited for their coffee.

Nigatu laid a thin iron plate on stones positioned around the fire. Bending back the tip of a bamboo splint, she held it ready as she poured the beans onto the plate. Immediately, she began to push and pull the beans across the hot surface. The muffled sound of wood on metal mingled with the scent of roasted coffee, a scent that grew stronger as Nigatu tipped the beans into a small wooden mortar and pounded them. Shaking the powdery coffee into her hand, she creased her palm and slowly poured the coffee down the neck of a round-bottomed clay pot. Closing the neck with a corncob fragment, she put the pot over the fire to boil.

Not until we had all drunk our fill of coffee did the man stand up to present his problem to Chimate. The baby began to cry. A woman reached out and took the baby, offering her dry breast. The baby quieted and began to suck as the man loosened the cotton cape around his shoulders. Taking the left end of his cape in his right hand and holding it in the air before his left shoulder, he bowed forward in Chimate's direction. Everyone grew silent as he made this claim for attention and mediation. Still slightly bent, he began to speak.

With my beginner's knowledge of the Dorze language I could follow only simple statements in the Dita dialect. Even my assistant had to strain to follow the ensuing conversation. I heard only the plea in the man's voice, the quiet probing of Chimate's questions, the stuttering comments of the big woman sitting behind Chimate.

My assistant explained to me later as we walked with Chimate to the marketplace, "The woman is pregnant by the man with the baby. She used to be his servant. She came to live with him when his wife quarreled with him and left the house. Several months later the wife returned home to give birth, and the servant went away. Yesterday the servant returned to the man's house. She said, 'I am pregnant and I want to deliver the baby in your house.' The man's wife was very angry. This morning she ran away and left the baby behind."

"What does Chimate advise?" I asked.

"She will invite the man's wife to a mediation. The servant woman will stay with Chimate until the matter is settled. The woman can help with the household work."

During the rest of our stay we saw the shy, silent woman aiding Chimate's servant. Months afterward I learned what had happened to her. The man's wife had returned to him. After persuasion the wife had permitted the servant woman to bear her child in the house and bury the placenta there in the child's father's house, according to custom, before returning to her own community with her baby.

With Chimate and her scribe we made an hour's slow diagonal descent along the valley wall to the market area. Clouds were drifting in and out of the valley; sunlight dappled through, warming us briefly. People kept stopping Chimate for advice. She told some of them to visit her at home and consulted quickly with others.

The market came into view. Around a clump of trees, perhaps five hundred people were gathered. Twice a week they came, their feet crushing a large saucer-shaped area of the surrounding meadow. Men and women spread their wares on the ground or tethered livestock at one end of the market. Traveling merchants displayed soap, safety pins, cheap manufactured clothing, salt, spices, and enamel dishes. A few men offered handwoven cloth. Farm women sat behind baskets or gourds filled with barley, piles of pulp from the false banana plant's stems and tubers, baskets of dried peas and beans, and gourds of beer. Under the trees, butter and *harake,* a colorless liquor distilled throughout Ethiopia, were being sold.

Chimate showed us where to cross the river on stepping stones. Turning right, she walked to a spot downstream at the edge of the crowd. There she stood until mid-afternoon, talking with the many people who approached her.

A young woman carrying two gourds filled with barley was the first to come up to Chimate. Putting down the gourds, with one swift movement she was on the ground kissing Chimate's feet. Chimate, steadying herself on her walking stick, bent and cupped her right hand under the young woman's chin to raise her. The young woman tilted her head back, eyes shining, mouth curved. Gently turning the young woman's face from side to side, Chimate kissed her on both cheeks. The young woman stepped back. Looking into one another's eyes, the two women smiled. Then the young woman scooped up the gourds, turned, and was gone.

A man took her place. As he bent to kiss Chimate's feet, Chimate said, "No, no!" and stopped him. She kissed his face, and the two had a brief conversation. Another man came up, rearranging his cape to hold it in the gesture of supplication I had seen that morning. Catching Chimate's attention, he bowed. "What is it?" she asked, and began to talk with him.

I watched in fascination, remembering what I had read about the etiquette of traditional Ethiopia, an etiquette now outmoded in the cities and in Dorze. People would rewrap their capes according to their respective social positions and what they wanted of one another. In greeting, it was common to kiss the feet of a social superior one had not seen for a time.

Observing Chimate, I could see all the nuances of the kiss of greeting. Some people aimed for her feet, others for her knees, others for her shoulders, her social equals for her cheeks. She allowed certain people to complete their movements and others she stopped. She even distinguished between those she allowed to kiss one foot and those she allowed to kiss both feet, according to her spontaneous reactions. As for the men and women who greeted her, some obviously expected to be stopped in their downward movement and they offered little resistance, while others could not be stopped by a stereotyped gesture but only by force.

Further downstream from Chimate a group of men sat on stones embedded in the earth. Their walking sticks, pushed upright into the ground, formed a spiky fence in front of them. These were the prominent elders who met every market day to mediate disputes. Chimate took me to them, and my assistant made his speech of introduction. The men eyed me with reserve, too proud to show surprise. Chimate spoke to several of them, urging them to come next morning and talk with me at her house.

In the evening, Chimate, my assistant, and I ate together. The servant brought out an enamel tray heaped with boiled potatoes and chunks of lamb. Smiling at me, Chimate picked through the meat, finding choice pieces and placing them before me. "Eat!" she commanded. Peeling potatoes, she offered them as well with the same energy and hospitality.

After the meal I got out my questionnaire, which I had been using off and on during the day. Chimate and her grandsons, who were now eating their meal, began to help me with my inventory of Dita culture and economy. Even after her hard day, Chimate showed an impressive mental tenacity and precision. I sat up straighter and breathed deeper; it was exhilarating to work with her. Not only did she answer questions thoughtfully and thoroughly, she extended them, pushed them to their limits, and tapped the knowledge of everyone in the room if necessary. It was this habit of mind that had generated her invitation to the elders earlier in the day. "They should come and talk with you," she had said. "They know things I don't."

The next morning, no one came to be interviewed, a clear indication that Chimate's influence was limited despite all the deferential behavior people directed toward her. Chimate went about her business, going out to visit people and supervising some of the household work, and I spent the day walking around Dita. As I reached the meadows cresting the mountain, I passed flocks of sheep being driven by little boys and girls. At the summit I saw for the first time the landscape to the northwest. I stared and stared at the dim silver gleam of distant rivers and the pale shapes of receding mountains. I knew that no outsider had fully explored that area and mapped the people living there.

I left the following morning. Back in Dorze, I decided to change my fieldwork plans. I would base my dissertation not just on Dorze economy and demography but on a comparison between Dorze, where farming was unimportant and income came from weaving and trading, and Dita, where farming dominated the economy.

In June I spent a week in Dita; Chimate had invited me to witness the initiation of a new king. The ceremony was modest. The young king was about my age, in his late twenties, and seemed to have very little influence. During one chilly evening I made my offer of a sweater to Chimate and she promised me a house. After I returned to Dorze, Chimate visited me there several times, once staying overnight. In January 1971, one year after I had met her, I moved to Dita and became part of Chimate's household.

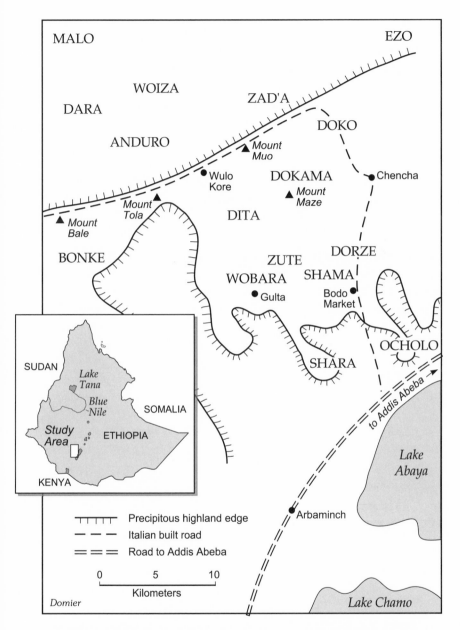

The Gamo Highlands and significant towns and communities. This simplified map indicates Arbaminch (the capital of Gamo Gofa Province), Chencha (the administrative center of the Gamo Highland), Gulta (an important village), and some of the Gamo communities, each a former kingdom.

A young woman kisses Chimate's feet and is kissed in return.

The central Dita valley, with houses mingling with farmland.

A Dita compound and surrounding farmland.

The author laughing with Dita friends. Photograph by James A. Sugar.

Chimate sits by her hillside household and looks out over the Dita valley.

Threshing grain and herding sheep.

3   Historical Background

It was only luck that a king's son saw me and married
me. Otherwise, my life would have been like that of
most women, carrying things on my back—water,
wood, children.

~

As a woman, Chimate operated in a political arena dominated by men. As a Dita citizen, she was part of a tiny kingdom conquered by the Ethiopian Empire during the late nineteenth century and seen by that empire as a source of labor and tribute. When history is written from the point of view of those most in control of political resources, Chimate and her community are seen as powerless, locked in static traditions, the passive pawns of forces beyond their control. Yet Chimate's life was full of action, opinions, and advocacy. She adapted as best she could to difficult circumstances, experimenting with different strategies. She worked hard to create the society she envisioned, lobbying Dita citizens and provincial administrators on such issues as extending landholding to women, regaining an important title for her branch of the family, and building an elementary school in Dita.

The choices Chimate made and the opinions she voiced cannot be understood without some understanding of Ethiopian history and society.* An early center of agriculture, animal husbandry, and empire building, Ethiopia includes great linguistic and cultural diversity. In the twentieth century, over a hundred different languages were being spoken in the country.

Geography provides a basic starting point for understanding the area. Ethiopia is crossed by a fault zone where the plates that form our continents

---

*In the text of this book, I will use "Ethiopia" to refer to the country I knew during the early 1970s. Since that time, a thirty-year war of secession has changed Ethiopia's boundaries: Eritrea seceded from Ethiopia in 1993. Eritrea lies to the northeast between Ethiopia and the Red Sea.

are slowly being pulled apart. As I stood on the eastern edge of the Gamo Highland I looked down into this Rift Valley and could imagine a time when the valley would become a sea and the highlands on the other side of the valley, a distant horizon.

The frequent volcanic activity associated with this movement of the earth's crust has created a jagged landscape that has eroded into flattened, table-like highlands through which major river systems have carved steep, narrow valleys. On a relief map of Africa, these central Ethiopian highlands stand out quite prominently, like a clenched fist on a table, separated from Sudan, Kenya, and Somalia by lowland areas. Ethiopia has been described as an easily defended fortress; indeed, Ethiopian independence from out-side colonization is unique in Africa. The country was occupied by a colo-nial foreign power—Italy—for less than a decade.

Travel in Ethiopia follows the high ground. The rivers are not naviga-ble, and they flood severely during the May to September rainy season. Highland areas could become islands unto themselves for part of the year. This fact has always affected political centralization—it has been much easier to create political units within a local physiographic area than across many other highland and lowland areas on the continent.

Yet another strong geographic influence is Ethiopia's location near the equator, which crosses Kenya to the south. At the same time of day, a low-land area can be hot and arid while the nearby mountaintop is cool and rainy. Throughout Ethiopia, highlands and lowlands are juxtaposed. Along the temperature and moisture gradient between high and low altitudes, different plants and animals are found. This has permitted a wide variety of local economic adaptations and has encouraged cultural diversity.

In general, people in the highland areas like Dita have relied more on agriculture, a higher population density, and greater political centralization. Lowland people have used various combinations of herding, agriculture, hunting, and gathering. Disease helped draw a boundary between highland and lowland areas, for malaria was found only in the lowland, an area high-landers often preferred to avoid. One of the sorrows of Chimate's life was losing a son to a disease he caught while supervising road construction in the lowland near Dita.

Connections across the different ecological zones were nevertheless quite strong. Throughout Ethiopian history, ecological diversity has encouraged trade and contact. A well-developed system of markets, with smaller ones feeding into regional centers, has been in existence for hundreds of years, in some places thousands of years. In the marketplace, people from a variety of local economies could meet and mingle. For example, a Dita woman with handspun cotton or barley to sell could easily range beyond the twice-weekly Dita market and attend any other market within a day's round-trip on foot. She would often choose a market in or near the lowland where she could buy honey or tobacco to trade for a profit back in Dita. Professional traders lived an itinerant life, each visiting a chosen circuit of markets. In this way items passed from hand to hand and market to market, sometimes over long distances.

Longer distance trade followed two corridors. One ran north and south, originating on the Red Sea and roughly following the Rift Valley. The second ran east and west, crossing the Horn of Africa on its way to the Indian Ocean. In times of active external trade, Ethiopian exports of incense, gold, and ivory reached as far as the Mediterranean and India, and slaves were sent to the Arab emirates.

Local political life and the political relationships among the Ethiopian people showed the same variability seen in other spheres. Before examining the political dimension, I want to reflect upon the underlying images we use to think about it. My discussion may seem esoteric, but I believe it can help us include, on that visceral level created by our imagery, the presence and contributions of groups of people like the Dita who are not politically dominant.

The earth's surface changes slowly, but the political ideas expressed by human groups upon this surface can change quite rapidly. A relatively new political idea is the concept of a nation-state with clear and arbitrary physical boundaries. We use maps to describe this political idea, with boundaries drawn boldly across what is actually contiguous soil and water. These boundaries represent social agreements among the nations involved, not physical facts.

Correlated with this arbitrary drawing of boundaries is a tendency to think of communities and cultures as pieces of a jigsaw puzzle, neatly intermeshed but distinct. A famous characterization of Ethiopia's great linguistic and cultural diversity refers to the country as a "museum of peoples"—an image that fixes these people into an undynamic, frozen time, an imaginary set of exhibits fixed in shape and extent.

I find it helpful to use a different image, an image that—like a map or jigsaw puzzle—is also made up of color and paper. Imagine a wet sheet of paper to which watercolors are applied. Each spot of color spreads and mixes with contiguous colors and the boundaries between colors may not be very clear or consistent along all the edges of a central color spot. Localized conditions on the page—a slight ripple, extra water, a raised section—will affect just how far a color spreads and how much it mingles.

In addition, each color has its own specific chemical properties, varying from batch to batch and manufacturer to manufacturer. Some colors tend to predominate over others. I have seen a particular yellow that, when added to a wet page, spreads like a shooting star.

It is this shifting dance of color that I use as a central image when thinking of the thousands of years people have lived upon that surface now called Ethiopia. The political ideas they have used during this time have ranged from egalitarian life in hunting and gathering bands to the inequality found in a stratified kingdom. People met, exchanged, and blended with one another in a variety of ways. The degree of political centralization found in any area was related in part to its participation in long-distance trade and its place along the two major trade routes for export to the Arab world, Asia, and the West.

The local variation in relationships among specific groups over many centuries would not only be tedious but impossible to describe. If we do not try to keep this variation in mind, however, it is all too easy to ignore local creativity in favor of the easy, overgeneralized summary. By following Chimate's story over less than a hundred years, it will be obvious just how many ways patterns can form and reform.

The watercolor imagery yields another useful analogy. With watercolor, colors can be laid over others. A thin wash of color can cover large areas, combining in unique ways with each color already in those areas. The variation may be large or small, but it is an intrinsic part of what has happened. Just so for tiny Dita, overlaid by and mingling with the Ethiopian Empire.

Three major colors have flooded across the Ethiopian landscape. The first has been a succession of multiethnic, Christian Abyssinian empires, originating at the northern end of the north-south trade route and gradually moving south. The first was the Axumite Empire, located on the Red Sea, which reached its height of power in the fourth to sixth centuries A.D. Axum controlled the Red Sea routes for exporting incense to destinations as far away as Rome and India.

Among the Abyssinian empires that followed Axum, the fourteenth- and fifteenth-century expansion is of particular interest: the medieval empire, under Amhara control, reached into the central, south central, and southwestern areas of what is now Ethiopia, including the Gamo Highland and Dita within its domain. Christianity spread south to some areas; during this time the Gamo Highland communities built, however temporarily, Christian churches. Amharic became the language of the political center and has remained so ever since. The ideas brought into the south—the mix of color laid on color—affected local people long after the Amhara empire had receded. In many communities political institutions took a different shape. Throughout the region, the elaborate New Year's celebration called Maskal dates from this time, taking many local forms.

The second flood of color dates back to the seventh century. The Islamic religion spread into the region; the decline of Axum was directly linked to Islamic control of Red Sea trading. Islamic states were created along the east-west trading route. At times, these states vied with the Christian empires for broad political control.

The third flood of color began at the southern end of the north-south corridor in the sixteenth century, when the Oromo people (also known as the Galla) expanded north. The Oromo were herdsmen and women with an efficiently organized expansionary military culture based on male age grades. By the 1560s, the Oromo had met and mingled with the Amhara people from the Abyssinian Empire in an area roughly at the center of Ethiopia, Shewa Province. These people eventually played an important role in creating the modern Ethiopian Empire.

Modern Ethiopia was created in the context of nineteenth-century Egyptian expansionism and European competition to establish spheres of influence and colonies in East Africa. The political and military leadership to fend off these challenges did not come from the most centralized areas, such as the coffee-exporting kingdom of Kefa. This leadership emerged in the north, where the Abyssinian Empire was in a phase of disarray and fierce internal competition. By mid-century a series of successful military leaders had emerged, each crowned emperor in turn: Tewodros, Yohannis, and Menelik. These three emperors ruled during the period 1855-1913. The newly revived Abyssinian Empire expanded its boundaries south and held off Egyptian and Italian attempts at conquest. The key victory that earned Ethiopia its unique independence from long-term colonization occurred at the

Battle of Adwa on March 1, 1896, when Menelik decisively defeated an Italian invasion.

The Abyssinian Empire proved, therefore, to be a phoenix for two thousand years, rising again and again from its periods of disorder. Certain features of organization made this society particularly resilient.* Built upon a military ethic with flexible, very open social classes, the empire held up to every man the possible prize of military victory, economic exploitation of subject people, and political superiority. Patron-client ties crystallized around an effective leader and dissolved as soon as that leader lost effectiveness, with followers sorting themselves out into new configurations around new aspiring leaders.

Over time, conquered people could assimilate to an Abyssinian identity, learn the Amharic language, add Christianity to their religious practices, acquire more control over their land, and adopt an ambilineal method of reckoning descent. With ambilineal descent, every person's relatives are counted back through all male and female ties. This prompts a great deal of ethnic assimilation. In patrilineal societies like Dita, where descent was reckoned only through men, a marriage by either a man or woman into another ethnic group could allow the descendants, if they counted their relatives through ambilineal ties and not patrilineal ones, to claim the most politically useful ancestors among thousands of candidates. The Abyssinian emperors, Haile Selassie included, gained their positions by force and legitimated them by genealogical winnowing.

The Abyssinian polity contained an inherent expansionary dynamic. Although nobles did not own the peasants' land, they were assigned peasant families as *gabbar* who owed labor and tribute to the nobles. The nobility was strongest in the core areas of the empire, benefiting fully from its extractive rights. This created an incentive for the emperor to expand his domain, creating new frontiers where he could exercise greater control and obtain higher levels of tribute. Over time, however, local people could become Abyssinians and thus unsuitable objects of extreme economic exploitation. After several generations, the nobles who had been assigned peasant families as gabbar would become more entrenched in this new frontier and less indebted to the emperor. This would transform a periphery into a core area and create a further incentive for imperial expansion.

*I rely heavily here on the excellent analysis by Donham, "Old Abyssinia and the New Ethiopian Empire."

At the start of the twentieth century, three methods were used to incorporate new subject populations. Local rulers in six previously independent kingdoms, all located in the most commercialized areas of the empire, were semi-independent and paid tribute directly to the emperor. Lowland peoples at the far margins of the empire were raided for cattle and taken as slaves. Most commonly, local people became the gabbar of the Abyssinian military leaders, soldiers, and settlers who lived among them.

Local people such as the Dita referred to their conquerors as the Amhara. The Amhara people have held a dominant role in the Abyssinian Empire since the thirteenth century, but the empire has always been multiethnic. As used in southern Ethiopia, Amhara generally refers, not to a specific ethnic group, but to all the people who have assimilated into this identity. During the time I lived in the Gamo Highland, the men and women there held a wide variety of opinions about those they called Amhara. Some hated or feared the Amhara, who had robbed them of political independence. These people adopted a stance of covert resistance that could flare into open opposition given the opportunity. Others, no matter what their feelings were about the past, wanted to be respected citizens of the Ethiopian Empire and sought assimilation. These were not fixed positions in any individual's lifetime; strategies could change.

At the time of conquest, Dita and the other Gamo Highland people were organized into small kingdoms and at the same time held passionately to their democratic assemblies of elders. Kingdoms traded among themselves, made treaties, and went to war when the treaties were violated. Highlanders ventured into the lowlands for occasional trade and warfare but returned quickly to their green fields and sacred groves. When the armies of Emperor Menelik II reached the Gamo Highland, the highlanders met guns with iron-tipped spears and hippopotamus-hide shields. They were defeated in a few days.

Within living memory the people of Dita have experienced five distinct forms of political organization. The period of local autonomy ended in 1897. Until 1935, they lived under the Ethiopian Empire as gabbar owing tribute and labor to the northern Ethiopian soldiers and settlers. Next, Ethiopia was a colony of Italy (1935-41), then returned to an indigenous monarchy supported by taxes and a bureaucracy (1941-74); after the revolution of 1974, it became a socialist state. When I lived in Dita in the early 1970s, many people chose to remember their independent past as a golden age.

Before the Amharas, the Dita men just sat around, polishing their spears and shields. We had many slaves and were successful in war. When we fought other countries, we took people as slaves if we won. The manure was thick on the ground and the land gave good crops. The slaves did all the work. We were so rich we ate butter every day.

Our Dita king was like God! If someone quarreled with him, when King Mijola looked at him, he would die. If he said, "Give birth," the woman gave birth. If he told a dumb person to speak, he spoke.

As intimated in the first quotation above, an important element of masculine identity in Dita was participation in warfare. Each man's goal was to kill an enemy in battle, take his penis as a trophy, and be honored by a series of special ceremonies including an elaborate funeral at death. This idealization of the successful warrior is found in many Ethiopian societies. At the time I knew them, the emphasis on warfare remained central for many Dita men. For some, it led to a willingness to join the armies of the state, while for others it was a motivating force for seeking local autonomy and reestablishing themselves as Dita warriors.

A song sung at the death of King Mijola, Chimate's father-in-law, captures the flavor of these cultural values:

> Leader Mijola Zante killed at Tsaithe Helo!
> Leader Mijola Zante killed at Zaise Busa!
> Leader Mijola Zante killed at Bonke Tola, Shagera's Bonke land!
> Mijola killed with a man named Gatara in Zaba!
> Leader Mijola is the one who killed in Doko Marzo!
> Leader Mijola Zante took a horse from Borodda and exchanged it for slaves!
> Leader Mijola Zante is the one who bought a horse named Wariyo with slaves!
> Leader Mijola Zante killed at Zaise Busa!
> He was brave as a vulture,
> As brave as a vulture,
> As brave as a vulture in battle!
> He killed with brave people!
> He killed an elephant in the lowlands!

He killed a leopard!
In Shelela Telo he killed gabbar!
He killed a leopard in Tsaithe Shelan!
He rode a horse Wariyo and he killed double!
Mijola Zante is the son of Orka from Goza!

As Chimate explained, "At a funeral, the people sing songs like this in turn. Half the group sings while the other half keeps quiet, then sings next. They sing back and forth. It is very nice when people sing like that."

Chimate might have been proud of King Mijola's exploits, but her own view of warfare was considerably more sardonic than that of many Dita men. Women could not become warriors, and that weakened their cultural and political importance. Female infanticide was practiced in the Gamo Highland until the second decade of the twentieth century, when people accepted the teachings of a prophet named Esa, who condemned it. As I observed it, Gamo Highland social organization was both hierarchical and egalitarian, simultaneously granting and tempering advantages. The local kings stood at the apex of a religious system that emphasized animal sacrifice. Only a king could sacrifice for the good of the whole kingdom. In the past, he had also taken the leadership role in battle. His very position as senior sacrificer, however, was expected to put him somewhat above the squabbles of internal politics.

The men and women of each neighborhood settled disputes through mediation whenever possible, each person being capable of taking the role of a third party facilitating agreements between disputants. Assemblies of male citizens met regularly within local districts and on a community-wide basis to adjudicate important disputes. Although a politically astute king, particularly one like the late nineteenth-century King Mijola who was successful in battle, could gain considerable influence, he had no separate power base such as a band of his own warriors. To call these ritual leaders "kings" is a convenience of translation; the phrase "senior sacrificer" would be more apt.

The relationship between men and women was unequal, with more resources in the hands of men, but again this inequality was tempered. Descent was reckoned in the male line, land was owned by men, and propitiatory sacrifices were performed by men. Men could take several wives, and in case of divorce the children stayed with their fathers. Women depended first upon their fathers, then their husbands, then their sons. Women had the option of dissolving their marriages and contracting second marriages at their own will. A single standard of sexual conduct, forbidding extramarital sex, applied to both men and women. Women had an important ritual role in their own patrilineages. They were called upon as witnesses and ritual experts at birth, marriage, and death. Women were active politically within their own neighborhoods. In mediating disputes they practiced the same techniques as the men did.

Within Dita there was nothing mysterious or remote about men's or women's lives that would increase a power difference between the sexes. The Gamo Highland was densely populated and people had constant contact with one another. Cultural mechanisms that could create areas of privacy and secrecy, such as underground kivas, the use of masked and costumed figures to represent authority, secret societies, or women's menstrual huts, were not utilized. On the contrary, high mutual visibility was promoted. Political assemblies, markets, funerals, and all important ceremonies took place out-of-doors; because of the hilly terrain, these events could be seen for miles. Men and women walked the hilltops to shout their grievances.

The religious system revolved around a set of taboos, with the most intimate aspects of one's personal life the subject of public confession and propitiation. Sheer physical survival into middle and old age was proof that men and women had acted, on balance, righteously. Otherwise, infractions of taboo would have sent them into an early grave. It was assumed that the actions of individuals could affect not only themselves and their relatives but could also bring prosperity or disaster upon the community. For example, sexual intercourse between a citizen and a member of a noncitizen craft group, such as a potter, might bring drought and famine.

The tenor of life in the Gamo Highland, therefore, was one of close monitoring of everyone's behavior and encouragement of high community morale. The nineteenth-century kingdoms had been small, ranging from five to perhaps sixty square miles. The warfare of which the men boasted was in fact quite unlike the extensive military campaigns of northern Ethiopia. War was carefully controlled and limited in scope. Confrontations took place at an agreed-upon site to which warriors came during the day, returning home at night. If neither side gained the upper hand, a peace treaty was sworn between the kingdoms. Should one kingdom gain the upper hand, its enemy became its vassal, owing either support in times of warfare or agricultural labor on the lands of the dominant kingdom. The proper way to refer to the vassal kingdoms was as the "children" or "wives" of the dominant kingdom. To refer to them as "slaves" was a bitter insult; in the twentieth century, this term was used as a deliberate form of provocation.

Contemporary Gamo Highland concern about who was or was not a slave in the past is ironic. The people of southern Ethiopia were incorporated into an empire that placed them at the bottom of a national system of social stratification. Extreme changes occurred in the scale of political life. The Ethiopian Empire occupies an area approximately four-fifths the size of the state of Alaska—or 11,400 times the size of Dita.

Though tiny, Dita had possessed the two hallmarks of an independent political entity. It had the right to wage war on its own behalf and the right to impose penalties for the most severe of crimes, such as murder. Both of these rights were taken over by the Ethiopian Empire in 1897. Decisions affecting Dita would henceforth be made hundreds of miles away in a language most Dita people would never speak by people whose behavior they could neither monitor nor influence.

The armies of Emperor Menelik were used to secure and govern the south. Garrison towns were established in the highlands, which were free of malaria. Consequently, the highland people had the most intensive contact with the new government. They became the gabbar of the soldiers and military commanders, owing them labor and tribute. Lowland people living close to the garrisons were expected to pay regular tribute, while those living farther away were periodically raided by the soldiers. Chimate told me,

> The Amharas from the North who settled in our area were given local families as gabbar. A low-ranking soldier would be given one family, a high-ranking administrator a hundred. Each family had to give four days of labor per week to the person it served. Every Sunday, people brought wood, water, and grass. A yearly tax was paid, in cash, and every month a thaler's worth of butter had to be given. For food, each family gave the Amhara barley, wheat, and chickpeas. If a family said, "We won't give," they were imprisoned. If there was not enough, a household member was taken as a slave.

Chimate's friend Halaka Halke had been a teenaged boy at the time of the conquest. He described the Dita reactions to defeat:

Before the Amharas arrived, a man named Bade Chulto said to us, "They come to conquer us. Pay them taxes and don't fight." But we said, "We don't want to pay." Taking our spears, knives, and shields, we went to fight. Many died in battle. After our defeat, when we returned to Dita we killed Bade. We tore out his heart and cut it into small pieces.

When the people realized just what sort of tax they were supposed to pay, they refused to give their hands and to pay the tax. They fought again, saying, "We aren't women even if we do tie our loincloths with a cloth belt as women do! We are not the wives of the Amharas, to serve them as they wish!" For a month they fought, and thirty or forty people died.

After this, for ten years we resisted. The people said, "Even if we do farm, the Amharas will take it all. They will kill us anyway, so we will have to kill them too, by not having food for them." The people ate tubers during this time. Many people left and went away. No one knows to this day what became of them. Although the people were very weak from the famine, the Amharas forced them to carry wood, and many people died in the road while carrying the wood. Finally we learned that there was no place to escape to. The people accepted the payments the Amharas demanded of them. For a short while we planted two crops a year to end the famine.

The kings of the Gamo Highland were quickly appointed balabats and held responsible for their people's compliance with the demands of the soldiers. Other local people were chosen as *chikashums* to help administer districts within each community. King Mijola was given fifty gabbar families from among his own people; each of the Dita chikashums received three gabbar families. The power of the local kings was increased by this change even as they were put into an ambiguous position, responsible for both protecting their own people and aiding in the extraction of food and services from these same people.

The members of the elite who had been adults in 1897 were much less accepting of Amhara rule than those who spent much of their adulthood under it. This was true of King Mijola as opposed to his son Masa and of Chimate's grandfather as opposed to her father. Chimate was born shortly after the period of passive resistance ended. Her approximate date of birth is 1910. During her childhood she lived in Tsela, a community five hours' distance from Dita on mule back. For her, the empire was a fact of life as she grew up and married. The following is Chimate's description of her childhood and marriage.

~

I am not from Dita, although I have spent most of my life here with my husband's people. The place where I was born is Tsela. My father's family is the family of elders for our kin group. My father's father before him, then my father, then my eldest half-brother were all *demutsa* priests who performed sacrifices for the good of our people. They were also known as rainmakers. In times of drought my father would slaughter a bull or a goat to bring rain; he did the same to cleanse the country in times of disease.

While I was a young child, my grandfather still lived. He didn't wear modern clothes; he was born before this area was made part of Ethiopia. He refused to wear Amhara clothing. He wore only a heavy cotton cape, or *buluko*, over a loincloth which he tied with a cloth belt. My father dressed differently. He wore pants and a light cotton cape, or *gabi*, with one colored border.

The two men didn't look alike either. My grandfather was short, dark-skinned, and had plenty of hair. My father was tall, light-skinned, and bald. They differed in their acceptance of our new rulers, the Amhara. My grandfather never left home to help the Amharas; my father was always among them. One of their settlements was near us, and my father knew them well. He acted as an intermediary between his people and the Amharas.

My father was one of five brothers. Living in one household under my grandfather were his children and his children's children. With young and old together, there were sixty-three people living in that household. Thirty of these had to wait to be given food by the others; they were small children who were never allowed to help themselves. They had to wait until others called them and filled their hands with food. Respectful children still do the same today.

We all worked hard. The women cut grass for fodder and chopped up the leaves of the false banana plant for fodder, too. We herded animals. We spun cotton. And in our house there were many slaves. Working with us around the compound were thirty households of slaves; their homes surrounded ours. We owned land in the lowland too, and there we had more slaves and many tenant farmers. My father was called the "king's son" because of his wealth. Except for salt, there was nothing which his fields did not give, lowland and highland together: peas, chickpeas, *teff*, sorghum, maize, wheat, barley, pepper, cotton, potatoes, sweet potatoes, yams, squash, false banana plants, shallots, tobacco, cabbage, garlic, flax—all were plant-ed. We paid a thousand dollars in tax. Every year, a thousand. Before the Italian occupation of Ethiopia, we paid by *wana* tax: ten wana. The slaves helped us pay. We traded some of our cotton in the Ezo market and in Chencha, using the money we got to help pay the taxes.

My grandfather and my father never went to war. Their position as priests forbade this. So when the Ethiopian armies conquered our people in 1897, my grandfather did not fight against them.

My mother died after I was born, and I never knew her. I was raised by my father's other wives. One of my elder sisters married a Dita man and then invited me to come and stay with her. I was ten years old. I attracted the attention of Masa, the son of the king of Dita, and when I was thirteen years old I married him.

My parents did not want me to marry Masa. When Masa's father sent an intermediary to them, they refused the proposal of marriage. "He has married many times," they told him. "We want our daughter to marry a man who has never married before."

Again and again the intermediary came to my parents. "The king's son wants to marry your daughter in order to have an heir," the intermediary said. "He has no sons." Begging and begging, at last he convinced my parents.

I rode a mule from my parent's home to my husband's home in Amhara fashion.* I entered a small house where I stayed hidden for many days. My husband's family gave a large feast for my husband's kinswomen, and in another house he feasted with his friends as well. After a few days, wom-en came and pierced my ears to show that I was a married woman.

Before me, Masa had had seven wives, but they bore him no sons who lived. I remained childless until I was eighteen years old; then I bore Amano, the son Masa wanted. I bore Masa seven children. Three boys and two girls lived to become adults. Today only one son survives, but both daughters are still alive.

It was only luck that a king's son saw me and married me. Otherwise,

---

*Riding "Amhara fashion" on a mule to her husband indicates partial assimilation to Amhara marriage customs. At marriage, a Gamo Highland girl would be kidnapped from the side of the road by her husband's friends and carried shoulder-high, struggling and screaming, to his house. A picture of such a kidnapping is included in my article on the Dorze people, "Ethiopia's Artful Weavers," 140.

my life would have been like that of most women, carrying things on my back—water, wood, children. I would have farmed the land along with my husband, milked the cow, swept out the compound, cleaned the animals' pens, and carried manure to the fields on my back.

Instead, other people worked for me, and I supervised them. I did some of the cooking myself, and of course I spun cotton into thread for buluko and gabi cloth. I asked my husband if I could go to the fields and supervise the men who cultivated the land for him. My husband was always going to the town to spend time with the government people there. He often went to the courthouse. "I can oversee the work of the fields," I said, "while you are away." He agreed, and I enjoyed that kind of work much more than working as most women do.

4   The Death of King Mijola

I am near death. Hear my will. I am near death.
Hear my will.

~

Chimate's account of King Mijola's death in the late 1920s would be recognized by her own people as a campaign speech, an active assertion within an ongoing political struggle. The struggle concerned matters essential to Chimate's position as Dita's balabat. Chimate's husband, Masa, was King Mijola's third son, yet two older sons were disinherited in order to make Masa king and balabat.

Why was this decision made? Was it the correct decision? The answers to these questions directly affected the degree of legitimacy Chimate could claim for herself, her sons, and her grandsons. King Mijola's deathbed will introduced an important element of controversy into Dita politics. It became possible for different Dita factions to back different candidates for leadership, all the while claiming the support of Dita values. Those who wanted the eldest son to be king and balabat could cite traditional rules of primogeniture. Those who favored Masa could cite the right of any father to disinherit sons as he chose. The mere acknowledgment that alternative candidates existed probably acted as a curb on the use of power by any of King Mijola's descendants. Chimate described the act of disinheritance.

~

While I was pregnant with my third son, Atumo, my husband's father, King Mijola, died. His grave is in the graveyard on the hill above my house. All the men of his clan are buried there.

Masa was Mijola's youngest son, but King Mijola made him his successor. King Mijola called people from this neighborhood and that one and that one, from this and that and that place he called the elders to witness. He called as witnesses men of his own age, his friends and peers.

"I am near death. Hear my will," he said. "I am near death. Hear my will. My eldest son, Tilinte, is now living with the Amharas. He married an Amhara woman, and he has had children with her. He doesn't respect our ways. Only the father may slaughter for his children, but when I slaughtered bulls, he slaughtered bulls.* When I killed sheep, he killed sheep. He didn't stay with our own roots, he married without my permission! Without any care for our seed, without growing from our roots, he married without my blessing and without a marriage feast. Let Tilinte not take the title! I have a piece of land behind my house, let him take that and nothing more.

"Akirso, my second son, is born of a woman who was bad to me. I married her, she gave birth, and I divorced her. I don't want Akirso to visit me on my deathbed. I don't want to see him. Akirso could be the leader but he took a wife without following our customs. He married a slave woman!† Let Akirso wander as a vagabond! I cursed him when he married, saying 'Let you be poor.' Again, 'Get out and don't return,' I said, cursing him.

"There were two [other] sons older than Masa who might have become king, but they have died. Masa is young but he has helped me. He has supervised my gabbar serfs, and he has never made trouble by bringing court cases against people. He has taken messages from me to the governor of this subdistrict. Neither Tilinte nor Akirso should wear my silver ring!"

The people asked, "What will happen to us when we say this to Tilinte? He likes taking cases to court. He will try to harm us. We would like to follow your will, but what shall we do?"

"Bring the governor to me. Bring him and a scribe."

The people spoke with the governor, who said, "Take my scribe, go, and write the will. Tilinte is a troublemaker. He not only takes your people to court, but Amharas as well. He sleeps with other men's wives when their husbands are away. *Hashu!* Prosper! Leader Mijola has made a good will."

The people brought the scribe to Mijola. The elders gathered around. "From today on, Tilinte has no right to my title," said Mijola, and signed with his fingerprint. The old men added their fingerprints. The scribe who had written down the will was given a sheep and went home.

---

*In the traditional religion of the Gamo Highland, a man cannot slaughter animals while his father is alive. Only the father can perform propitiatory sacrifices.

†The early twentieth-century prophet Esa tried to erase many of the social distinctions that governed traditional highland life, including the barrier between slaves and masters. Akirso seems to have been a sincere follower of Esa.

When Tilinte came to Dita, he said, "Since my father disinherited me, I won't live here." Akirso returned to Dita after his father's death. He left his wife and children, washed his body in the Aba pond, slaughtered a sheep, and wore the wet skin. When he saw the Dita people at the funeral, he said, "I wore a skin, I left my wife, I left my children, I washed my body in the Aba, and came to Dita. My father disinherited me. From where will I take land and live?"

Tilinte gave Akirso his own land, and Akirso lived there. Today the title of king is held by Akirso's son, but my husband's branch of the family has kept the title of balabat.

One section of Dita did not want Masa to take the title. There are four divisions of Dita. One section said, "Why did his father disinherit Tilinte? We will make him our leader." But the other three sections said, "We will make Masa our leader."

~

One element of interest in Chimate's account is King Mijola's decision to use the government to reinforce the disinheritance of Tilinte. The second noteworthy element is that King Mijola accuses his two oldest sons of having made improper marriages. By implication—Chimate is too subtle to state this outright—she, Chimate, daughter of a Gamo Highland rainmaker, is the right and proper woman to bear Dita's future kings. Masa's marriage to her shows that he accepts traditional Dita values. Tilinte is depicted as being too acculturated, too much on the side of the Amharas. For good measure, even the Amharas are said to be displeased with him. As for Akirso, he is a visionary who has overstepped local tradition and married a slave woman.

The dispute over the kingship was still alive at the time Chimate recounted her family history to me. It will appear again in this account. The kingship passed from Mijola to his son, Masa, but then was taken away from Masa's son Amano and given to another branch of the family, leaving Amano with the title of balabat.

The separation of the title of king from that of balabat occurred in many Gamo Highland communities. The highlanders did not appreciate having the senior sacrificers of their communities under the control of an external political administration. By separating the two titles, the balabat became a secular agent with considerable political power, the king a ritual leader.

Yet another step, making the acting balabat separate from the balabat who officially did the work, was taken in many communities.

In continuing to describe King Mijola's death, Chimate talked of the funeral ceremonies with zest and detachment. It was the timely death of a man who, as the Dita people say, had "eaten much."

Forty years later, I attended funerals for such old men and women and found a quality of celebration. People cried out sorrowfully, it was true, but there was an elasticity in the tread of the men marching round and round the public meadow, a spark in people's eyes as they sang the praise songs. I find no other word for this but pride—pride in the deceased, in themselves as actors in this lively spectacle, in the songs and movements with which they greeted death.

For Chimate, there was an additional source of pride, the special funeral rituals accorded to a king. Only a king is displayed publicly, sitting in a chair. Only a king is given such a lengthy funeral involving representatives from many Gamo Highland communities. The funerals of kings therefore legitimize and publicize their and their descendants' importance. Chimate's intense interest in the details of the ritual is revealed in her account of the events following King Mijola's death.

～

When King Mijola died, everyone mourned. His body was seated on a large chair, and a white scarf tied around his forehead. His male relatives tied white scarves around their foreheads and at the ceremonies wore ostrich feathers at the back of their heads.

People put butter in a lump on the hair of the dead man, tied a white scarf around his head, and seated him on a chair. As he sat there, people from all over the highland came and cried, cried, cried. They began mourning early in the day. At nightfall the relatives spent the night in King Mijola's house, mourning with people who had arrived from other communities. All the neighbors bought butter and milk and brought them to the dead man's relatives.

The next morning the king still sat on his chair. Everyone went to the funeral field and mourned. A coffin, a big coffin, was made. The carvers cried as they made it. They cried, they cried. They sang, "Wo-o-o ka'o, wo-o-o king, our king is gone, our king is gone." Singing that, they made the coffin. Mourning, mourning, mourning they made the coffin.

When the coffin was finished, quickly! it was brought. The neighbors dug the grave. Masa went and watched. He measured the grave by lying down in it to see if it was too short. It was well dug, and he said, "Good, good. This is suitable for my father."

The neighbors asked again, "Isn't it a good grave?"

"Yes, it is good."

King Mijola's wife took a *gozda* necklace and put it around the dead man's neck. Beforehand, one of the neighbor men had taken the silver ring of office from his finger. He concealed it. After hiding it, he kept quiet, quiet, quiet. "Our silver ring, where is it? The ring, where is it?" asked the sons.

No one will tell them where it is. If a man tells them, the people will kill him.* The man who took and hid the ring was rewarded. The people gave him a cow and a buluko blanket, too. He took a buluko and a cow. He got the ring while King Mijola was sick, slipping it from his finger when he didn't realize it. The king died, and everyone forgot who had the ring.

"Where is the ring? It's been lost," they said, and the man who had it kept silent. The neighbor man kept it hidden. Then, after the body had been taken, buried, and mourned a second time, the neighbors came in a group to the relatives. They stood in a line in front of the relatives and said, "Don't mourn. We have something to say to you."

The relatives stood up. "What do you have to tell us?" Getting up and standing there, they asked, "What does the country have to tell us? Our master has died. What do you want to say to us? What did he say in his will? Whom did he choose as king? Our water, our grass, what did he say about them? Our crops, our milk, what did he say about them?" So speaking, they questioned the neighbors and sat down again.

Next, the elders of the country asked the neighbors, who were still standing in front of the people, "What did the king will?"

They replied, repeating the dead king's words, "I took care of my own father when he became old. Now death is taking me away. If death is coming, listen to my words. Don't quarrel with those countries with which we have treaties. Don't break the Bonke treaty. Don't break the Zegets treaty. Don't break the treaty with Dorze, or with Zad'a, or with Doko. Don't harm any of the treaty countries. Don't touch them.

---

*This detail indicates the degree of control that the people expect to have over the succession to the kingship.

"If you are milking your cows, let them give a lot of milk. Cultivate the land with profit. Let the crops produce abundantly. Let the ensete plant grow well. Let starvation stay away from my country. Let everyone prosper.

"As for my children, the eldest I give this much land, the younger, this much; I have spoken. My brother, this much land, my married daughter, this much land! I have spoken. Let this servant work for my daughter. If my daughters visit their brothers, let them be treated well. Feed them; give them drink; don't take away the land I assigned to them. And let our country keep its treaties. Don't break them."

The relatives asked, "Is this what he said?"

"Yes," said the witnesses.

"Have all our customs been followed?" asked the old men.

"No," said the witnesses.

"Has the coffin been made well, and has he been properly buried?" asked the elders.

"Yes. We have buried him in the coffin we made."

"But have the customs been followed?" asked the elders.

"The sacrifice for the ghost has not been made. A feast for the neighbors who made the coffin has not been held. The cleansing of the house has not been done. We have only repeated what he said in his will," said the witnesses.

Then the elders ordered, "We will be sitting in the assembly by the marketplace and will hear when the house has been cleansed. Cleanse the house!"

After this, the neighbors who made the coffin and who cooked food for the relatives of the dead man were fed from King Mijola's house. A feast was made for these neighbors. An ox was killed for them to eat.

King Mijola was a great man. When he died, the people sang many praise songs at his funeral:

> To whom did you leave your big country?
> To whom did you leave your country?
> Mijola is a great king who governed wisely.
> He governed from the heart.

They sing this back and forth. After the funeral was over and the house had been cleansed, the neighbors said to Masa, "Call the women of your lineage quickly. Our leader was respected by all, but now he is dead. We will make a new king."

The neighbors called the clanswomen, "Come, bring necklaces to make the new leader."*

The clanswomen replied, "If you follow all our customs, we will do it." The senior woman had to be given a big buluko cape to wear above and a second one to wear below. Then she called all the other women. A special feast was made for them, and they arrived wearing new clothes. I was required to wear new clothes, as was King Mijola's widow. All the relatives were called, given a feast, and then there was a ceremony in the marketplace.

All the women relatives arrived wearing gozda necklaces around their necks, like new brides. They put these around my neck and the neck of Masa's mother. When we reached any water on the way to the marketplace, the kinswomen carried me and Masa's mother across on their backs. The necklaces were many and very heavy.

When we reached the marketplace, we moved through it, right through the people who were buying and selling things. Masa sat down and first drank our local beer from a calabash with his mother, lip to lip; then he drank with me. All the elders and the *halaka* leaders whose fathers were dead participated. The halaka leaders whose fathers were still alive stayed away. The halakas and the people sat and drank beer. The kinswomen borrowed more gozda necklaces from the people and put them on me and on Masa's mother. Everyone walked through the market together. After this was finished, Masa was called "*dana*" or "leader." I was called "*mishe*" by older people, and younger people called me by the respectful form, "*mishinto.*"

After the ceremony was finished, the elders instructed Masa about the treaties Dita had with other countries. To illustrate what is meant by such a treaty: Doko is a treaty country with Dita. If a Dita man takes five cents from a Doko man or does something bad, the Doko man comes and complains to the elders, saying, "There is a treaty between our countries." Quickly, the people tell the person at fault to return the stolen property. If someone steals and refuses to return what he steals, his relatives pay for it; and if the relatives refuse, the whole country pays for it.

When the old men who witnessed King Mijola's will were dying, they called the people. "Come to hear what our king said to me. I don't wish to die without saying it again to you." From among those who witnessed the

---

*This is a good example of the ritual importance of the women of a patrilineage. Without their expertise and participation, the installation of a new king could not take place.

king's deathbed will, when one falls ill, he calls the people of his neighbor-hood, who then call people from other neighborhoods. "In the past, our king said this, and this, and this to me. Don't disobey these words. Don't disobey these words. He said this to me, what I am telling you now. What he said to me, I am living long enough to tell you."

"Wo-o-o-i! The dying man spoke the words of our former king!" the people say. People who hear it tell the words to their neighbors who did not hear. When a middle-aged man later dies, he tells people what he heard from the old men, who heard it from the king.

King Mijola's eldest son did not become king. Masa became the king. Tilinte didn't mourn when his father died. He didn't come to mourn when Dita people died. He was angry with our people, thinking that they had told Mijola to disinherit him. He didn't attend the funerals of the men who had witnessed the will.

The kingship belongs in our branch of the family. If God so wills, the title will return to us one day.*

---

*Appendix 1 contains a genealogical chart of the various branches of King Mijola's patrilin-eage in which the two titles were held.

5   Warfare

I am a woman. Shall I prance around? Shall I boast?

~

Two of Chimate's frequently told stories describe times when her husband Masa traveled north to take part in warfare, first in 1930 when the northern governor, Ras Gugsa Wale, engaged in a power struggle with the man who became emperor later that year, Ras Tafari Makonnen, and then in 1935 when the Italians invaded Ethiopia. Both times the military personnel administering and guarding the south were sent north, leaving behind skeleton forces of older men in the garrison towns. In the Gamo Highland, many men of the local elite like Masa were required, not asked, to travel north.

Ostensibly, the Gamo Highlanders increased the number of soldiers available to fight on the side of the central imperial government. In fact, their removal from the highland also kept them from stepping forward into the power vacuum, reasserting local autonomy in the absence of the northern soldiers and administrators. The Gamo Highland leaders, instead, traveled across much of the empire. For months and sometimes years, they lived in the company of the men who governed them. The two groups fought side by side in battle. Highland men who distinguished themselves in battle were awarded the same military titles held by the northern Ethiopian administrators. All of these experiences encouraged the male elite of the Gamo Highland to identify with the empire and its rulers, helped them to understand and speak the national language of Amharic, and taught them Amhara customs and values.

While the military personnel and many Gamo Highland leaders were absent in the north, other individuals stepped forward. Masa's absences provided Chimate with opportunities, however unwelcome, to expand upon the leadership role she had begun to take within his household. Other persons who, like Chimate, later became acting balabats may also have begun to exercise leadership during these times.

Chimate had two favorite stories about this period. The first describes her husband's experience in war. In this account, Masa uses a medicinal herb called *kosso* before going into battle. Kosso is used against tapeworm and acts as a powerful laxative and purgative. Many Ethiopian cultures, including the Amhara and the Gamo, can be thought of as cultures that emphasize self-restraint. The use throughout Ethiopia of kosso as a purgative before battle is an organized way to let go, intended to cleanse and free a man for battle.

The successful warrior is thought of as being like a woman—one partially out of the control of culture, somewhat unruly, outside the domain of masculine self-control. The use of kosso makes a man temporarily more like a woman.

There is a subtle comedy and irony in Chimate's telling of this story, for it is a woman who speaks. Men in Gamo Highland culture claim superiority over women in part because they are the warriors. Yet, to be successful, they must make themselves like women for a time. In this story, Masa fails to become like Chimate, and he fails to kill an enemy in battle. In recounting Masa's anxious musings and his irritation at his failure, Chimate, without underlining the fact, is looking at masculine values with the skeptical eyes of a woman.

Fitawari Masa, my husband, got his title after going to war.* On his way home he met Dejazmach Gezaheng, who governed many of the highland communities near Dita. The dejazmach had also been to war and had returned without being defeated. He returned with his followers, unharmed. From our people, two men died in battle.

After returning home, Dejazmach Gezaheng invited everyone to a feast for the founding of the Gabriel church.† He bought special shirts for the people he planned to title fitawari. In the past, titled people wore special shirts. At the feast, Dejazmach Gezaheng put these shirts on the men whose conduct in battle pleased him. Thus, Fitawari Masa and two other men received their titles.

*The holders of military titles also had administrative responsibilities. See the note on military titles in Appendix 1.

†Churches of the Ethiopian Orthodox Christian faith were being built in the highland.

The first war they went to was the Gondar battle.* Masa was the king at that time. He was ordered to go north with his servants to fight the rebellious Ethiopians in the area of Gondar. Masa's older brother Tilinte went, too, and stayed away for five years fighting.

To go to war, Fitawari Masa took two mules to ride alternately. When one tired, he rode the other. He also took one mule to carry his tent, one mule to carry other things, and two pack horses. All in all, there were six, yes. Servants? Six men went too and carried three guns. No, there were more than six servants, but I can't remember them all.

Halaka Halke went with Masa and carried wheat flour in a sack to the Gondar war. On the way, he saw a water pipe and drank as much as he could from it and added water to the flour. By the time he reached the battlefield, almost a month later, the water and barley had brewed beer.

I sent with Halaka Halke kosso medicine for tapeworm which I had ground myself. I carefully ground it. "When you reach the battlefield, give this to my husband, give it in a glass to him," I said, and put it in a small cloth pouch.

Early in the morning of the battle my husband said, "Give me the kosso." It was early, when the birds were beginning to make sounds. He drank it and sat there. People at the time did not know how to make coffee, people didn't know how to roast the beans quickly. So Halaka Halke gave my husband beer. My husband said, "I don't want beer." The kosso didn't work as a purgative, it just sat there inside him.

Fitawari Demse Asefa was in those days our district governor. He died just this year in Addis Abeba. He marched with our men to the battle. He was very brave. In the battle he encouraged people, "Stand firm, stand firm."

Halaka Halke went to get water for our camp. "In the morning after getting water, I was returning and saw all the tents being taken down and everyone getting ready for battle," he later told me, "and Fitawari Demse was speaking to the men."

When Halaka Halke came to my husband's camp, Masa told him, "Let war kill you! This kosso isn't working, it hasn't purged me." He was very angry.

"Ay-y-y! I don't know the reason!" said Halaka Halke.

*The former husband of Empress Zawditu, Ras Gugsa Wale, governed in northern Ethiopia and through a series of local campaigns was becoming a rival of emperor-designate Ras Tafari (later Emperor Haile Selassie). Wale was defeated at the Battle of Anchem on March 31, 1930.

There was a horn, the old-time horn for war, blowing "Tih-tih-tih-tih-tih!" and warning people to gird themselves for battle. They came out, ready for battle, and went to the battlefield.

Who led the enemy? Ras Giorgis. Fighting, fighting, the kosso didn't take effect and sat in Fitawari Masa's stomach, fighting, fighting, until night fell and everyone went back to camp. They had fought hard with Ras Giorgis and finally pushed his troops back and were victorious, killing him. They came back singing "*Hailana, hailana!*"

"Come, eat," people told Fitawara Masa.

"No. What happened? The kosso has dried up in my stomach!" he said angrily. He feared that this was due to cowardice. "Give me more kosso."

This time the kosso purged him. The next morning he said to people, "Yesterday I drank kosso and nothing happened. Was that because I was frightened in the battlefield? Was it because I carried a gun in the battlefield?"

People said, "Don't talk about it; now you are purged. What would have happened if it had worked yesterday, and you had been seized by diarrhea in the middle of the battle? You would have run away!"

And Kenyazmach Eldo said, "Hashu, the kosso has cleansed you!"

Kenyazmach Eldo killed an enemy in the battle. He was honored in Chencha. People put butter on his head and called him "the Killer." Fitawari Masa was angry. "I didn't kill an enemy in battle. The kosso dried in my stomach, I wasn't purged, I didn't achieve anything."

But our neighbor Aga was a killer, he killed an enemy. He shared a tent with Fitawari Masa. "Are you leaving without having killed an enemy?" asked Aga.

"I haven't killed an enemy. I don't care, there's no reason why I should mind not having killed," Fitawari Masa replied, all the while feeling irritated and unhappy.

After a while, the food they had taken with them ran out. One of the Dita men was sent to me to tell me this. In seven months' time I collected from our gabbar money for food, twenty Maria Theresa thalers. I also sent them ground barley mixed with butter and a skin sack of barley flour on a pack-horse. When they finally returned, everything had been used, and only one of the three guns remained.

There wasn't a second battle. The men left and went south to Addis Abeba. They stayed there until they received the order, "Go home, go to your own community!"

"Okay," they said, and began to prepare. "Now we will go home, after we buy trunks for our things we will go." But the horses and mules were no longer with them. Some had strayed, some had died. Airplanes were a new thing and some animals were frightened by the sound "Wun! Wun!" the airplanes made. Even the mules that people had begged from their relatives' houses were dead.

"How are we to return?" they asked. My husband sent me a message, "I must buy a mule. Send me money for a mule." I sent him ninety Maria Theresa thalers.

By that time I had given birth to my daughter, Alimetu. My husband came back from the battle and a month later an invitation came to all the Gamo people. Balabats, chikashums, district governors, governors, all the important figures were called to the coronation of Haile Selassie.*

"We will make a new king!"

"Who will be the new king?"

"Haile Selassie!"

So after just a month's stay, Fitawari Masa went back to Addis Abeba. Ay-y-y-y! Just after he had returned, he was called back!

Fitawari Masa had no food for the journey. Nor did the other people. "Just what can we take with us to eat?" the people asked.

"Go to your houses and grind barley and take it with you! Go!"

He took a hundred dollars, just one month after his return, and went to Addis Abeba. They all arrived in Addis Abeba dressed in uniforms. Nine months after the birth of Alimetu, when she was beginning to walk, they returned home.

~

What Chimate does not explicitly state is that Fitawari Masa was using his twenty-year-old bride who failed to prepare good kosso medicine as a scapegoat for his own failure in battle. Masa could not become like Chimate, but it was all Chimate's fault. This fact gives the story an added comic twist as Chimate recites it.

Chimate's second story is also a gloss on male values and behavior but in a much different vein. In 1935, Masa was fighting the Italian invasion in the north. During his absence, a war began between Dita and an adjacent

---

*Empress Zawditu died in April 1930, and Ras Tafari was crowned Emperor Haile Selassie in November 1930.

community, Wobara. This reversion to local warfare was an assertion of political autonomy that could not be tolerated by the Ethiopian government.* Such challenges were common throughout southern Ethiopia in periods when most of the soldiers and military leaders had been transferred north.

The immediate cause of the war was a quarrel between two men, but the underlying cause was a long-standing rivalry between the two communities that had led to warfare in the past. The Wobara men were not successful in battle and acted quickly to obtain support. They went to the garrison town of Gulta, accusing the Dita of refusing to pay taxes. This was a spurious issue, since all Gamo Highland people were unhappy about the feudal obligations imposed upon them. By phrasing the conflict as if Dita, not Wobara, was acting against the Ethiopian government, the Wobara men were able to enlist on their side the Gulta soldiers and administrators. Later, the men of other highland communities joined in the war against Dita.

Chimate tried to bring the dispute to mediation before combat began. Twice she left Dita and crossed Wobara territory to reach the town of Gulta. The first time, the administrators there told her that the group of Dita elders she had brought was too small to make a settlement. The second time, the forty Dita men who had agreed to accompany her to Gulta deserted her.

There is no question of the great personal courage of this twenty-five-year-old woman, fresh from bearing a child, who tried to stop a war that brought much suffering on Dita. The Dita men accepted her leadership briefly, then preferred to enact their ancient code of male virtue, the warrior's code. They sought glory on the battlefield. Chimate could not control them, but her bitter speech that begins "I am a woman. Shall I prance around? Shall I boast?" shows that she thought them fools.

As in the kosso incident, there are several layers of meaning. Chimate is referring to the boasting songs and mock combat that take place at a warrior's funeral. It is a major infraction of taboo for a woman to sing these songs, even in jest. Some Gamo Highlanders believed that the Italian invasion of Ethiopia came about because women in Dorze broke this taboo. Chimate is commenting both on the foolishness of men and on the fact that the strictest rules of Gamo Highland culture forbid women to be equally foolish.

---

*This remark applies specifically to the highland communities that were the empire's major source of labor and tribute. Remote lowland tribes could engage in warfare with relative impunity.

~

Once I tried to end a war between Dita and a neighboring community, Wobara. At that time, the Italians were invading Ethiopia. My husband, Masa, and other local men had gone north to join other Ethiopians fighting the Italians. I was home alone when the war with Wobara began.

The Wobara went to the Amharas living in Gulta, which was then the district capital. Gulta lies at the edge of the highland. The Wobara people accused the Dita people of refusing to pay their taxes and enlisted the Amhara on their side. The Amhara called upon other highland communities to join them in punishing the Dita people, for only the older Amhara soldiers and administrators were in Gulta. The rest had journeyed north to fight the Italians.

"We don't care about those old men in Gulta. We aren't afraid of them, we'll fight them!" said the Dita men.

I had just borne a child ten days before, but I decided to act in my husband's absence. I took some of the Dita elders and went to Gulta. I called on one of the Amhara leaders, Fitawari Getachew Wombara. "Have you come with the elders to make a settlement?" he asked.

"Yes," I replied.

"If you want to make a settlement, you must bring forty men," he told me.

I agreed and returned to Dita. I gathered forty men and began the half-day's journey back to Gulta. While traveling we had to cross the marketplace of Wobara. There the men of Wobara were seated with the men of two other communities. They were all armed with spears, knives, and shields. As I came toward them with the forty men, they said, "Dita is coming to fight us! How can they be so foolhardy?" From among them, five Wobara men, catching up their spears and riding their horses, shields raised, came forth.

"Are you coming to me? Are you coming to fight with me?" I asked. "Will you fight with a woman? Will you fight against someone who came as a mediator?"

"We didn't come to fight you. Dita has many shields and spears, but the king's wife has come instead. Dita is truly great." And they climbed down from their horses, put their shields and spears on the ground, and were ready to accept mediation.

But the men with me said boastingly, "Mandose!" This is the name of one of Dita's great kings who conquered many Gamo Highland communities. The men said, "Mandose! Even if you put down your spears and shields and get down from your horses, we won't make a settlement!"

The Dita men with me caught up pistols and spears and stones, saying, "You're our former slaves." This was a terrible insult. "You're our former slaves. Slaves won't fight with us. Slaves don't fight their masters. We didn't come to sit around like all of you. We came to fight!"

I could do nothing. The men started to fight. I left the Dita men there, men who had promised to come for mediation. As I left, only four of the forty men came with me as I headed toward Gulta.

"I am woman," I said to the others. "Shall I prance around? Shall I boast? The Dita men came to make a settlement but left me at the battleplace and began to fight. My husband was not there. My children were not there. The men left me at the battleplace! Why? Yes, the Dita men began to boast and left me very quickly!"

"Now what will you do?" one man asked.

"I will go ahead to a place where there is the rule of law, to Gulta. I don't want to turn back to Dita!"

"You want to leave those men?"

"Yes! I won't go back!" I said, and went on my mule to Gulta. On my way I had to pass through Wobara, and the women saw me. They took their fodder-chopping knives, which are over a foot long, and shouted, "Chimate! Chimate! Chimate!" and ran toward me. The men still in Wobara didn't come out, only the women did.

"War will kill your fathers! What can I do? I am only Chimate!" I shouted at them. "I am Chimate! What will you do to me? Don't leave! Go ahead and insult me!"

But two men carrying rifles were with me. The women clustered in front and in back of the mule and threatened to kill me with their knives. The men who were standing by said to the women, "Stop! Stop! Stop! Leave it!"

The old men, men too old to go to war, repeated, "Stop! She came to mediate but the people of Dita didn't cooperate. You young women, stop!" While they spoke, I hurried on and entered Gulta.

I was very worried. "Where will my children go? My husband has gone to fight against the Italians; I have been looking after the children. Now I am not in my home in Dita. I'm not with my husband." I comforted myself, saying, "If I die, if my children die, when my husband comes home he will avenge my children's blood! He will avenge them and avenge me. And since we're in three places, we won't all die."

I stayed in Gulta in a house with three people. On the first day of the battle two Dita men were killed, there in the Wobara marketplace. One Amhara of Gulta also died. On the second day they fought again. When the Dita were defeated, the conquerors ran through Dita, burning houses. But two Amharas sat in my Dita house, holding rifles. They saved my house and that of one other person, but the rest of Dita was burned down. Everyone fought. The old people sitting at home were killed. Many died.

After two weeks, I came to the hill overlooking Dita with men carrying seven rifles. I pleaded with the people, making our traditional gesture of peace. I held out my arms with my cotton cape draped over them, covering my hands. Holding this white cloth to the sun, I shouted, "Enter your houses, enter your houses, there is no more fighting, go home!"

The people said, "We will enter our homes, and we will pay our taxes."

The Amharas who came with me took the two Dita officials who served the government under my husband, the chikashums, and the Dita elders to prison for a while. After the war was over, I saw my children again. The Dita people cleaned up the ashes, rebuilt their homes, and paid the tax to the Amharas.

Six months later my husband Masa came back. He got into a quarrel with one of the administrators, Dejazmach Gezaheng, and was imprisoned for a while. He was soon released. The Italians were coming into our area, and he was released to join the other people in fighting them.

Before the Italians reached Dita and while Masa was still in jail, many retreating Ethiopian soldiers passed through the area. They lived off the land, confiscating clothing, food, and livestock from people. One group came when I was sitting quietly with the elders, stripped the men, left me alone, and killed the elders.

When I got home, I hid my husband's guns and ammunition by strapping them to my body. I did not want the soldiers to take them. Then I put on my finest cotton buluko cape and prepared a feast. I invited the soldiers to the feast. Very politely I offered them food, to this one wheat beer, to this one honey mead, to that one milk, to that one barley boiled in milk and running with melted butter, to this one barley porridge, to that one white wheat flour. Like this, I served them all, smiling politely.

In this fashion I saved myself, my animals, my possessions, and the guns. The soldiers were ruthless. They took people's boxes and broke them open. They stabbed people with their knives, killing them.

Dejazmach Gezaheng took my husband to prison and didn't send him back. In the meantime, I fooled the soldiers with food. I saved two guns and two ammunition belts.

At times I feel I have no measure for this woman, no common ground. I have walked in heedless safety. How can I ever know how it feels to watch soldiers kill the men around me, then to arrange a feast for the murderers? I have seen Chimate tell this story many times. Always she enacted the drama, handing the food to this imaginary guest and to that one. She acted it with pride; yes, she was advertising her own courage and cleverness. She acted it with humor, mocking the gullible soldiers. I tremble as I remember this, for underlying it all was a dark, bitter, passionate tenacity, strong and heedless, the gnarled roots of a human life.

6   The Italian Occupation

Life was very, very hard for me then. Those days were
like night to me.

～

"Masa was called to do battle with the Italians who were invading Ethiopia
from the north," Chimate said to me. "He was told, 'Come!' and with five
men, three animals, a scribe named Demse, and a gun, he went to Addis
Abeba. They joined the army there, and traveled north again, a fifteen-day
journey.

"The war took place. The Italians were in the air. From the airplanes,
bombs, bombs, bombs were spilling out on our people, who had only guns.
Two of our Dita men fell. The battle continued. The bombs were killing
people, killing them all. People were dying far from home, in places they
had never expected to see. People were running for their lives. Half of them
hid in the forest and under bushes.

"People fled to Addis Abeba. Another of our men died on the road while
going to Addis. My husband and Demse, a brave man, did reach the city.
They had no food, their clothes were all worn out, and people there all
robbed one another.

"The government ordered people to go home. 'The spear from Gamo
should return to its country,' they said to my husband. Night and day, the
Gamo Highland people began the journey home, walking. It was when they
were almost home that the Italians entered Addis Abeba, and the Emperor
left, wasn't it?"

I fulfilled my role as listener and nodded in agreement.

"People said, 'Our Emperor Haile Selassie has left. He has betrayed us!'"
Chimate paused as the door of the room opened and a young man, the
household cook, came in carrying a tray with a cup of tea for me and coffee for Chimate and my assistant. I reached out and turned off the tape
recorder, moving it aside so that the tray would fit on the little table.

We were in Addis Abeba, sitting in a large house built by the Italians during their occupation of Ethiopia. I was living there with other Americans, and Chimate was staying with her daughter in another part of the city. She had come to Addis Abeba in order to tell me her life story far from the demands and distractions of Dita.

The Italian invasion of Ethiopia began in October 1935. In the spring of 1936, the Italians started to use their air power. By May 5, 1936, they occupied Addis Abeba, the emperor having fled. When Chimate resumed her story, she explained that when the Italians had reached the Gamo Highland, most of the people living there had refused to fight against them. "The Italians won easily," she said in disgust. "Three of our Amhara leaders, Fitawari Getachew, Kebede, and Dejazmach Gezaheng escaped and spent three years in England. They learned a lot in England while my people were under the Italians!

"The Italians killed many people. Along the road to Dorze there is a place called Awa Geloso, the 'Place Where the Sun Enters.' You know where that is, don't you?"

"Where the river crosses the road, right outside Dita?" I asked.

"Yes. There seventy Amhara men, tied together, were put into a large hole in the ground. The Italians shot a cannon into them, killing them all. They killed only men. They didn't harm women! They never killed women, they went to bed with them. No Amhara women were killed, nor were children."

The Italians, I knew, had abolished the feudal system under which the Gamo Highlanders had been ruled, killing many of the men who had administered this system. I recalled a conversation I had had with Halaka Halke, who had protected Chimate during the Italian occupation. At the time, he was building a fence around Chimate's compound. I asked him, "Were you happy to see the Italians come?"

"Keep quiet!" he hissed at me. "*She*"—by this he meant Chimate—"is an Amhara!" He meant this to be taken figuratively, not literally. Throughout southern Ethiopia, members of the local elite who were powerful and closely identified with the government were often called Amhara.

Halaka Halke lowered his voice. "Yes, I was happy. Who wasn't? We hated being serfs." His voice was emphatic and bitter. "To the Italians we paid only taxes, not service, which made life much easier for us. They destroyed the record books that assigned our lands to the Amharas."

Chimate was continuing her story, and I pulled my attention back to her words. "The people began to rob the Amhara women, cutting off their clothes, leaving them naked," Chimate was saying. "My husband asked the people, 'Why are you stripping these women? Why are you robbing them? There are no longer taxes on you! Why strip these women naked?'"

By this time I was leaning forward, curious. I had heard Chimate recount the incidents leading up to her husband's death before, but never had she mentioned the Amhara women. She's changing the emphasis, I thought to myself. She knows now that I have a special concern with women. As a good narrator, she's bringing out details she knows will capture my attention and hopes will direct my sympathies toward Masa.

"The Amhara brought boxes to our house containing guns and clothing. We hid them. After this my husband said, 'Just go ahead and try to strip the Amhara again! Just try to touch the women again!' But this only led to more trouble.

"'What, he's preventing us from taking the Amhara's possessions!' people said, and decided to take revenge in other ways. The leader of the Wobara people, with whom we had been at war, hated my husband. He began telling the Italian governor in the town of Chencha, 'A black king is telling people not to pay their taxes!'"

Chimate's story had resumed its familiar contours. I sat back absorbed, as Chimate's voice carried me along.

~

Many Dita people sided with Fitawari Mamo of Wobara. They met with him and said many things. "We won't support our leader." "We want the Amharas' possessions!" "We will kill him!" "We, we will kill our master." "Let us have him killed."

Two of King Mijola's former slaves went with Fitawari Mamo to the Italians. They said, "Our master, Masa, says, 'Don't touch the Amharas, don't strip them, don't hit them. He has been speaking at the public meetings, forbidding that.'"

The Italian they spoke to was a young, unmarried man. "Who is this black king? Who is this black king?" he asked.

"Masa Mijola."

"Masa Mijola?"

"Yes."

The foreigner became angry. "All right, show us those Amhara possessions!" he said.

Relatives of my husband heard about this and sent a message, "Hide the Amharas, hide them!" My husband told the Amharas, "The Italians are coming to kill you. Escape to the lowlands."

From Chencha an order came, calling my husband to that town. I had a dream, and said to Masa, "Don't go! Don't go to Chencha! Go to the lowlands with your friends! Don't go to Chencha!"

"No, I'll go," he said. He took the upper road. With him he had a milch cow and a sack of barley flour. In the meantime, along the lower road, six soldiers were coming from Chencha.

We were sitting at home with our head scribe, Demse. In those days, I wasn't thin as I am now. I was so fat I couldn't come out of our door unless I turned sideways. Not only was I fat, I was pregnant with my daughter, Almaz. I couldn't get onto my mule by myself; two men had to lift me.

The six soldiers arrived. "Where is your husband?" they asked me.

"He has gone to Chencha. He was summoned."

"He was called, and he went?"

"When the government calls him, does he suddenly become lost?"

"Okay, okay," they said, and began to search the house.

Our house was filled with the belongings of the Amharas. There were seventy boxes, all in our house, filling it. Demse, the scribe, knew that we also had fifty sacks of bullets, and he took an old sack and covered them. Then he quietly left; he joined the others in the lowlands. The soldiers lifted a cloth off a box. Underneath they found a bullet. A shield was hanging on the wall. They saw it. "Aha!" they cried, and took the bullet and the shield.

"What will they do to my husband after he reaches Chencha?" I asked myself.

The soldiers went outside and picketed their mules on the grass by the house. They entered the sheep pen, took a sheep, and cut its throat. Returning to our house, they sat down, preparing to eat.

Where was I to sleep? I went to a neighbor's house to spend the night. The next morning the soldiers took the bullet, the shield, and seventy buluko cloths from the seventy boxes. They had a hard time picking them up, they were so heavy. No one was there to help them carry their spoils. They returned to Chencha, taking prisoners from among our household servants. The prisoners' feet were chained together, and the soldiers held one end of the chain.

My neighbors helped me mount my mule. I took the lower road toward

Chencha, avoiding the soldiers. On the way I reached Doko. I asked the people of Doko, "What has happened to my husband?"

"He took the other path," they said. Everyone was afraid to tell me that he had been killed.

The day before, when Masa arrived in Chencha, he was questioned. "Ah! Fitawari Masa has come! Are there any Amhara in your country?"

"Yes, there are."

"Didn't you tell your people not to rob the Amhara?"

"Without your permission, how can I allow people under me to be killed and robbed? How can I allow women to be stripped naked? If you order me to allow that, all right, I will allow it!"

Masa was thrown into jail with many others. The next morning, soldiers came to get Masa.

"Are they taking me out in order to kill me?" asked Masa.

A man who knew Italian said, "They are taking you out in order to kill you."

Masa turned to the men with him. "Listen!" he said.

"Yes!"

"Listen!"

"Yes!"

"The foreigners have called me to kill me. If any of you survive, tell my wife, 'I know your heart. Don't leave our home. Don't separate my sons from any sons you may bear later. Don't separate my children from my other wife, Shawaye. I know your heart. My heir is my son, Amano.'

"Tell this to the people of Dita. 'I inherited my land from Mijola. Let my son, Amano, take my house, and no one else. I have a gun, let Amano take it. Let my sons and daughters divide my land equally. If my sons won't give my daughters land, let it be taboo for them. And let it be taboo for the people of Dita if they do not share land equally between sons and daughters.' Some of you won't die. Look to this, my children! Tell this to the people!"

As Masa was being taken away to be killed, he said quickly, "The Italians have killed me here treacherously and without reason. They will die in the same fashion!"

The Italians took Masa and shot him. They shot him in a meadow near Chencha and buried him there. I never reached Chencha. The people told me what had happened, and I returned to Dita to mourn.

The people of Dita were afraid of the Italians. They refused to have a big public funeral for Masa. I took my children and hid them.

Eleven days after Masa's death, the men who had been in jail with him found us sitting and crying over his loss. They said, "Bring people to hear what we have to tell!" They stood in front of us and said, "Masa told us this, and this, and this."

The people said, "We agree to follow his will."

"Masa said, 'Let the Dita people take care of Amano. Let them keep my houses in repair. My wife has a knowing heart. The work may be too difficult for her, but let her try her best.'"

I stayed for two weeks in Dita. I heard that the Italians were saying, "Let Masa's wife and oldest son come here. I went to talk with Captain Kanzi, the Italian in Chencha. I took our friend King Kare of Ezo with me. Ever since men have been king, there has not been one like King Kare! He was a very brave man. He was not present when Masa was killed, and when he learned in Chencha of Masa's death, he shouted, "If I had been here, no one would have dared to kill him!"

I said to the Italian, "My husband has been killed. I'm still alive. If you killed my husband, it would be easy for you to kill his children. Where can I raise my children in safety now?"

"Is this his son?" asked the captain.

"Yes."

"How many children do you have?"

"I have given birth to six and am about to bear a seventh. Where can I raise them? I will catch them up and run away from this area."

"Don't run! No one will touch you and your children. Raise your children. But give the oldest boy to Fitawari Kare, King of Ezo, to raise."

Turning to Kare, the Captain said, "Kare, buy a horse for this boy Amano."

"Very well."

"Buy him clothes. Take him and educate him."

Kare brought Amano trousers, a coat, a shirt, and a cap. At that time boys liked to wear a special kind of Italian cap. I told Amano, "Go with Fitawari Kare. If you stay with me, someone will kill you."

So that nothing would happen to me, the captain declared that the title of balabat would go to Kenyazmach Saira. The captain was sorry for me. He saw that I was pregnant. "Stay here in Chencha, in your friend's house!" he urged me.

But I hated Chencha. My master died in Chencha. His blood spilled out there. After I left Chencha that day, I didn't return for many years to that town.

At home in Dita I gave birth to the baby in my womb, Almaz. When she was a year old, the title of balabat was taken away from Kenyazmach Saira, who had allowed me to live in peace. It was given to an ambitious man from the Dorze community, Fitawari Sono. He came to live in Dita, and one day he sent two messengers to my house. They told me that Sono wanted to marry me.

"He wants me?"

"Yes."

"After taking my title, he will marry me?"

"Yes."

As soon as the messengers left, I walked all the way to the town of Gulta. There I sought the protection of Fitawari Getachew Wombara. Sono came to speak to me a few days later.

"Listen, my master," I said. "I will marry you if I can be sure of just one thing."

"What is that? What is wrong with me?"

"There is nothing wrong with you. But if I marry you, on the day on which I die, there will be no funeral for me."

"And just why should there be no funeral for you?"

"Just listen."

"Yes."

"My sons will ask me about the title. I bore many children in Masa's house; if I marry you, I will also bear your children. The children I have by you and the children I have by Masa will quarrel about the title. I will take away the title from all of them by doing this, take away the land. The children will curse me. When I die, my bones will dissolve quickly in my grave.

"Don't wish to marry me!" I pleaded. "Wish to become my relative. Take one of my children, feed it, and become my relative."

"All right! I don't want to marry you! Go away! Will you dare to live in Dita after this?"

With that, Fitawari Getachew broke in, asking, "Haven't you heard enough? Keep quiet, and leave her alone!" Later, Fitawari Getachew asked me, "What will you do now?"

"If Sono allows me to live in Dita, I'll live there. If not, I'll leave." I then said to myself, "I don't think that he will allow me to stay."

Life was very, very hard for me then. Those days were like night to me. Back in Dita, I went to Halaka Halke, who had helped our family in the past. "I have no place to live in safety," I told him.

"Why not?"

"My husband is dead. My children are thin. No one tills the land for me. Now Fitawari Sono will take revenge on me for refusing him. How can I survive?"

"Listen. I will feed your children by tilling your land. I'll bring crops to your house and guard it. I'll leave my house and live in yours; let my wife live in my house with my children. Don't allow yourself to go downhill. Don't allow your clothes to become dirty. Don't let your children grow thin. And marry whichever king of this region pleases you. Marry someone, be his wife. Marry!"

"If I marry, what will happen to my children?"

"I cannot bear to hear people insulting you and reviling you. If you were a married woman, when you returned here to live, no one would touch you. A powerful husband would be your protection."

So I allowed Fitawari Kare of Ezo and Fitawari Kircho of Bonke to court me. I chose Kare and went to live with him. Yes, he married me and hid me in Done.

After I left, Fitawari Sono was very angry. He called Halaka Halke, accused him, and refused to release him. But my new husband Kare heard of this, and he sent a paper to Sono, and they set Halaka Halke free. But Halaka Halke was still forced to pay a fine of seventy dollars to keep out of prison. I couldn't help him. At that time he was rich and I was poor.

For just three months I lived hidden in Done. Fitawari Kare's wife suspected that he had married me. She asked around until she was sure. In those days my two eldest sons were living with Kare, and he was caring for them and teaching them.

"She married my husband. I won't raise her sons!" said Kare's wife, and sent them away from her house. Mago went to live with a priest in Gulta, and Amano came to me.

I thought, "Am I not Fitawari Kare's wife now? Who will dare to touch me?" I decided to return to Dita with my children. There I found out that I was pregnant, but in the seventh month I miscarried.

My children and I had many troubles. I begged people to work for me. I petitioned them to pardon me for any troubles I had caused them. I had many enemies, for while Fitawari Sono held the title, no one wanted to help me.

~

"Enough!" Chimate said briskly. The rain had stopped. "I'll go home now and tell you more tomorrow."

I brought Chimate her new coat, a gift from the Dita people living in Addis Abeba. They had feasted her, bought her clothing, and were now coming to her with many disputes to mediate. "The subdistrict governor of Dita arrived in this city the same time I did, but the Dita people feasted me first," Chimate told me proudly. She cited a Dita proverb, "When you sweep your compound, sweep inside the houses first, then sweep the ground outside."

My assistant was waiting outside the gate with a taxi. Chimate and I went down the rickety wooden steps of the old house and crossed the muddy courtyard. I helped her into the taxi. Smiling at me bravely—she was afraid of cars and buses, barely consenting to ride in them—she said good-bye and was gone.

7   Chimate's Career Begins

I came by the lower path, crying in a shrill voice, "Li-li-li-li-li!" My tears were falling from my eyes like hail.

∾

"The Italians left our area after three years, no, not even three years. We waited for a governor from the north to come and rule again. The Amharas who had been in hiding in the lowlands became outlaws, living off the highland people." Chimate's tone was disapproving. "Many of them stayed near Dita and gave us a hard time. From my five mules, they didn't leave me even one. They took them all.

"I was determined to go and speak to the outlaws. 'If they kill me, they'll kill me, and I'll stay there forever with them. I don't know how to travel on foot. Let the outlaws return my mules, or kill me!' I said to those who told me not to go.

"I went to see Fitawari Demse, the head of the outlaws living near us. I wept." Chimate smiled wryly as she said this. "He spoke sternly to his men, 'If you men have pulled even one hair from her mules, don't eat food here any more, and leave my camp! Didn't her husband die because he protected us?'

"I brought back my five mules. I sold four, each for fifteen dollars. I was afraid the outlaws would come again," she concluded, "so I kept only the mule I needed to ride on." The smile lingered for a moment on her lips. Then she grew serious and began to tell me how she had regained the title of balabat for her family.

∾

During the time of the outlaws, Fitawari Sono was still balabat in Dita. At last I heard that a governor had been assigned to our province—Dejazmach Gebre. I went to Ezo to consult with Fitawari Kare. Sono remained in Dita.

Kare asked me, "Will you travel north with me to meet the dejazmach in Borodda?"

"Of course!" I replied

"Be brave, don't be afraid. I will help you talk to Dejazmach Gebre."

"Good," I said. The next day we set out, Kenyazmach Saira going along, too. When we reached Borodda, I was granted an audience with the dejazmach.

"Because he was keeping the Amaharas' clothing and ammunition, the Italians killed my husband. After killing him they took the title away from me. I had a lot of trouble. There was no food to feed my children."

I could hardly speak. I cried and cried. Dejazmach Gebre told me, "Don't worry, don't worry."

Then I joined his party, which was traveling south to the place he had chosen for his capital—Chencha. Thus, I reentered the town where my master died. We reached Chencha on the second night, and the next morning I went with Kenyazmach Saira and Fitawari Kare to the meeting place where Dejazmach Gebre was sitting. I brought my three sons with me: Amano, heir to Masa's title, Mago, who was short and fat and deaf as a stone to my advice—he became a priest—and Atumo, the only one still living, then only nine years old.

I came by the lower path, crying in a shrill voice, "Li-li-li-li-li!" My tears were falling from my eyes like hail. The dejazmach looked at me, and I began to speak. "The Italians took out my heart, only my skin is left, and that is why I cry 'Li-li-li.' They took my heart, only a shell is left. Only now do I see light after years of darkness!"

So speaking, I recounted my story. The dejazmach listened and questioned me for a long time. Then he turned to the men with him, saying, "Call Sono quickly! Go!"

Fitawari Sono came; he arrived the next day. Dejazmach Gebre was there at the meeting place before him.

"Fitawari Sono!"

"Yes, sir!"

"Was the title which you hold your father's title?"

"No, my master."

"Whose was it?"

"Masa Mijola's. When Masa died, his heir was Amano, but the Italians took the title and gave it to me."

"Did the Italians govern here?"

"Yes. The Italians gave it to me."

"How were they able to do that?"

"It was work, so they gave it to me."

"Masa Mijola, where is he now?"

"Since he was our enemy, the Italian government killed him."

"*You* were his enemy. Now will you leave the title, or will you go to court with the young man?"

"I won't go to court."

"Isn't the title his?"

"It's his."

"Is that sure?"

"Let Emperor Haile Selassie die if it's not true."

"Leave this title."

"Let Emperor Haile Selassie die if I have not left it."

"Sign."

Fitawari Sono signed. "I won't keep their title," he declared.

I cried again, "Li-li-li-li-li," and caught Dejazmach Gebre's two feet. Everyone told me to stand up, but I didn't. Tears flowed like water from the eyes of Fitawari Kare.

Dejazmach Gebre took the title from Fitawari Sono and gave it back to me. That was the last that Sono had to do with our title. My son, Amano, inherited the title. The Italians took it away, and then we got it back.

~

Chimate's voice rose. "From that day on, Fitawari Sono and I have been constant enemies! We hate one another!"

"And yet your eldest daughter married Sono's brother, Shela," I commented.

"Yes, and right now Sono is trying to take my daughter to court!" she retorted. "While Shela was in prison, Sono gave her seventy dollars to pass on to Shela. Now that Shela is out of jail, he hasn't repaid the money. Sono isn't accusing his brother, he's accusing my daughter! That's how Sono treats our family. He hates us, and we hate him."

During my months in Dorze I had often seen Fitawari Sono at political gatherings. An old man who moved slowly, he wore a pith helmet and an olive-drab wool coat as signs of his wealth and status. Someone always carried a chair to him while the other men sat on the grass. Upon seeing me, he would call me to his side, offering me his chair. I would, of course, decline his offer.

Sono was said to be the highland's cleverest politician, a man who had always landed on his feet with every change of government. Chimate's refusal of him—he obviously liked women very much—and her reclaiming of the title must have been quite galling to him. The year Sono stepped down as Dita's balabat was 1942. In January 1941 the British had begun sending military forces into Ethiopia from Kenya and Sudan. By May the emperor had returned to Addis Abeba, and by the end of the year Britain controlled both Ethiopia and Eritrea. Britain set up a protectorate and took an advisory role in both areas. The British presence was never obvious to the Gamo Highlanders, who thought in terms of the restoration of Amhara rule. By 1944 Ethiopia had been returned to the emperor's authority, and in 1952 the British left Eritrea.

Amano was fourteen years old at the time the title was returned to him, too young to do the work. Chimate at thirty-two was rather young as well, for in the highland a person over forty is growing ripe for responsibility, a ripeness that increases with age until senility sets in. Nonetheless, with the backing and support of her friends among the highland leaders, Chimate assumed the work of balabat on Amano's behalf.

Dita had now been part of Ethiopia for more than forty years. Local political autonomy, though a cherished dream of some Dita citizens, was no longer a possibility. All of Africa had been organized into large-scale political units. It is clear that without the emergence of an indigenous Ethiopian Empire, Dita would have been incorporated into a European colony.

The newly restored Ethiopian government had changed since the days of Mijola and Masa. Emperor Haile Selassie was interested in centralizing power and modernizing the nation. He turned to his advantage the fact that throughout Ethiopia the Italians had put to death members of the former ruling elite. Bureaucratic administration was substituted for personalized rule by military leaders, taxes on land for feudal obligations, police stations for garrison towns. Each administrator's salary was paid from the national treasury. As in feudal times, administrators were transferred regularly to prevent them from gaining a local power base.

The political arena in which Chimate won and kept a place was dominated by unstable coalitions of groups and individuals. There were factions within each Gamo Highland community (for example, only three out of Dita's four divisions supported Mijola's appointment of Masa as his heir), factions among the various highland communities (a Dita-Wobara faction brought about Masa's death), factions within the governmental bureaucracy, and factions that included both governors and governed. One person, of course, could belong to more than one kind of group.

Were not the permutations of these factions enough, two other factors that have already been mentioned added fluidity to the scene. First, government officials changed frequently. Second, the position of balabat was stable on paper but could be unstable in fact. In many Gamo Highland communities the titled balabat was a figurehead and someone else did the work. As alliances shifted, this work could be transferred from one person to another without the central government being any the wiser. Even barring such transfer of responsibility, the effectiveness of the acting balabat as community leader, dispute arbiter, supervisor of public works, and supervisor of tax collection could fluctuate over time.

Such fluctuation is not surprising. Among all the political roles in the province, that of balabat was the most ambiguous. The primary accountability of the local elders was to their own community, that of government officials to the empire. Chimate and others like her were accountable in both directions and had to act as living bridges between two different political systems and cultures. Among other things, this meant understanding both the national language, Amharic, and the Gamo language, having a knowledge of courtroom procedure and of Gamo mediation techniques, fostering an ability to affect decision making within a bureaucratic hierarchy and within a democratic assembly striving for consensus, and upholding conformity with both the religion of the Ethiopian Orthodox Christian Church and the complex Gamo system of taboo.

Chimate, as we have seen, was born into one high-ranking Gamo Highland family and married into another. Her background prepared her for factional politics in two ways. First, the elite families throughout the highland were in communication with one another. Their intermarriages often crossed community boundaries, unlike those of lower ranking highlanders, and reinforced their ties of friendship with ties of kinship. Witness Chimate's marriage, which created a link between Tsela and Dita. Second, even in childhood Chimate participated in both Gamo and Amhara cultures. As a native of Tsela, Chimate learned Gamo Highland customs from her family, kin, and friends. The process of assimilation into Amhara culture began as the northern Ethiopian administrators and settlers actively cultivated friendships with the local elite, urging northern Ethiopian food, dress, religious customs, and the like upon them.

I saw this process still at work in Chimate's life when, after a two-year absence, I returned to Dita in 1973. Chimate had become close to the new subdistrict governor and his wife. "We've become relatives," Chimate said proudly. The couple came from the Gofa Highland and were native to the province, like Chimate. Their acceptance of Amhara custom was more advanced than Chimate's, and they pressured her to follow their example.

"I eat *duro wat* now," Chimate told me, referring to a dish made with chicken and hard-boiled eggs, both abhorrent foodstuffs in Gamo culinary tradition. "The governor's wife told me, 'If you won't eat this food I've prepared for you, I won't be your relative!'" Chimate doubtless had similarly pressed other northern Ethiopian customs upon her Dita friends.

If Chimate's social background gave her access to certain resources necessary to the work of balabat, her special personal characteristics won her the position. What she has recounted of her history amply demonstrates her ability to take initiative in moments of crisis. In her everyday life, she consistently sought out responsibilities beyond the normal woman's role, as when she began to supervise the laborers in Masa's fields. During Masa's long absences as he fought in northern Ethiopia, she assumed some of his role as balabat. Inserting herself into leadership positions, she must have had a great deal of conviction and a firm sense of identity. These qualities alone would not have been sufficient. She also would have needed a talent for assessing people accurately, asking of them only what they could give and avoiding those confrontations she could never win. Intelligence, beauty, eloquence, wit—these were hers as well.

Chimate enjoyed her work. She moved about the countryside incessantly, visiting not only the various Dita districts but also the administrative centers—whose locations tended to change. She received a fee every time she mediated a dispute, a sum of money at the end of every tax year ($40 U.S., in 1973), and various gifts and services from people. For example, the men in her district cultivated and harvested the fields belonging to her household but charged only half the fee they would normally charge. Her main income came from this farmland.

Over the years Chimate's three sons and two daughters married, and Chimate had a brief affair with the king of another highland community. She gave birth outside Dita. The child had to be abandoned to the care of an Amhara woman living in Chencha before Chimate could reenter Dita.* Chimate's daughters, like Chimate herself, left their local community in order to marry important men. Alimetu moved to Dorze, and Almaz moved to Addis Abeba. Amano and Atumo remained in Dita and embarked upon unstable marital careers. Mago, the stubborn son whom Chimate could not influence easily, became a priest in the Ethiopian Orthodox Christian Church and moved to Gulta.

Mijola and Masa had held two titles, those of king and of balabat. Amano became balabat but not king. As Chimate indignantly told me, "When Masa died, the people said, 'Masa's older brother, Tilinte, was cheated out of his title. Now we will make Tilinte king.'" The kingship never returned to Masa's designated heirs within Chimate's lifetime.

Two of Amano's wives gave birth to sons, assuring the family's hold on the title of balabat. Amano himself died in the early 1960s, victim of a fever caught in the lowland. He had been supervising road work for the government at the time. His brother, Mago, died several years later. Chimate continued as acting balabat, now on behalf of her grandson, Wombara. That was how things stood when I met her in 1970.

Chimate shared the strengths and weaknesses of all women in patrilineal societies. These women are suspended between the lineages of their husbands and of their fathers and brothers. Generally, they have responsibilities to both groups, as in Dita where women farmed with their husbands and acted as ritual experts for the lineage of their fathers and brothers. Women in situations like this must learn to use influence rather than authority. They must be persuasive and observant, able to express their point of view at just the right time and in just the right manner. These skills served Chimate well in her role as intermediary between two mutually suspicious levels of government.

Competence and structural vulnerability are important criteria in the choice of an intermediary. Chimate's position as a member of the local elite in a patrilineal society contributed to both. In Dita, women did not have

---

*Any intercourse outside marriage was taboo in the Gamo Highlands. Illegitimate children had to be abandoned before their mother could reenter her community. In earlier times, such children were killed by leaving them in certain forests to be eaten by hyenas. Chimate talks about her illegitimate daughter Ababe briefly in chapter 10.

organizations through which they could exercise collective power. Traditionally, women were completely excluded from the sphere of external politics, the wars and treaties among the Gamo Highland kingdoms. Women's marginality in local politics could help make them acceptable intermediaries, less threatening than their male counterparts.

Chimate as a native of Tsela, not Dita, was doubly vulnerable. The two basic sources of political support in Dita were kinship ties and territorial ties. Chimate could draw upon these only indirectly. Her own patrilineal kin and the place where she grew up were located far from Dita. But as a woman, by bearing children, Chimate was able to create ties where none had existed. Her children's birth and survival enabled her to become partially assimilated into her husband's patrilineage and community.

At the time I knew her, Chimate spoke of "our neighborhood," "our lineage," or "our ancestors," meaning her adopted community and kin. In one angry speech, however, she articulated and exaggerated her isolation as a woman and a stranger. She made the speech five years after the death of Amano.

~

The people of Dita came to me and said, "This silver ring which makes a man king of Dita, allow us to give it to Bele."*

"It is well. I agree," I replied.

They completed the ceremonies to make him the king of Dita, and then disease entered the country. Like a broom it swept people to their death— sweeping, sweeping, sweeping! The people came to me again. They were afraid that they were being punished for making the wrong man king.

"Bless Bele for us!"

"Why should I bless him? Just what could I say to bless him? I don't have the mouth from which blessings can issue. Only men can do that! What could I say? Just what words would I find? I'm a woman. I'm not powerful! I have no relatives here. I have no friends here. Apart from the emperor and God, what powers protect me from danger?" Thus I refused them.

Within two years, Bele was dead. The ring does not belong to his branch

---

*Bele is Chimate's husband Masa's grandfather's brother's son. The title of ka'o next went to Masa's older (but not oldest) brother's son, Wata. He is the man I knew as ka'o.

of the family.* From his house, men should not enter the kingship. The ring of our family does not enter his house. My son, Atumo, should get the title.

~

As in the Wobara-Dita conflict, Chimate's speech emphasizing "I am a woman" came at a time when she was thoroughly disgusted with the Dita men and eager to emphasize her estrangement from them.

Chimate faced the same problem as any other acting balabat who did not hold the actual title, the need to legitimate her position. Chimate's role as Amano's mother validated her work as balabat. She could claim to be a temporary regent, helping him until he could work alone. As such, she did not pose a threat to the principle of male domination of Dita's external political relationships. It seems probable that only under such conditions would a woman, however qualified, have been tolerated. Chimate's two female counterparts in other Gamo Highland communities were also close relatives of the titled balabats—one a sister, one a mother.

The price Chimate had to pay for this kind of legitimation, which a man would not have had to pay, was celibacy. Chimate's marriage to King Kare and her affair years later were similarly brief. She chose to remain single. Marriage would have started the process of assimilation into her new husband's lineage, which would have obliterated Chimate's role as Amano's regent.

Chimate occasionally used tactics different from those of men. She could not take on the quintessential Gamo Highland male role of warrior. She went into the Wobara-Dita confrontation as an unarmed conciliator. Had she been a warrior, she might have been able to control the men with her. As a woman, she felt that she could not threaten direct physical harm in order to intimidate the men with her. Although she occasionally allowed others to form a bodyguard around her, my impression from living and talking with her is that she disliked the use of violence to solve problems.

Conversely, Chimate may have been more comfortable and successful than most men when manipulating a situation in terms of dependency. Recall her successful approach to the Italian captain, her plea to Halaka

---

*To understand the various family relationships and the inheritance of the ka'o and balabat titles referenced by Chimate, see the genealogical chart in appendix 1.

Halke, her marriage to King Kare, and her tears with the outlaws and with Dejazmach Gebre. She undoubtedly could sense when to approach men in this way and when to employ other tactics. If she was capable of crying in front of one governor, she was also capable of taking another governor to court. She phrased her demands as pleas during a period of great personal vulnerability, and she survived.

When Chimate began her career as acting balabat, she was expected to relinquish control to Amano as he matured. By the time he was in his thirties she was still in charge. He died young, and the transition was never made.

Who would have predicted that Masa's child bride, newly come to Dita from Tsela, would spend many years as Dita's balabat? Certainly she could have had no such ambition. She lived her daily life as many courageous and talented young women have, creating opportunities for herself, exercising and honing her skills. If, at last, fate left a door ajar for her, she herself opened it and stepped through.

Part Two

Chimate's Two Worlds

8 The Harvest

*Now I want a quiet life of my own. Wombara is
working as the balabat now.*

∽

Stars clung like frost crystals to the cold January sky. The door had been
barred and we were all preparing to sleep. Chimate sat on her bed under a
thick cotton blanket and pulled her dress off over her head. I undressed
inside my sleeping bag. Chimate's grandson, Seyum, lay down on the floor
beside my new assistant, Gida, sharing a blanket.

It was 1971. I had been living in Dita for two weeks, and this particular
day had been quite tiring for me. All of Dita had celebrated the Epiphany—
January 6, the day on which the infant Christ was baptized, witnessed by
the wise men from the East—with songs, drinking, horse races, and religious ceremonies. To the joyous crowd, I had been one more entertainment.
I had soon sought the relative quiet of a house where liquor was sold. There
Bele's Mother, a handsome middle-aged woman who was fond of me, had
given me coffee to drink and roasted barley to eat.

"I'm going to make Judy my daughter!" she had told the men sitting
about the room. "Here, Judy," cupping a hand under one of her breasts,
"nurse on my breast and become my child!"

I was glad that tomorrow would be an ordinary day. I reached for the
kerosene lantern I had brought with me, about to blow out the light. Sud-
den shouts and pounding on the door interrupted me. "Our Mother, our
Mother, come witness! Come witness! Dombas has killed a boy!" came a
man's voice. A second voice cried, "*Gene* [outrage]! Gene! Gene! Gene!"

Chimate sat up in bed, pulling the blanket over her bare shoulders.
"Seyum, open the door!" she commanded.

A man entered and went over to Chimate. Bowing his head, he explained
in a quiet, tense voice, "Our Mother, there's been a fight among the tanners.

They're all drunk from the festival. Dombas said Sedho's son hit his son, and then he himself hit Sedho's son, and Sedho hit Dombas. The boy is lying on the ground covered with blood."

The second man remained outside shouting. Chimate's voice was hard to hear. "I can't come with you this time of night," she protested. "Wombara is working as balabat now. He's sleeping in another house. Take Wombara's brother Seyum with you tonight. He will witness, write down what everyone says, and escort you home. Bring everyone here tomorrow morning."

"Yes, Our Mother," the man replied. Still bent forward, he backed to the door, pausing outside to wait for Seyum. Seyum dressed hastily. As he pulled on his shoes, he turned to Gida. "I'll borrow your flashlight. Bar the door behind me, Gida, and let me in when I return!" He picked up the flashlight with one hand, grasped a heavy walking stick in the other, and was gone.

In the morning I asked Seyum, "Is the boy dead?" "Oh, no, Judy," he laughed. Fifteen-year-old Seyum looked lively and rested despite his night's work. "He'll be all right. One of the men there grabbed *me* by the neck and almost hit me when I arrived with the flashlight. When he saw who I was, he asked my pardon."

This was the day Gida and I were to move from this compound, which Chimate shared with two of her grandsons, to her new compound. As the two of us began carrying our possessions away, we passed the group of men who had gathered for mediation. Chimate spent the morning talking with the men, then went to a funeral; Wombara and Seyum stayed with them all day.

Gida and I followed the main path for a few minutes, then turned left on a steep uphill path and climbed to a platform of tamped earth cut stepwise into the hillside. Three houses stood in a row, the first for storage, the second a cookhouse, the third the reception house where we would live with Chimate. Two men working on a partly completed fence bordering the platform greeted us as we arrived.

I had many things to move—a duffel bag full of clothing, bedding, a typewriter, a heavy camera bag, a tape recorder, books, paper, a small wooden typing table, a chair, cooking utensils, and eating utensils. Chimate had asked me to bring some of my household goods with me from Dorze, and a young man who was a neighbor of hers, Sando, had spent a week moving them to Dita. Now he helped us again, and when we had finished he began to bring Chimate's possessions to the house.

My aim in Dita was to duplicate work I had done in Dorze. My time was limited; I had to leave Ethiopia by April. This gave me three months to make an intensive study of the district in which Chimate lived, which covered about half a square mile. I began by making a sketch map of the area, then surveyed the fifty-odd households located there. I chose at random twenty households for my two-month intensive observation. My main emphasis was on economic and demographic data, but I also gathered information about funerary rituals and questioned two old men about their memories of Dita history. Chimate and I were usually quite busy during the day, heading in separate directions and meeting in the evenings.

This day was no exception. I went back to the old reception house and met Chimate over supper. Turning to her grandson, Wombara, Dita's ostensible balabat, I asked, "Well, Wombara, what decision did you come to?"

"Dombas was in the wrong because he hit Sedho's son. Dombas paid me three thalers, Chimate three thalers, and Seyum one thaler.* Because Sedho hit Dombas instead of coming to mediation, Sedho paid one thaler. We bought three bottles of liquor with that and everyone drank together."

"And what will you buy with your money on market day, Wombara?" I asked. "More liquor?"

Everyone, including Wombara, laughed. Wombara, Seyum, and their cousin Kebede were relatively idle young men by the Dita farmers' standards. They seldom did agricultural work. Chimate had sent all three to school outside Dita. Although none had studied for long, they had returned to Dita in a restless frame of mind. They tried as best they could to amuse themselves, but there was little to do except go to the market twice a week and get drunk. This they did, getting into fights and coming home to swagger noisily around their relatives' compounds. Seyum and Kebede were especially troublesome. More than once I noted in my diary "Seyum drunk, insults Chimate" or "Kebede drunk, threatens to burn Chimate's house down." Their adolescent struggle with authority figures, particularly with a woman who had an unusually high degree of influence in the community, emerged in such moments.

"Young men are difficult to live with," Chimate had said when explaining her decision to build a compound of her own. "I built this compound when Amano died and raised his children here. Now I want a quiet life of

*One thaler equaled $1.50 in Ethiopian currency; thus Chimate got $4.50.

my own; Wombara and Seyum can live here in the old compound. Wombara is working as balabat now. I'm old, I'm ill, I don't want to do the work."

That evening Chimate looked very tired and ate in silence. As Gida and I retired to sleep in our new quarters, she said, "I'll move in with you in a few days. We'll come to the house for coffee tomorrow, and Nigatu will build you a fire."

Nigatu carried a live coal to the house next morning on a twist of straw, and Wara's Mother came with her, bringing us hot barley porridge sprinkled with ground fenugreek, a bitter, pungent spice. Soon Chimate and a large group of people had joined us and we were all drinking coffee.

One of the men turned to me. "Are you coming to see our work this afternoon?"

"What work?"

"We're harvesting Our Mother's barley."

"I'll come."

Gida and I spent the morning working on our household survey. Chimate's only living son, Atumo, came by the house after lunch, carrying his five-stringed lyre. "Will you play some music for us?" I asked.

Atumo sat in the door, where the light was strong, and began to play, head turned away from us. He was an excellent musician, touching the lyre gently and strumming out first one rhythm, then another. His expression sad, he stared at the ground and softly began singing the names of his ancestors. Suddenly he stopped, stood up, and left without saying good-bye.

Atumo always seemed subdued when I saw him, but he had a violent streak. I once asked Chimate why a man named Zeto was blind.

"Atumo blinded him," she replied.

"What! Why did he do it?"

"You know that Atumo has had many wives." Indeed, I knew that. When I had surveyed his household, Atumo had given me the names of his four current wives—most other men had only one or at the most two—and his twenty-four divorced wives. "Well, he was mistreating his wife, Amo. Another woman kept urging Amo, 'Leave Atumo, he's bad for you!'

"One day I was sitting at home with Atumo. Zeto came in. Atumo asked Zeto, 'Isn't it true that your wife has been telling my wife to leave me? Isn't that true?'

"'Yes, it's true. How can I control what my wife says? Maybe she's right.'

" 'You shouldn't meddle in my affairs!' And Atumo took out his knife"—
Chimate's face contracted in disgust—"and rushed over to Zeto. Woi! Woi!
Woi! I couldn't stop him!" Chimate sat, eyes closed, shaking her head back
and forth.

"Atumo stabbed Zeto on each temple," Chimate resumed, "and ran out
of the house. I don't know why he stabbed him there. I went to Zeto, who
was bleeding, and said, 'Come with me to the Chencha hospital. I have two
mules. Come with me, ride my mule, I'll take you to the hospital.'

" 'No! Atumo will pay for this!' shouted Zeto. Revenge, revenge, revenge,
that's what Zeto wanted, he didn't think about his eyes. Zeto and his relatives brought a court case against Atumo and won. I paid a large fine for
him. Zeto's wounds healed, but over a year, slowly, his vision failed. Now
he sits at home and does nothing and begs money from people like you."

Just down the hill from Atumo's large, fenced, prosperous compound
with a sacred tree by the entrance, Zeto's one little house stood naked on a
square of earth. On clear days Zeto sat outdoors, right by the main path that
followed that side of the valley. The path connected the two households, and
Atumo must have walked it often.

As Gida and I took this path on our way to the harvest, I wondered if
Atumo and Zeto ever greeted one another. How did Atumo feel about the
silent figure below his household, so still and so depressed? Was Zeto's presence a continual reproach, a continual revenge?

We passed the sacred tree and started downhill. I called hello to Zeto and
laughed as Zeto's twelve-year-old son chased a rooster around the house.
"I'm going to sell my rooster at the Dorze market tomorrow!" the boy told
us. He sold his chickens and eggs in other communities, bought honey or
tobacco or butter, sold that in Dita, and bought more chickens to raise. Every
week he visited at least two markets, struggling as did his mother and his
older sister to keep the household going.

"Don't forget, I like eggs," I told him. "I'll buy any more you bring me."

Farther downhill, Gida and I took a side path. Nigatu and another girl
passed us, each bent double under the big bundles of straw and weeds they
were taking back to Chimate's animals as fodder. "Let me be the one to die!"
I said.

They giggled at my use of this respectful greeting. In the highland there
was a phrase of greeting for every type of work. They replied in turn, "You
mustn't die!" They hurried uphill and we hurried downhill, crossing an

already harvested field in which cows, sheep, mules, and horses were grazing on the stubble. We pulled blades of grass from the ground and threw
them in the direction of the harvesters, shouting, "Prosper! Prosper!"

A line of thirty men working side by side was advancing uphill, backlit
by the sun, which dissolved the barley they were harvesting into a shifting
golden sea. With gentle tugs they loosened the plants from the soil, gathering them into small bundles that they tied with a straw and cradled on one
arm while continuing the harvest with the free hand. Girls and women
standing nearby came to the men, took the bundles, and laid them flat on
the barley stacks, stems pointing toward the center of the pile and furry tips
waving in the air.

The men sang as they worked, one man yodeling out a phrase and the
rest answering with an enthusiastic vibrato chorus. A tanner blew his horn
intermittently, a choked braying sound. Little boys and girls sprawled on
the ground, jumping up when some animal in their charge left the cleared
field and wandered over to the standing grain.

Chimate stood at the edge of a clump of bamboo. She directed two of
her small grandsons, both Atumo's children, as they cut bamboo for building the fence around her new compound and carried it uphill. She wore a
faded gray dress with a rip in the hem and a pair of cracked plastic shoes.
Her black scarf was sliding off her hair and her thin white shawl curved once
around her shoulders and slid nonchalantly down her back.

Something further downhill caught Chimate's attention. She put one
hand on five-year-old Gosho's shoulder and pointed with the other hand.
For a moment he stood in outline against her wide skirts, looking solemn-
ly in the direction she indicated and flexing a stick in his hands. His little
shirt just grazed his belly. Then he ran off shouting after his grandmother's red cow, his shaved head with its one central crest of hair glistening in
the light.

On a stone wall of a terraced field sat the young king, Wata, with Halaka
Halke, Chimate's friend and one of Dita's elder statesmen. They were supervising the harvest for Dita's balabat; only Chimate and the two chikashum
officials under her were entitled to have a group of men work for them at a
reduced fee, tilling the fields, sowing the grain, and harvesting.

More accurately, the two men were witnessing the harvest, for they sat
benignly smoking a water pipe. I greeted them and joined them for a time,

getting out my camera. The harvesters grinned up at me and began showing off, throwing their heads back in exaggerated tremolo as they sang and breaking into little dances.

I put down my camera and shouted laughingly to them, "I don't take pictures of men dancing, I take pictures of men working!"

Chimate, carrying a great sheaf of barley, walked slowly uphill. "Welcome!" she said to me, and sat down beside Halaka Halke. She began jesting with the two men, cupping one hand under her chin and tilting her head to catch their eyes.

Cool shadows advanced on us from the opposite hillside. The harvesters reached Chimate's feet, where one triangle of barley remained beneath the stone wall. In silence they completed their task, then pulled weeds from the field and began scraping the dust from their bodies.

Now the petitions and discussions began. First, a man approached and said to Chimate, Wata, Halaka Halke, and a fourth man who had joined them, "Halaka Tulumo came to me and took a sheep from me. He never paid me for it!"

The fourth man, who seemed to be Halaka Tulumo, retorted, "I didn't take that sheep for my own use. We sacrificed it in the marketplace for the good of all Dita. The whole community should pay for it!"

Chimate told them, "I don't know anything about this sheep. I never saw it and this is the first time I have heard of it. Come to me tomorrow morning, each one of you with a witness. Then we can discuss the matter."

A woman pointed angrily at one of the harvesters, claiming that he owed her money. People argued, but no decision was reached. Next, one of the harvesters said, "My Mother, six of my neighbors didn't come to help with the harvest. This is the balabat's district! Everyone should come!"

A second man added, "Seven of my neighbors didn't come either." Turning to face the maximum number of people, he continued, "We are all from one district, aren't we? We all cooperate with our leaders, don't we? Those people who did not come should be set apart from the rest. We shouldn't help them in any way. They are not of us!"   .

The young king changed the subject. "My neighbors, bear witness. My brother has insulted my wife! He told her, 'I'm not going to hit you, but someone certainly should hit you.' She had failed to mourn with him when his sheep died, but that's still no way to talk!"

The young man in question was disappearing over the hill. People called out to him, "Come back! In the name of your neighbors, come back!" He heard them, for his body stiffened, but he kept on going.

There were no other matters to discuss. Each complaint would be aired again when Chimate and other elders were at hand and eventually would be dropped or settled. In the twilight we scattered to our various homes. I pulled on a sweater and Chimate wrapped her shawl carefully around her body. The western edge of Dita, where the river is born and the hills are highest, hid the setting sun. Pale orange stained the sky. Chimate, Gida, and I trudged uphill toward that final glow and were glad to exchange it for the lively flames of a hearth fire and some warm food.

Men harvesting Chimate's barley.

Women carrying bundles of barley and straw from the harvest to Chimate's house.

Chimate with Halaka Halke and another man, overseeing the harvest.

Chimate with a bundle of barley plants.

Chimate walks across the field of harvesters.

Chimate instructs a grandson (probably to herd a straying sheep).

9   Political and Economic Context

If we have a school, some day the government would
open a clinic in Dita. If the students would learn
about farming in the school, and if there were a
tractor to cultivate the land, we would begin to get
other things, too.

~

In order to understand the role Chimate played during the early 1970s, it is necessary to examine the relationship between Dita and the Ethiopian Empire. With the restoration of Haile Selassie in the 1940s, a land tax had been substituted for the gabbar obligations that had caused so much hardship. The attitude of the government, however, remained predominantly extractive. Emphasis was placed upon the taxes paid to rather than the services rendered by the government. For example, Gamo Gofa Province had an estimated population of 700,000 but only one high school, which was located in the provincial capital and largely served the children of the immediate area.

At the same time, Gamo Gofa Province contained both people who were eagerly taking part in the emerging national culture and people who scarcely knew the empire existed. The latter predominated. Nomadic pastoral people living in the southern part of the province, where ecological conditions were variable and precarious, might not even recognize the name of the emperor. The Dorze weavers, representing the other extreme, traveled constantly between Addis Abeba and the Gamo Highland. They often had a Dorze wife in Dorze and a second wife from another ethnic group in Addis Abeba. Many Dorze people spoke Amharic, gave their children Amharic names, observed carefully the traditions of the Ethiopian Orthodox Christian Church, and campaigned against injustice by attempting to change the government rather than by attempting to secede from the empire.

In the emerging system of regional differentiation, Dita's place was closer to that of the Dorze weavers than the nomadic pastoralists. Gamo Gofa Province had two economic activities that tied it to the national and world economy. The first, of importance since the inception of the empire, was weaving. On their frequent visits to the area, the weavers brought home money earned in the urban setting where they spent much of their lives.

In the form of special taxes, this money had been siphoned off to help in the development of the second economic activity, commercial farming of the lowland. The warm lowland climate is suitable for cash crops that will not grow in the highland, such as high quality coffee and Egyptian cotton. The level, fertile tracts of land offer an opportunity for the kind of mechanized farming not possible on the hilly slopes of the highland. Development of the potential for commercial agriculture required an expensive infrastructure of roads and irrigation systems. In the 1960s this development had its start in the lowland just south of the Gamo Highland. A new town, Arbaminch, was built and became the provincial capital. The road between Addis Abeba and the Gamo Highland was extended south to Arbaminch, using the labor of Gamo Highlanders as well as lowland people. While supervising Dita men working on this road, Chimate's son, Amano, caught the fever that eventually killed him. Land suitable for irrigation was then expropriated from local people, including Gamo Highlanders who had been living in the highland and migrating daily to their lowland fields in order to avoid the malaria there. Some of this land was used as a government farm, in part to attract settlers from northern Ethiopia.

The late 1960s and early 1970s were a time of economic enterprise and expansion in the province. The Dorze people played an important role in this accelerating economic activity. Merchants' associations, whose members included Amhara traders from the highland town of Chencha as well as Dorze men, owned buses and Toyota Landcruisers that traveled the roads linking Addis Abeba, Arbaminch, and the Gamo Highland. Dorze was located along the highland road that ended in Chencha, and entrepreneurs exported fiber, rawhide, and lowland maize to Addis Abeba and then imported manufactured items. They built and ran bars, hotels, and one-room stores around the Dorze marketplace. Men traded in thread and cloth. Women traveled to the nearby lowland to buy maize, butter, and honey in the highland markets. Some Dorze men—a very small proportion—were becoming teachers, soldiers, truck drivers, and lawyers. One was a diemaker in an Addis Abeba factory, another a conductor on the train between Addis and Djibouti.

An example of the quickening pace of change is the migration between Addis Abeba and the province. In 1969 when I first visited Arbaminch, four buses a week left Addis Abeba for the ten-hour, 250-mile journey south. Sister buses left Arbaminch for Addis at the same time. By 1971 there was a daily service in both directions. By 1973 two buses started at each end every day, and passengers had to reserve space in advance.

Dita was marginal to these changes but not completely outside them. The people remained subsistence farmers, utilizing the sophisticated intensive agricultural system of the highland to provide the major items in their diet. They sold some of their barley to pay their taxes and to provide for their minor household needs, such as salt. Those short of money might travel to Dorze during the planting and harvesting seasons to be supervised by the Dorze women, earning room, board, and wages. Others went to Arbaminch to work as laborers on farms or as day laborers in the town. A small proportion of the Dita men had learned to weave, and many of these men lived part of the time in Addis Abeba like the Dorze men.

The degree to which Dita and Dorze were dependent upon the existence of the Ethiopian Empire colored their political attitudes. The Dorze weavers' lives were linked to national and international factors. The customers for cloth were found throughout the empire. National policy had created the roads along which the weavers traveled and had banned both the import of competing cloth and the local construction of cloth mills to imitate handwoven cloth. Although the handwoven Dorze cloth was not exported, the yarns used in weaving were imported from countries such as Japan, India, and Germany. As well as affecting the price of yarn, the international economy also affected the buying habits of Ethiopian consumers. A drop in the price of coffee, Ethiopia's principal export, could impact negatively on the demand for cloth.

It is not surprising that the Dorze weavers saw themselves as legitimate citizens of Ethiopia. They actively used the channels open to them to express their political dissatisfaction with the provincial governor. They went to the courts, appealing some cases all the way up to the emperor, and in parliamentary elections they sometimes supported opposition candidates. Conversely, the Dita citizens tended to view the government as an alien and intrusive force. They did not seek political engagement with the empire.

It was precisely Dita's partial isolation that made Chimate's career possible. On the one hand, the Ethiopian Empire had been a constant presence in people's lives for seventy years. Government representatives had been largely absent in the lowlands. Until the recent use of antimalarial medicine and the creation of Arbaminch, they had established their garrison towns in the highland.

On the other hand, nothing had attracted northern settlers in large numbers into the highland, nor had the government made much effort to integrate the area into the empire. The Gamo Highland agricultural system employed intensive techniques unfamiliar to northern Ethiopians, such as the construction of terraces, the use of manure, and the use of two-pronged hoes for cultivation, and it yielded no valuable cash crops, not even the favorite grain of the north, teff.

As for the services the government could have rendered to the people of Dita, these were notable by their absence. Only once did I hear a Dita citizen protest this, and he did so with an urgency born of the fact that few other Dita men and women shared his perceptions. I had been administering a questionnaire to the Dita households in a particular district. In one house, a man sat weaving. He wore a handsome wristwatch and had recently returned from Addis Abeba. When I had finished and was leaving, the man stood up, told his friends who were sitting with him, "I'll be back soon," and walked off with me.

When we were out of earshot of the others, the man turned to me and asked me to stop and talk. He held my eyes with a passionate, bitter stare but his voice as he spoke had a pleading note. "Look at us here in Dita! We are poor. Just look at my hand!" He offered a calloused palm. "We till the earth and eat only false banana plants, potatoes, and barley. We have no hospitals, no schools, no factories." With the pain of one who has seen his homeland through new eyes, the man continued, "We are poor. We are ignorant. Can't you help us? Tell important people about us. Ask for help on the radio. The government has forgotten us! People are dying in Dita right now, disease is using up our people, and no one comes to help us!"

I asked him if he had tried to obtain help from the government officials, and he said, no, in Chencha they didn't listen to people like him. I asked if he knew of the Gurage people and the self-help associations they had formed.

"Our people are ignorant," he replied. "They sit here in the mud and do nothing! They're happy like this!"

In her darker moments Chimate would have agreed with this man, but her images of change were different. She stressed education, land, and clinics, not weaving and the building of factories. These are her words.

~

Studying and farming are better than weaving. If many people come to Addis to weave, the land isn't used. If a man stays in Addis, his wife in Dita cries. The land remains fallow. Instead of this, learning in school is a good thing. If we have a school, some day the government would open a clinic in Dita. If the students would learn about farming in school, and if there were a tractor to cultivate the land, we would begin to get other things, too. The emperor would send us other things.

These days, just look, Tapara hasn't even had any children. He has built houses in Addis Abeba. If he dies, there are no sons to take his land! He has no children! He just stays in Addis quietly, just look at him! Addis is full of this kind of Dita men, just look at them!

~

Chimate's values placed her within the conservative elite of the highland and of the empire, who viewed the world of commerce with suspicion and who classified artisans as a stigmatized lower caste. Rural farmers therefore ranked higher than merchants and craftsmen. Chimate's rejection of weaving reflected both her attachment to rural life and her hope that Dita citizens would retain a relatively high status as farmers rather than being tempted by the material rewards of weaving.

Chimate and the weaver saw themselves as part of the empire and agreed that education was important. But many Dita men and women had no use for it. The services that governments offer are double-edged. Education can be seen as a benefit or as a forcible means of indoctrination and assimilation. It is too simple to state that the government neglected Dita by not building a school there. The government could not be troubled to invest in schooling as one way to entice and coerce the population into the mainstream of national culture.

When Chimate lobbied for an elementary school, which was finally built in 1973, she was sending messages in two directions. To the government, she was saying that her fellow citizens were valuable and worthy of assimilation. To the Dita people, she was saying that the life of the empire was valuable and worthy of participation.

Chimate's complex and ambiguous identity drew upon Gamo Highland

and Amhara elements. This was true of all Gamo Highlanders; what varied was the balance of elements that were accepted, rejected, and sought
after but never achieved. From the Dita point of view, Chimate was more
assimilated into the national culture than most other Dita citizens, and
therefore she could form a useful bridge between Dita and the government.
Nonetheless, while Chimate understood the national language of Amharic, she refused to speak it, and she could neither read nor write. She feared
all mechanized means of transportation and avoided the long-distance jour-
neys made easily by many highlanders. On these and other counts she was
less assimilated than many Dorze citizens. This was probably one of the
reasons why Dita citizens, who, so to speak, wished to turn their backs on
the empire, tolerated her as Dita's acting balabat.

To be effective in influencing people, it is necessary to demonstrate that
in some ways you resemble them. A key element in Chimate's relationship
with northern Ethiopians was her Christianity. To Ethiopia's ruling elite,
participation in the Ethiopian Orthodox Christian Church was a mark of
civilization.* I saw this clearly in the reactions of Amhara acquaintances.
When I told them that many Gamo Highlanders were devout Christians,
their surprise and increased respect were evident. Throughout the highland
this reaction was taken very seriously by members of the elite like Chimate
and by citizens of communities like Dorze. These people looked upon themselves as Ethiopians, and their Christianity demonstrated to them and others
that this was the case. They claimed high status within the highland on the
basis of their strict observance of the fast days and various Christian ceremonies. Most Dita citizens were relatively unengaged with the Christian
religion, although a church was being built with the support of Chimate
and a few others.

Chimate's husband had been put to death by the Italians for protecting
Amhara settlers and administrators. This gave Chimate legitimacy in the
eyes of northern Ethiopians and was a fact she used to advantage in factional struggles. Masa's execution doubtless had strengthened Chimate's
personal identification with the Ethiopian Empire. This identification had
also been strengthened by certain features of Amhara social organization.
It had been possible for a woman to rule the empire during the early part

---

*At the time, the central government was dominated by Ethiopian Orthodox Christians. Chris-
tian beliefs provided a legitimation of the emperor's role. Islam was also an important religion in
Ethiopia; its adherents probably outnumbered Christians.

of the twentieth century, when Emperor Menelik was succeeded by his daughter the Empress Zawditu. More fundamentally, according to Amhara custom, women as well as men could own and inherit land, and this right was established in the legal code of the empire. Chimate wholeheartedly supported this alteration in Gamo Highland customs of male ownership and inheritance. The government, however, did not try to impose all aspects of its legal code on a relatively peripheral area like Dita. It was up to the people who believed in new laws to lobby for change.

The way in which Chimate expressed her support is worth noting, for it illustrates her ability to translate external policy into locally acceptable terms. One feature of Gamo Highland social organization is the ability of prominent highland men to change local custom by so ordering in their wills before death. Chimate emphasized in her account of King Mijola's death that he had left land to his daughters and that her husband Masa before being led to the firing squad had said, "Let my sons and daughters divide my land equally. If my sons won't give my daughters land, let it be taboo for them. And let it be taboo for the people of Dita if they do not share land equally between sons and daughters." By using the words of Dita's former kings rather than her own words, yet repeating these words often, Chimate kept up pressure for change. Such change did not automatically follow from a deathbed will and indeed had not occurred in land tenure despite Chimate's support. Some changes might be accepted with alacrity. In Dorze it took only a few years to institute a dying elder's command that Dorze men need no longer go barefoot at funerals, because their feet were soft from living in cities. Other customs might not be altered until community members became convinced that indeed they had broken a taboo.

The notion of taboo, or *gome*, was central to Gamo Highland thought and social interactions. Chimate could not have been accepted by the Dita people as a full participant in community affairs without a thorough understanding of gome. Every aspect of local politics was colored by gome, from the rules of mediation to the imposition of sanctions.

In Dita the quality of personal relationships assumed great importance for economic survival. This importance is difficult to imagine for those of us living in highly monetized societies with a complex division of labor. The Dita farmers were dependent on local conditions and relationships. During my first visit to Chimate, a man whose wife had left him because he had impregnated a servant woman sought mediation. His wife had abandoned their young infant to his care. What was at stake was whether the baby would live or die, whether there would be enough labor to till his farmland, and whether the man would even eat. The man, like other farmers, had very little cash income. Moreover, there was very little that cash could purchase. Dita had no restaurants; cooked food could not be bought. Lacking the labor of a wife, a man could count on the help of his neighbors only if he had maintained good relations with them. He might not be able to find a wet nurse, milk was scarce and very expensive, and the child's survival would have depended on finding a woman to move into his household as a second wife or servant.

In Dita, access to land depended on father-son and neighbor-neighbor relationships, not on money. Land was transferred primarily through inheritance, but any son could be disinherited if he displeased his father. Even if land were sold, it had to be offered first to one of the people owning adjacent fields and that person might be chosen on the strength of a good relationship.

Furthermore, all the kinds of help that aid in survival could be refused to someone who had offended the community. After this person had officially been pronounced *hilo* by a local assembly of elders, ostracism began. If the person's cooking fire went out, no one would share a live coal to start the fire again. If his house was burning down, no one would help put out the fire or provide housing after it had burned.*

Mediation of quarrels among people therefore was very serious business in Dita, and skilled mediators like Chimate were constantly sought out. Her role was broader than that of simple mediation. Through her cautionary tales and outright lectures on proper behavior, she was one of the moral arbiters of the community, reminding people how they should behave toward one another.

The way the people of Dita thought about and acted upon their mutual interdependence was strongly colored by the notion of gome. Poverty, infertility, illness, death, epidemics, drought—all these could be caused by an infraction of gome. The taboos numbered in the hundreds; some, but not all, prescribed proper forms of social behavior. It was gome to have intercourse outside marriage, to allow blood from a cut finger to fall into food, to bear false witness, to marry within one's own clan, to kill a certain kind

---

*At the end of the preceding chapter, a man proposes that people who have not come to harvest Chimate's barley be shunned, that is, made hilo.

of snake. There were so many taboos that everyone broke them from time to time, often taking a risk knowingly. Only after misfortune fell would the search for the cause begin with the help of the local experts in divination. Public confession of one's misdeed was necessary, followed by a sacrifice to end that particular taboo. If misfortune persisted, the search for further infractions of taboo continued.

Throughout the Gamo Highland, gome helped motivate people to conform to certain standards of conduct. Every serious illness led to a review of past behavior and relationships. In order to save a dying child, a parent might be required to make peace with a cherished enemy or inform the community of an act of adultery.

One result of the belief in gome was a pragmatic and flexible approach to human relationships. A second result was the moral vindication of success and power. To survive was a sign of proper conduct. This interpretation of events gave the living a sense of self-confidence about their activities. For the Dorze weavers and traders, gome may have acted as a kind of Protestant work ethic, encouraging economic innovation.

Chimate illustrates gome in the following narrative. She describes the normal course of events, including the initial indignation and refusal to forgive on the part of the person wronged. While living with her I had occasion to observe just how faithfully she followed this cultural script when she herself had been wronged.

~

After a young man marries he knows gome; before he marries he does not know gome. If his child doesn't grow, if the child dies, if he doesn't have enough money to celebrate with his friends, if he doesn't have enough money to buy clothes for his family, he thinks, "Is there gome? What kind of gome?" and he goes to the diviner's house. He asks the diviner, "Why has thus-and-so happened to me?"

"If you have done something bad when you were young such as stabbing people's animals, if you have slept with someone on your father's bed, if you have sat on your wife's father's bed, if you have killed people's animals, confess!"

"Yes. I have taken someone's property."

"What did you do with it?"

"I kept quiet about taking this thing, and that thing, and that thing."

Next the man may confess, "On my father's land, on the earth belonging to my father, I had intercourse with a woman."

"Go to the *woga's* house.* Go to your father and tell him, go to your elder brother and tell him. After they have forgiven you, your children will grow, and you will be rich in coffee. Confess! When you have confessed, kill a sheep and bring its intestines here for me to see. I will look at the intestines and tell you if the gome is finished."

"Okay," says the man. He leaves, and to finish gome finds two elders or three elders and goes with them to his father's house.

"What is this?" his father asks.

"I did such and such when I was small, I did thus and so and thus and so."

"Woi! You slept with a woman on my land?"

"Yes."

"In my house?"

"Yes."

"Did you do bad things?"

"Yes."

"Get out of my house! Don't speak to me! Get out! Get out! Get out!"

The neighbors say, "Listen to us. Settle this quarrel!"

"And just how am I to forgive this? I refuse," the father says. "Didn't he confess he slept with a woman on my land?"

"Yes, he did."

"I will not forgive him. Did he confess before that he had slept with a woman? No, only after it has become gome for him."

The neighbors reply, "No, he did not confess. He had a problem, went to the diviner's house, and now needs to kill a sheep. But when he says '*Wog*'† to you, who are you to refuse pardon? That is gome."

"I refuse because he did bad things on my land. He took my sheep. He had intercourse in my house. He had intercourse on my land and spoiled it. Do you refuse to admit that he did these things?"

"He did them. Stop this! Listen to our laws! This has now become taboo for you," say the people, who have looked in the meantime at the sheep's intestines.

---

*The woga is the man who knows local customs well.

†That is, when the son invokes tradition and asks his father to forgive him, the father should do so.

"Is that the case?" asks the father.

"Yes. You must send an elder who is of your age to your son to ask his forgiveness, saying on your behalf, 'When you came, I refused you, now it is gome for me. Come back, and go with me to the house of the man who knows our customs, go with me to Kanko's house.'"

"All right," the son says, and comes to his father's house, and they consult the wise man.

The wise man says, "You spoiled your father's land. If you want to end the gome, give him a sheep to sacrifice."

The boy gives his father *edha,* a fine. If his father slaughters sheep to end gome, the boy gives a sheep, and if his father throws honey to end gome, the boy gives honey. Seven elders are invited to the father's house. They say seven times, "The boy is wrong." They say, "Eat together, drink together, let gome not enter here." The sheep is sacrificed, and the gome finishes.

&

Chimate lived her life in the belief that the two worlds of Gamo Highland culture and Amhara culture could coexist. Like many other highlanders, including those who had become priests of the Ethiopian Orthodox Christian Church, Chimate experienced no contradiction between her Christianity and her use of gome to explain and manipulate the world around her. She referred disputes both to the Dita elders and assemblies and to the Ethiopian courts. As an agent of social change, she was selective in the changes she advocated, and she was fiercely attached to Gamo Highland institutions such as the kingship her husband and father-in-law had held.

The various roles Chimate played were not sharply demarcated by time and place, as such roles tend to be in more modernized societies. On the morning of the harvest she had simultaneously been a householder organizing the day's first activities of food preparation and livestock tending and a government representative discussing a serious crime with people who had come to meet by her compound. She then had gone to a funeral, kneeling like any highlander in front of the bereaved, crying out and beating her breast. As she moved to the sidelines, she was caught up in discussions with various people. Funerals were key times to share information and lobby for one's special interests because all adults of the community were expected to attend and because funerals occurred so frequently. Later at the harvest Chimate was a householder, a balabat for whom the men showed respect by turning out in force and by working for a reduced fee, and a Dita elder sitting side by side with other elders to hear complaints.

Kinswoman, tax collection supervisor, local historian, householder, moral arbiter, Christian, believer in gome, mediator, road construction supervisor, godmother, Ethiopian citizen, Gamo Highland citizen, advocate of education and of the right of her one surviving son to be Dita's king— Chimate was all of these. In 1971 she tried, and failed, to give up her role as acting balabat. In 1973 her career was flourishing as never before and the pace of change within Dita had quickened. By then the revolution was just one year away, and Chimate's life was on the brink of yet another transformation.

10   Chimate and *Gome*

I won't open my door to you! . . . When Seyum
caught you, did you scream for help? Many people
live there and could have stopped him. No, you
brought gome on our house!

∼

After Chimate and I moved to her new compound, our household consisted of nine people. Three were linked to me—my assistant, Gida, an elderly woman named Balaye's Mother whom Chimate had asked me to hire as my cook, and a little girl who aided Balaye's Mother. With Chimate were two granddaughters, the twelve-year-old Nigatu and two-year-old Katse, and two servant women, the aging Wara's Mother and the teenaged, flighty Tije. These two servants still spent much of their time in Chimate's former household, helping Wombara and Seyum, and slept there at night.

Only two days remained in January. Most of the household was away. In a field near Chimate's compound, two women and three children harvested barley. A boy returning from market walked the path below, a basket turned upside down on his head, another basket filled with grain dangling from one hand, and a black lamb tucked under his arm. I sat typing information about Dita history into my field notes. Gida had the tape recorder and was playing and replaying a funeral song, trying to transcribe the words. A man whose toe I had just bandaged was helping him.

In the cookhouse Balaye's Mother was baking *injera* bread, a northern Ethiopian dish she would serve that night with a spicy meat sauce made from the lamb someone had just sold us. Flames fanned out in a blazing halo around a clay plate balanced over the fire. The bread she pulled from the griddle looked like an oversized pancake two feet across. Dropping it on a tray, she dipped out more fermented batter—it was made from teff, a grain first domesticated in Ethiopia—and began again.

Chimate, Gida, and I ate together that evening. While the others took the remaining food to the cookhouse for their meal, Chimate started to tell us a story. "I was once falsely accused of arranging a theft!" Her expression was amused rather than indignant. "I was staying in a certain man's house in Chencha for the night. . . ." Loud crying from the cookhouse interrupted Chimate. It was little Katse.

Chimate and Nigatu executed a familiar maneuver. Chimate called out, "Nigatu!"

"Yes!"

"Do I hear someone crying over there? Is somebody making trouble?"

Katse's crying stopped abruptly. Nigatu called back heartily, "Nobody's here. Nobody's crying." And indeed, Katse remained silent, allowing Chimate to continue her story.

～

I was staying in a certain man's house in Chencha for the night. I had brought a teenaged girl with me, a girl about Tije's age. I was tired and lay down at nightfall. I was tired and before I slept the girl sat near me and washed my feet and then lay down also. I had taken off my trousers, which I had worn while riding my mule. Into the trousers I had tied an old silver thaler, a big heavy Maria Theresa thaler. The woman servant of the man said, "Buy us food for dinner."

The man said, "You're a stranger, don't buy food. You've just arrived."

I tied the money into my trousers; I was very tired. The servant of the man was spinning cotton by the fire. I was lying on a bed. The girl was lying near my feet. She was scratching my body where the fleas bite me. Then we all fell asleep.

Without our knowing it, a hole opened by our feet and a thief came into the house. The house was a rich man's house. The thief had dug a hole and entered. Slowly, the thief entered near our feet, digging and entering.

I awoke and called to the girl. "Yes," she answered.

"Get up and help me. I want to go out to urinate," I said.

She got up and when she stood up she fell into the hole. She screamed, "Wi-oo-oo! My Mother, I'm in a hole!"

"What hole? What hole?"

"I'm in a hole!"

The servant was sleeping near the fire pit. She didn't sleep with the man.

She tied some pieces of wood together and lit a torch from the coals of the fire and began shouting, "Woo, woo, woo, woo, woo!" The man kept crying, "My guns! My guns! My guns!"

His gun was gone from above his bed. His pistol was gone. The spun cotton and some other things were gone. Some newly washed clothes which had been left hanging in the house to dry were gone. The new buluko cloth I had brought as a gift to the subprovincial governor was gone. I had bought it for twenty thalers to give him as a gift. We shouted and shouted and the neighbors came out in the night to see what was the matter. The man was waving a torch and shouting, "My guns! My guns!"

I thought, "Maybe if I hadn't come to his house this wouldn't have happened." What could I do? I wished I hadn't come. The man was crying, "Yi-yi-yi-yi-yi-yi-yi!" crying and crying for all he had lost.

In the morning I learned that the thief had also taken my trousers. The man said, "The thief entered near your bed. Did you invite someone in to steal? Who came with you?"

I was young. I was beautiful. The man thought someone had come to sleep with me and had taken things as he left.

"If a man wanted me, why wouldn't he come before I slept? He wouldn't dig a hole under my bed! Am I a slave? Would someone dig a hole under me in order to get me? God knows what happened!"

They agreed to use me and my girl as witnesses. I stayed there for a week mourning for the loss and then I heard that in Dita some buluko cloths were stolen from my house, and I went home.

Later, the police called me as a witness. They took me into a dark room to ask me questions. They closed the door. One man, a captain, was sitting there. The man had told the captain he had lost his property plus a hundred dollars.

The captain said, "Probably you know who the thief is. Isn't it impossible you couldn't have seen him? He entered under your feet. He entered at the foot of your bed, the man tells me. Be sure to tell everything you know!"

"Me? I don't know anything. I came to stay in a relative's house, a man who is said to be a good man. I came to stay there and for nothing else. I was tired, and I lay down. When I am lying down I have a habit of sleeping. A girl came with me to wash my feet. I brought her with me. We had drunk a lot of beer, good beer. In his house we drank a lot of beer and I awoke in the night and needed to urinate. I awakened the girl to tell her I wanted to go outside."

I told them about what happened then. I explained, "That man whose guns had been stolen was thinking only about 'My guns, my guns!' but my trousers which had been at the foot of the bed were stolen too. What! My trousers stolen! But I didn't say anything to anyone."

"Didn't you see the guns up there on the wall?" the policeman asked.

"When I was staying in the middle of the house, and the man was sleeping behind a partition on his bed, just how would I see the guns hanging over his bed? As my heart beats, I didn't look closely at the things in his house, as my heart beats! When the man called out, 'My guns, my guns,' I learned about his guns."

They had put the girl who was with me in prison. She was just the age for marrying. I said, "I want to see what happens to her now."

She came and witnessed, "I was called by My Mother and I got up and fell in the hole."

"You fell in the hole?"

"Yes. I screamed. I don't know anything else."

We were set free. The man said, "She brought someone to steal my things in order to share them with him."

I said to the policeman, "Ay-ee! If my friend came to steal your guns, would he come through a hole in the ground? Why not come riding to your door? And how would he know to dig a hole under the bed which you chose for me?"

The man acted very badly. The policeman said, "Stop! Don't bother her! She witnessed with her own breath. Don't bother her!" The policeman became very angry.

~

"After that I refused to look at or greet the man," Chimate concluded. She had enjoyed our surprise and amusement at her strange experience, and now she added wryly, "Ay! I avoided him! That kind of man I wouldn't look in the face a second time." She stood up slowly and, as she went to the cookhouse to sleep, turned toward us a final time. "I wouldn't greet him, and now he is dead."

Balaye's Mother soon joined Gida and me, and we barred the door and sat on cushions around the fire. Gida and Balaye's Mother began a rapid discussion that I couldn't follow. I sat and watched their gestures and faces.

Balaye's Mother stood about four and a half feet tall. She was at least seventy-five years old. Her face was one of the most extraordinary I have ever seen. To a delicate oval, nature had added two huge and beautifully sculpted ears and an enormous bulbous nose. She looked like a mask of comedy despite a perpetually sad expression lingering in her eyes.

She had explained that sadness to me. "I have only one son, Balaye. He's in the army and I almost never see him. The girl I have with me was given to me by her parents to work for me."

She had paused, looking so unhappy that all I could bring myself to say was a sympathetic "Mmmm." As I watched her quietly, she burst out, "I bore nine children, nine children, and eight of them died! Other women have families, other women have grandchildren, I have none! I held my babies and they burned my heart, I loved them so!" Tears slid down her cheeks. "Eight babies. Eight babies."

This evening Balaye's Mother seemed almost cheerful as she talked. Gida, the earnest young student, was arguing with her, poking at the fire as he talked. Then we heard a familiar cry from outdoors. "My Mother, bear witness! Gene! Gene!" It was a woman's voice.

Gida opened our door and looked out. "It's Wara's Mother," he said in surprise. "She's come from the other household." The door of the cookhouse opened and Wara's Mother went inside. On our doorsill Gida stood listening until an attack of laughter made him step inside and slam the door shut. He sat on the floor, trying to stifle any sounds that might carry the twelve feet to the cookhouse. Loud snorts escaped him. "It's Seyum!" he choked out. "Seyum—slept—with—Tije," here he succumbed for a moment, "in—the—*cowshed!*"

Balaye's Mother and I covered our mouths with our hands and began laughing, too. Gida joined us by the fire, almost out of control, laughing with adolescent excitement. When he calmed down he whispered, his eyes bright, "Seyum was sitting in the cowshed tonight and Tije brought him his food there. He caught her and had intercourse with her. Wara's Mother sleeps every night in the cowshed; she came in and found them. She says she'll never sleep there again!"

Chimate's voice reached us. "It's gome. It's gome, bad gome. My cow stays in that house! Her milk will dry up! My sheep are down there! Woi! Woi! Woi!" Then she made a characteristic change of emotion, standing back and observing herself humorously for a moment. In a penetrating tone guaranteed to be heard in our house, she said, "What must Judy be thinking about us? How Judy must be laughing at us!"

"My Mother, My Mother, give me shelter!" It was Tije's voice.

"I won't open my door to you!" Chimate shouted. "I don't want to see you ever again! When Seyum caught you, did you scream for help? Many people live there and could have stopped him. No, you brought gome on our house! I won't give you any help!"

By breaking the rule of gome that forbids intercourse outside marriage, Seyum had put himself and others associated with him in danger. Illness, a broken leg, poverty, even death might now befall not only the pair at fault, but also Wombara, because the cowshed belonged to him, and Wara's Mother, because the bed they used was hers. Chimate's animals were also in danger, especially the cow, which so to speak had witnessed the act.

Balaye's Mother began whispering. "Seyum is just like his father. When Amano was dying, he killed many sheep for gome. 'Is gome killing me?' he would wonder, and sacrifice a sheep. The diviner would look at the sheep's intestines and say, 'There is gome. There is gome of fornication. Confess!'

"Amano would confess, 'I had intercourse illicitly with so-and-so.' Then he would kill another sheep to finish the gome. The diviner would look at the sheep's intestines and say, 'Yes, the gome you confessed is finished, but there is more. What else have you done?' 'I slept with so-and-so.'

"On and on this went. Amano killed many sheep before he died. He confessed to things no one had suspected; he confessed that he had stabbed and killed Bele's mule. But he didn't confess everything and gome killed him."

The next morning Sando, our neighbor, told me, "Tije spent the night in my house, but she left before my wife and I woke up. Maybe she went to live with her sister." We never saw her again.

Later in the morning Chimate and I sat and talked. She had just returned from an attempt to confront Seyum. His door had been barred and he had pretended to be asleep. "All the young people break the rules of gome and have intercourse when they shouldn't!" Chimate told me indignantly. "Only married people should sleep together. If you commit adultery, it can make the rain fall without stopping for many days.

"In the past, children born out of wedlock were never allowed to remain in Dita. In the nighttime, such a baby would be abandoned in the forest where no one would see. But now people keep such children; they go to town where they think gome will not affect them. I think it's good not to kill children. It was our own flesh we threw away in the forest. Can killing ever be good?"

Chimate was growing calmer as she talked. Forgetting Seyum for the moment, Chimate continued, "In the past when girls were born they were buried alive. People said, 'I won't raise a girl,' and buried them. People didn't like girls. 'If there are many girls, what good will they bring us? They will leave for their husband's houses,' they would say, killing them.

"But rules of gome can change. Killing girls became gome and women began to inherit their father's lands." Here Chimate stated the exception, not the rule; in general, women were still discriminated against. Chimate went on to admit, "One of my daughters was born out of marriage. Ababe. She was born out of lawful marriage. Even now she doesn't enter our house. Outside, outside, outside Dita she was raised because I couldn't raise her. I gave her to someone whom I hired."

"You were forced to give her away?" I asked, stopping myself from pointing out the parallel with Seyum.

"If I hadn't abandoned her, the people of Dita would not have allowed me to enter Dita again," Chimate replied. "I gave money to the person who raised her to feed my daughter. You know, gome sometimes affects Amhara people as well as Gamo people," Chimate said reflectively, changing the subject. She started to tell me about Nuguse Seyum, an Amhara man who had been in the Italian prison with her husband, Masa.

~

Nuguse Seyum was in prison with Masa and heard Masa's will, but he did not come to us and repeat the will as Masa had asked. "I'm an Amhara, I won't speak," said Nuguse Seyum, and left it, left it, left it.

Nuguse was the only one who did not speak. Three years later, he became poor. He became ill. It was gome for him because he did not tell the will. Before that he had taken cases to court and never lost them. Now everything was lost to him.

It was the period when the outlaws ruled. Each outlaw took things from the people as a tax, and everywhere they traveled they carried guns. But Nuguse, who was also an Amhara like the outlaws, did not profit during this time. He went to the house of a *maro*, a seer, to find out what was wrong.

"Men weaker than I am are able to rob people. Men the same age as I am manage to steal. They take cows, clothes, and money. I go with other men but I don't get anything. Why don't I get things too? Wo-o-i! I will take my gun and kill myself! I'm sorry I wasn't killed with my friends in battle!"

He went to the seer's house; she was a woman. The woman danced because her *ayana* spirit rode her* and said, "If I tell you your gome and make you rich like your friends, what will you give me?"

Said Nuguse, "I will give you a buluko cloth big enough to reach from your head to your feet. I will give you a buluko."

She said, "Why didn't you tell the message of the black man? Why didn't you tell the message of the black man?"

"What black man?"

"A black man called a king. A king who put a silver ring on his finger, or a gold ring. On a bad day he spoke to you. Why did you run away?" Thus she spoke.

Quietly Nuguse Seyum thought, thought, thought, thought, thought, thought, and finally understood. Standing up he cried out like a woman, "Li-li-li-li-li! I know now! I will give you the buluko. It's right, the black man spoke to me. Thank you, thank you, thank you, thank you!"

"Who was that man?"

"The Dita king who died was in jail with me. It has been three years since he died and told me his will, but I haven't spoken."

She advised, "Go to his wife and children and speak to them and tell them what Masa said before he died."

Quickly, he left and called some of our neighbors without going back to his own home. They told me, "An Amhara has come!"

I invited him, "Drink some beer in my house."

"I won't drink it. I forgot to tell you what our master said and it has become gome for me. I don't take things like other men, I don't eat other people's cattle. I have become poor. Gome is hurting me. That's why I came."

"Just what are you talking about?"

"When Masa died, this, this, this, and this he told me, saying I should be sure to speak to you, in case the other men did not. He said, 'Let it be gome if you don't do this.' And I have not spoken and now it is gome for me. Now I am speaking. Please forgive me!"

I said, "The other three men have spoken to us. We have heard his will. Let his children grow! We have had no problems; the three men told us his will."

"I'm the only one left. It is gome for me."

---

*The ayana spirit possession cult is discussed in chapter 14.

"May the gome leave you!"

"So be it," he said, and left and went straight out and stole seven cows and returned. He returned and spoke to us, asking our pardon again. One cow he exchanged for a buluko and gave it to the woman seer. The other cows he then took to his home. After that, he took people's animals and clothes and money and became very rich during the period when the outlaws were in power. He stole clothes, he stole animals, he stole money, he stole sheep. It had been gome for him, and he asked our pardon. We pardoned him. He became very rich after that and died just this year.

~

While Chimate had been speaking, her friend Halaka Halke had entered. Through his help she had survived the period of Italian occupation. It was he who had advised her to marry a powerful man, and she had complied. He was old now, but almost every morning I saw him striding past our compound as we were getting up, a crook-necked axe or a cultivating hoe over his shoulder. With his massive balding head, skeptical gaze, and coarse querulous voice, he was an imposing man.

Halaka Halke exchanged a few words of greeting with Chimate, then told her, "I've been to see Seyum's Mother. She will bring Seyum here tomorrow morning to beg your forgiveness."

"I don't want any mediation with Seyum!" she cried. "My cow gives good milk. It's hard to find a good cow. Now her milk will dry up!"

"Stop that! Stop now!" Halaka Halke shouted at her. "You're putting yourself in the wrong, talking like that!" He rose in disgust and went outside, where he worked for the rest of the day building Chimate's fence.

Early the next morning Halaka Halke and Chimate went to a child's funeral. After they had left, Seyum appeared with his mother and a close kinsman named Unka. Feisty and disrespectful, Unka had probably been invited to bolster Seyum's morale. They sat in the cookhouse waiting for Chimate to return, and when she did so, Seyum hastily left and went to sit alone in the reception house.

Only after Nigatu had served coffee and the second cups were being poured did Seyum reappear. He sat down, head lowered, and stared at the floor. Eventually Halaka Halke began a speech. "Anything can happen in this life," he said, "for man is capable of doing anything. But anything that man does can be finished with the sacrifice of a sheep. Here we have Seyum, who slept with his godsister. He confesses this deed and asks you"—here he addressed Chimate—"to forgive him. When you forgive him, we can go to the woga's house. He will tell us what sacrifice must be made to end the gome."

Seyum's Mother got up and bowed low before Chimate. "Seyum is in the wrong," she said. "You built the houses for the boys. You had the fences woven. You pay the taxes for them. You till their fields and do not ask for money from them. Seyum is in the wrong. He made gome for your animals and for Wombara's house."

Chimate replied indirectly, choosing this moment to air a grievance before she spoke about Seyum. "Wombara decided to take a wife this month, but he didn't tell me anything about it. A week ago he told Wara's Mother to prepare barley for porridge, and she told me about his request. I said, 'All right, go ahead and prepare it. If Wombara asks me to find him a wife, I can find one, but if he doesn't, I cannot stop him from finding one for himself. But if he marries, I won't take coffee again in his house.' But after all that, he didn't marry."

She paused. No one took up this topic of conversation but waited, watching her. She continued, "All three boys"—she meant Kebede, Seyum, and Wombara—"do not work but go to market and get drunk. When someone builds a house, they don't help, they don't carry bamboo. They don't harvest grain. They don't till the fields. They don't plant the fields. They carry nothing on their backs or their heads.

"I was living in Wombara's house but the boys insulted me and made the house bad. I want to keep my dignity; I moved here. Their father, Amano, never asked me to give him the household furnishings, though he could have asked, but Wombara and Seyum have asked for them all from me and, except for one box, I have left them all in their compound.

"In the past, their compound was very beautiful. Now the fences are falling down and aren't being repaired. They even used one house for firewood! I don't care if they destroy that place completely! I don't even care if they destroy my new home!" Chimate looked angrily around the room, paused briefly, and then went on.

"I used some of their false banana plants while I was living with them, but I replanted them. The moles have eaten some. Except for those plants, I didn't use anything that belonged to Seyum and Wombara.

"If Seyum dies, it's his gome that will kill him. What he did is gome for him, not for me. Now Wara's Mother is going to leave his compound.

The girl, Tije, has already left. Who will prepare food for Seyum and Wombara? Wara's Mother is saying, 'Tomorrow I will leave.' Yesterday she did not sleep on her bed, but on the floor beside it, by the animals.

"If Seyum slept with Tije, tomorrow when his sister grows up, he will sleep with his sister, too!" Chimate concluded bitterly.

Seyum's Mother and Unka stood up. Bowing before Chimate, Seyum's Mother said, "You are *tsilo*, you are in the right."

Everyone stood up. Chimate remained sitting, a sign that she was not ready to forgive Seyum.

"You are tsilo," Unka said.

"Seyum confesses he's in the wrong," Seyum's Mother said in a pleading tone of voice.

Chimate turned her face to the wall. Halaka Halke admonished her, "When forgiveness is asked, it should be granted. It is gome to refuse!"

Seyum's Mother gave her son a push. In a faint voice, Seyum said, "I'm in the wrong."

Chimate kept her head turned. Everyone pleaded with her; Halaka Halke became quite stern. Chimate reluctantly said, "It is finished."

She stood up. Seyum and his mother bowed before her, heads drooping. Everyone said, "Forgive him!"

"I have forgiven you," she said to Seyum.

"I have been forgiven," he replied.

"I have forgiven you."

"I have been forgiven."

"I have forgiven you."

"I have been forgiven."

We all chorused, "We have witnessed." Everyone sat down. Chimate turned to Halaka Halke. "How should Seyum finish the gome?" she asked.

"I don't know," he replied. "We must go to Kanko, the woga, and ask him."

I never saw the sacrifice of a sheep, for I left Dita the next day and went to Dorze. By the time I returned ten days later, the saga of Seyum had taken a new turn. Gida told me, "While you were gone, Seyum, Unka, and Kebede killed one of Chimate's sheep! She looked for it for a whole day before someone told her the truth. She went to the new church and vowed to God, 'If you kill the person who killed my sheep, I will give you a sheep!' and then she went to Seyum's cookhouse, broke the lock, took out all the food that belonged to her, and brought it up here."

At first, Seyum had been unrepentant. Then, discovering a sore on his penis and interpreting this as the result of gome, he had petitioned Chimate so desperately for forgiveness that at last she had pardoned him once again.

I found Seyum living in Chimate's household, using penicillin powder from my medicine kit on his sore. When it seemed to heal but then recurred, I gave him money and sent him to the Chencha hospital for treatment.

As for Seyum's accomplices, eventually they, too, begged Chimate's forgiveness. They lay down on the floor and kissed Chimate's feet in a most humble way, but I doubted as I watched the young men of Chimate's family if things would stay quiet for long.

Chimate mediates a case.

Chimate addresses
the males-only
assembly of elders.

Her face animated,
Chimate stands to
the side of the
assembly of elders
and mediates a case
with a disputant.
(right and facing
page)

Carrying a house to replace one that burned down.

11   Mediation

There is no false banana for me! There is no bamboo!
I walk the roads a pauper! My brothers use the
inheritance! I have nothing!

~

The first morning I spent in Chimate's household, people waited for her
and served up their disputes with the first coffee of the day. Men and women
stopped her as she walked the paths of Dita and sought her in the marketplace. When I brought her to Addis Abeba in 1973, the Dita weavers and their
families rushed to her with their problems and kept her busy for several
days. She seemed to have a reputation for untying difficult knots.

Such a reputation was earned under critical eyes. Mediation was a constant part of life in Dita. Every Dita man and woman played the role of mediator from time to time, if only among immediate neighbors. The Dita
people preferred to settle disputes among themselves with a minimum of
governmental interference. Anyone turning first to the Ethiopian courts and
not to Dita mediators would be reprimanded and fined by the Dita assembly of elders, or sometimes penalized by being ostracized. For its part the
government had no interest in urging the people to use expensive court
services, except in the case of serious crimes such as murder. Generally,
people settled their disputes within their own neighborhoods, appealing
sequentially to Chimate, to the Dita assembly which met twice a week on
market days, and finally to the Ethiopian courts if no agreement had been
reached.

Personal relationships were important for survival in an immediate and
obvious sense. Your neighbor was not only your kin or friend but also your
fire brigade and labor source. The belief in gome added further urgency to
these relationships, for wrong conduct might bring about a drought, a
smallpox epidemic, or a rain that fell continuously until the crops were

ruined. At the same time, this sense of intense mutual interdependence could both cause friction among people and motivate them to settle any quarrels that arose.

Every Dita child grew up learning how to mediate disputes, watching from the sidelines as Katse and Nigatu did while Halaka Halke persuaded Chimate to forgive Seyum. As a young adult, each man and woman could act as a chima, or elder, among neighbors and kin of the same age. Those who showed special talent for the role would be called upon with increasing frequency over the years to act as mediators. Chimate described the learning process.

~

Sitting, watching, hearing falsehood and truth spoken, doing this many times—that is how one learns to mediate a quarrel. To mediate a quarrel, concerned people bring the disputants together in the house of one of the persons involved. As we sit there, we say, "This one is in the right, this one is in the wrong." Gathering everyone and sitting down, we repeat what each disputant has said. We observe the behavior of each person and from this we can tell who is tsilo, right, and who is *wordo,* wrong.

To make an agreement, "So-and-so, come here. This person fought with that person. Let us mediate their quarrel." Thus speaking, then listening to the problem, we decide that this one is wordo and that one is tsilo. This one made a mistake.

"Okay."

"Yes, all right."

The person admits the mistake. According to our country's tradition, he or she pays a penalty. We sit, examine each person, and mediate; then they kiss one another on the cheek. That is how we end disputes.

~

Chimate earnestly practiced Dita techniques of mediation. Usually she worked as part of a team rather than alone. Halaka Halke, for example, might join her, or she might press someone who was passing by into service. She mediated cases only in the presence of witnesses, responsible community members who observed and remembered what happened, substitutes for the written records used in the courts. Chimate believed it was gome to refuse mediation, gome to be a false witness. She would explain,

"When a pardon is asked, if you refuse it is gome. People do not refuse such a request. And it is gome to receive a fine when a pardon has been asked."

As a woman with a powerful position in the community, Chimate was able to offer refuge to women involved in marital disputes. The pregnant servant woman returning to Dita to bear her baby had come to live with Chimate. Other women over the years had turned to Chimate, often helping with the household work, sleeping in the cookhouse, and staying until divorced or reconciled with their husbands. "I don't always succeed in settling quarrels between husband and wife," Chimate admitted to me, and proceeded to tell about one of her failures and one of her successes.

∾

Once a man named Sobo and his wife quarreled. She had given birth to one child. She said, "I won't remain with you. I won't stay in this house!" and came to stay with me.

"Stop, reach an agreement with your husband. Stop, be reconciled with him."

"No, no. I won't go back to him."

I said to him, "Since she doesn't want to reach an agreement with you, why not divorce her?"

"I won't divorce her! I love her very much! I would never divorce her!"

"I don't want him!" she said, although he begged and begged her to return. For about fifteen days she stayed in my compound. I asked her, "Just what is it you want?"

"Let him give me clothes to wear. I came from my father's house with many clothes!"

He said, "I won't give you clothes. You refused to stay with me, and because of that, I'll give you nothing."

I said, "If we called a group of elders and asked their opinion, would you abide by their decision?"

"All right."

"She gave birth to a daughter," said the elders. "It is true that he asked her to return, but she refused to stay with him. Give her one buluko cloth. She brought three buluko from her father's house, and you should give her one. She gave birth to a child."

"Okay," he said, and took an unsewn buluko and sent it to her to wear, and divorced her. "Marry someone else," he said.

"I will," she said, and left him and wore the cloth. Then she entered Ure's house. She was there for a long time, but then she left him too and went to Bonke. There she married and divorced someone else!

Sometimes I trick people in order to finish a quarrel. For example, a woman named Lembete was the wife of Nuguse. She gave birth to a daughter, yes, in his house she gave birth to a black-skinned little girl. He was a merchant and was away from home selling cloth. She took his radio, his gun, and clothes, and came to me and sat down in my house.

"What's happening? What do you want?" I asked her.

She said she wanted a divorce from her husband.

"He's good for the child!" I said. "Before you married him, you were having many problems, wandering from place to place. With God's help you married him. He gave you a child. Stop this! Stop this foolishness!"

"No, no, no, no, I don't want him!"

"Stay with him; it will be good for the child," I said, but she took the baby and went away.

Her husband came crying to my home. "She took everything from me! I want to make money in trading, but she took all my property! My radio, my clothes, she rolled up in a sheet and took away with her!"

He fell to the ground in front of her, but she still said, "I won't come back," even though he pleaded with her. I took her to Asefa's Mother's house and told her, "I will persuade him to give you a divorce and to give you money."

But I said this in order to trick her. I made her bring back the clothes and the radio. I told my scribe, Ketema, to write out a contract. In that contract her husband promised never to hit her again and to give her a new dress every year. Every year, a complete set of new clothes.

I brought her husband, Nuguse, there and took everything back from her and gave it to him. He signed the contract and she was satisfied. And to this day, the two of them live together. They are in Addis Abeba now. The daughter is still living with them.

~

As a mediator, Chimate was educating her people about the legal methods of the Ethiopian Empire when she used written contracts or cited laws from the legal code. She bridged two legal traditions, those of Dita and of Ethiopia. She knew what the interior of a courthouse was like, what a lawyer did, and how the courts functioned.

Chimate, at times, invoked Ethiopian law seriously; at other times she ridiculed it. She, like other Dita elders, tried to persuade people to use Dita custom first before turning to the courts. One day I saw her influence a man and a woman to accept her mediation by instructing her scribe to read out what he claimed to be the Ethiopian penalty: "Government law says you must pay five hundred dollars or spend five years in jail if your animals eat another person's crops." Another day she exclaimed, "You want a guarantor? Guarantor! Are there guarantors in our ancient laws, laws from the dawn of time?"

One tactic used in local mediation was simple delay. This was sometimes frustrating to me, for I could seldom follow a case from beginning to end. Chimate might ask that witnesses be brought to testify on another day. She might say that not enough people were present to witness the mediation. The introduction of written documents into an illiterate community was useful to her here. "I can't read that; come back another day." "We ought to write that down. Come back when one of my grandsons is here."

The cases brought to Chimate most often had to do with land. During my return visit to Ethiopia in 1973, I watched one stage of such a mediation. It was fascinating to watch as Chimate shifted ground, here invoking tradition, there claiming the backing of the district governor. She and this governor were on very good terms. He trusted her judgment, and when Dita people brought him disputes he often referred them back to Chimate, just as she herself often referred the disputants back to their own neighbors.

Unka, the kinsman who had come with Seyum for the mediation of Seyum and Chimate, had stopped by Chimate's compound to say hello. As we sat talking, we were interrupted by a young man who greeted Chimate respectfully, said hello to Seyum and me, and turned to Unka. "Please help me, Unka," he said. "Please go call my brothers to mediation here with Our Mother."

"Why do you need me, Hemo?" Unka asked.

"My brothers owe me my share of our father's land!" cried Hemo. "Seyum tried to call my eldest brother, Babo, to come to mediation. He gave my brother a paper but my brother refused to come!"

Chimate and Seyum joined Hemo in persuading Unka to help. Unka loved a good argument and resisted for some time but finally agreed and left with Hemo.

"Hemo wanted his inheritance," Chimate explained to me later when discussing the case with me. "He is the youngest son. He grew up in Addis Abeba. He left Addis after he was unable to learn how to weave well. He worked in Arbaminch as a coolie, carrying things for people, and he worked as a coolie in Dita, too. He has been working recently on the construction of our new primary school in Dita."

Hemo's position was a difficult one. In Dita most transactions in land and labor were nonmonetary, through inheritance and exchange. A project such as working on construction of a government building was very rare. Without land of his own, Hemo would be left to a life as an occasional laborer in Arbaminch and perhaps in Dorze.

When Hemo and Unka returned, they had Babo and Bulje, Hemo's older brothers, with them. The three brothers sat down in a row on a bench built into the wall, facing Chimate. Unka, Seyum, and I sat on the opposite side of the room, leaving Chimate alone in the middle by the fire.

Chimate immediately seized the initiative. "Why are you refusing to obey me, Babo?" she asked. "If someone summons you, do you make a joke of it?"

Babo objected, "I'm not making fun of you!"

And Bulje added, "If you tell us to come, don't we agree?"

"Well then, why didn't *you* come?" Chimate asked.

"Me?"

"You, yes, you."

Bulje explained, "Our neighbors came to us saying 'Stop your quarreling!' and as we were starting the mediation your letter arrived. We discussed the case, although we didn't reach an agreement, and I didn't come to you."

"Was Hemo with you?" Chimate asked.

"Yes," Bulje replied.

Turning toward Hemo, Chimate said, "Hemo, they say you were with them." Her voice held an implied question: if he had been so eager to receive his inheritance, why hadn't the matter been settled then?

"I didn't reach an agreement with them, My Mother," Hemo told her.

Babo spoke, blaming Hemo for the failure of the mediation with the neighbors. "'I won't go to mediation,' he said, and went somewhere else."

Hemo jumped up. Almost shouting, he cried, "The animals are in his hand! The money and the land are in his hand! I didn't get my share of the inheritance!"

Chimate asked in a steady, calm voice, "Bulje and Babo, didn't your father tell you to share with Hemo?"

Seyum spoke up; still in his teens, he was trying out the role of media-tor. "They say, 'He didn't take his share. He didn't ask for it.'" This tactic, allowing a neutral person to make a statement on behalf of another, some-times cooled tempers.

This time the tactic didn't work. Hemo continued passionately, "There is no false banana for me! There is no bamboo! I walk the roads a pauper! My brothers use the inheritance! I have nothing!"

"Didn't the elders tell you to share equally?" Chimate repeated.

"They did just that," Bulje agreed.

"What did they say?" Chimate prodded.

Hemo answered. "'Make an agreement with Bulje, divide the land. All three can eat from it.' Now I've spent a lot of money on this case! They should return the land to me!"

Everyone shouted at Hemo, "Stop it, Hemo! You're getting too angry!"

Chimate said incisively, "If you want to make an agreement, do so. 'Babo, give this amount to Hemo; Hemo, you take such and such,' this we will say." With an admonishing tone in her voice, she turned to Hemo. "On the day I sent the summons, Hemo, you took it and said, 'Yes, I'll make an agree-ment,' and kissed Babo's feet."

Bulje made two attempts to divert Chimate's attention. First, he made a brief claim that he had paid Hemo for his share of the land, a claim that he quickly dropped and did not refer to again. He then orated on the subject of "Hemo always insults me, saying that I wear old clothes."

Chimate ignored both attempts. When Bulje paused, she returned inexo-rably to the main question. "What's preventing you from dividing the land?"

Bulje, again evasive, retorted, "And where will I get the barley, beer, and liquor to give the neighbors when they witness this? And what about our other brother?" This fourth brother came up several times in the course of the mediation. He had probably been born in Addis Abeba, like Hemo, during a period when his father had been trying to make a living as a weaver there. Most Dita people, including Chimate, had never seen him.

"I've told you, Babo should bring him here. If you want him, bring him," Chimate told him firmly.

"Look here, My Mother!" Hemo exclaimed, impatient at the idea of postponing the mediation further.

Chimate, eyebrows raised, glared at him. "Stop that! I'm interpreting the law! Be respectful and don't say to me, 'Look here!'"

Babo said quietly, "Why doesn't Hemo just live and eat with us until our brother comes?"

Chimate turned from the three brothers toward Unka. Under the pretext of explaining the case to him, she began to invoke the authority of the district governor. "Unka, listen. Hemo didn't write his petition to me. He wrote it to the district governor. The governor stamped it and gave it to me, saying, 'You deal with this. I've stamped it. The paper is being sent to you. You can act as the lower *atsiba* court. Your grandsons can write for you. When you make your judgment, write it down and give it to me.'"

Acidly, Chimate continued, "With such a small case, what else should be done? 'Such a case will be easy to mediate. Bring the judgment to me!' 'Okay.' Saying that, I took the case. After I took the case from him, I had Seyum write out a paper summoning the brothers here to me."

I noted that even as Chimate was underpinning her authority with that of the Ethiopian government, she was using a Dita technique of mediation. Rather than make an assertion to the three brothers and lay it open to argument, she made it indirectly to another person. But now she returned to the attack.

"Bulje?" queried Chimate, looking directly at him.

"Yes!"

"Forget about the other brother; the eldest son can take his share and give it to him when he appears. Make an agreement here and now! Babo, Bulje, Hemo, I don't choose one of you and hurt him, another and help him. I'm speaking the law here. I like all of you. Am I not listening to all of you and speaking to all of you?"

She had convinced Babo, the quietest of the three. "You settle it!" he cried. "Let Hemo and Bulje go to court if they wish."

Chimate reiterated her point. "Listen, Babo. The men who came from Addis Abeba and spoke to Bulje didn't know the law." Here, obviously, she was addressing Bulje indirectly. "If you say that your neighbors in your district will take money from you, don't forget that in court they will take money, too. Hasn't Hemo spent some money on his petition? When you go to court, won't you spend money, too?"

Bulje broke in, convinced. "We'll spend a lot! I have problems with money. I can't go to court. I'll listen to you. On the day I spoke to the governor, our neighbor Era was there and said, 'Aren't you from the same father? Why are you writing to make a court case? Stop fighting! The neighbors aren't related to you. Let them judge!'"

Firmly, Chimate said, "Please listen to what your neighbors tell you."

All three brothers had their reservations. "Hemo isn't paying taxes," Bulje said. "I pay them, but he's always insulting me, and I can accuse him for this!"

"Bulje, listen to this," Chimate said. "He may insult you but the law won't stop him from getting his fair share of land."

Now Hemo spoke up. "I just want the land our father gave me! They're living in his house! They have refused to give me anything from the house! They're using up all the false banana plants!"

"If he wants false banana plants, why doesn't he pay tax?" Babo cried. "Pay tax! What's the reason for paying except to have the right to use the crops?"

Chimate ignored this new objection. "Listen to what I tell you. The law says to divide the land."

It seemed that Chimate, through persistent repetition and refusal to be diverted, had won her point. Babo and Bulje knelt on the floor before Chimate. "All right," they said together.

Chimate spoke sharply. "And is Hemo different from the rest? Hemo, you're bringing gome by not kneeling with your brothers!"

Hemo joined his brothers. Chimate spoke again. "The law tells you to divide the land. Without dividing it and putting up the boundary stones, you won't eat well."

The three brothers stood up. Bulje began talking of his other brother again, and Chimate suggested that Babo, the eldest, take the missing brother's share. They agreed. Then Hemo suggested that Chimate divide their land for them.

Chimate said she was unable to do this. "Only your neighbors know your land well, whether it produces lentils, wheat, barley, or false banana plants. The ones who know this are your neighbors. If you wish, I will send someone to witness and to write it all down, but you must pay him some money. If this is written down, your missing brother can see that you have taken his share temporarily."

A problem emerged. Hemo had recently called the neighbors to divide the land, but the other brothers had not come. The neighbors had left angrily. Now Babo insisted that Hemo call the neighbors again, and Hemo objected, afraid of their anger.

Chimate told Hemo, "You yourself should invite the neighbors." Turning to the others, she commented, "He was the one who did it without consulting us beforehand!"

"My Mother, live long and grow fat!" cried Babo.

"My Mother, the neighbors went back home insulted," objected Hemo.

"Well, finish this quarrel with them," Chimate recommended. "I'll give you someone from here to help divide the land. Wombara can go, and I'll send people like Era and Unka as witnesses. They won't favor one of you. If they do, they know it will be gome. Your leader will watch! Your balabat follows the law! Come to an agreement with the help of the neighbors! And don't be angry if they ask more money from you than usual. Just pay them."

Bulje now admitted, "I don't cooperate with the neighbors." He was being ostracized, they would not help him.

Hemo snapped, "Okay, okay, let my money be finished!" The situation was deteriorating.

"Stop, stop!" Chimate cried. "You can go to court after the land is divided, if you're not satisfied with the division."

"Whether I have money or not, you accuse me to Our Mother!" exclaimed Hemo, referring to Bulje's comments about his insulting words. "If you have witnesses, fine!"

Chimate said emphatically, "If he has crops, give them to him. If he has animals, return them."

"He doesn't even have five cents!" said Bulje loudly.

"I sowed crops, left them, and went away. He knows that!" cried Hemo.

"I'm not going to help either one of you, Bulje and Hemo!" Chimate cried, exasperated at last.

"My potatoes are gone!" Hemo blurted angrily.

"Don't talk like that to Our Mother!" Unka hissed at him fiercely. "If you were in the courthouse now, they would stop you!"

Seeing that Hemo and his brothers were growing increasingly irritable, Chimate diverted the course of the mediation. She dropped the matter of the land division for the day and turned to a quarrel between Seyum and Babo. This was a matter that could be settled quickly, so the encounter would end on a positive note.

Seyum described the incident in full. "When I came to the funeral, you were sitting at the edge of the field, by the fence by the cabbage. You weren't with the relatives of the dead person, so I approached you. I said, 'Come and take the paper!' and 'I won't come!' he replied." Seyum was now addressing the whole group. "The people told me to give the paper to him. 'By your father, I won't come,' he said." This was a deadly insult. "It's true! That's what he said! That's all that happened; because of this we fought."

Babo admitted, "Seyum is more tsilo, in the right, than I am because I insulted his father."

Looking at Seyum, Chimate added, "Seyum is also in the wrong for forcing you to come quickly."

"That's true, " admitted Seyum.

"You are in the right," Babo said to Seyum.

"Pardon one another!" Chimate commanded them.

"Pardon me, am I not the younger?" Seyum said.

"I pardon you," Babo replied.

"I am pardoned," Seyum answered.

"I pardon you."

"I am pardoned."

Now it was Babo's turn to request, "Pardon me."

"I pardon you."

"I am pardoned."

"I pardon you."

"I am pardoned," Babo finished.

"We have pardoned. We have pardoned," everyone else said. Before the topic of the land dispute could be discussed again, Unka said, "Open your tape recorder, Judy! Let them hear some Dita songs!"

I obliged, and after listening to a tape the brothers insisted that I record their singing. The results were ragged, but they listened with delight to the playback and left in a good mood.

A few days later, this is what Chimate told me about the end of the quarrel. "The brothers came to me again," she said. " 'The neighbors won't help us anymore!' they said. 'I can see why!' I replied. They begged me, 'Let old men of your choice divide the land.' "

" 'All right,' I replied. 'Let Kanda, Malka, and Kinfa divide the land among you. Give the work to them.' I called the three elders and, putting the land in the elders' hands, I mediated the quarrel among Bulje, Babo, and Hemo."

12   Factional Politics

*Wombara sent us to jail. He sent us to jail! . . . If you
had been asked, you wouldn't have sent us to jail!*

~

It was Saturday, a market day. Gida had returned from the marketplace in
a state of excitement. He told Chimate and me, "The police tried to arrest
Wombara this afternoon!"

"Was he drinking? Did he hit someone?" Chimate asked.

"No, the police were angry because the Dita people haven't brought bamboo to rebuild the police station. They came to Wombara to arrest him,"
Gida replied.

Chimate did not seem surprised. Jailing a balabat in order to pressure
the balabat's community into conformity was a common police tactic. Now
that she was trying to shift the work to Wombara, he was the target, as she
had been in the past.

"Wombara told the police, 'It's not my fault, don't take me. Take the
halakas. They're sitting with the elders. They're the ones who have refused
to build the police station!'"

Chimate's expression changed, and she cried angrily, "Wombara should
have gone! He is young and doesn't know how to do the work of balabat!"

The halakas were men who held executive and ritual responsibilities
within the Dita assembly of elders. They stayed in office for a year or two,
then retired and kept the title "halaka" for the rest of their lives. Three men
at a time held active office. The Dita people believed that the health and behavior of the active halakas directly affected the welfare of their community. Among the taboos these men should never violate was one against
spending the night outside Dita, as they would be forced to do if jailed.

"Wombara wrote down the names of the three halakas," Gida continued,
"and gave them to the police. All the Dita people who heard about this were

very upset. They told Wombara, 'Your grandmother would not have done this!' And they begged the policemen to let the halakas go. Even people from other communities pleaded with the police. The police started for Gulta with the halakas"—Gulta was a two- or three-hour walk away—"but they changed their minds and let them go."

"Wombara is wordo," observed Chimate, "he's in the wrong."

"Wombara apologized to the Dita people. He said he was wordo, but his voice was very angry."

"Unless you apologize from the heart, it doesn't mean anything," Chimate stated emphatically.

"After the halakas were freed, the police came and arrested Wombara after all and the two chikashums who work under him. Wombara is in the Gulta prison now."

Two men came to the door, two of the three wronged halakas. Each carried a walking stick made of brass and wood, and each wore a sheepskin on his back like a cloak. In the ear of one man, whose hair was very short, glinted an aluminum stud, a sign that he had killed an enemy in battle.

"Welcome, halakas," Chimate said, as we all rose respectfully from our seats. Gida took their walking sticks, carried them outside, and planted them upright in the ground; as halakas, they could not drive anything into the earth.

The man with the earring glared at Chimate, saying, "Wombara sent us to jail. He sent us to jail!"

The second man, his long hair streaming in all directions from his head, leaned forward in agreement. "If you had been asked, you wouldn't have sent us to jail! We don't want Wombara as our leader. We want you to be balabat."

The first man repeated, "Wombara sent us to jail!"

These complaints were heard many times during the following days. On Monday two policemen came to Chimate's compound. They sat stiffly in our two wooden chairs, self-conscious in the presence of this strange foreign woman, and drank the liquor poured out for them. Outside in the dreary gray afternoon hail began to fall. Hailstones the size of lentils bounced through the open door and formed a white line on the grass-covered floor.

Staring out the door, one policeman spoke in the local dialect. "Amano's Mother," he addressed Chimate, "why have you stopped working as balabat? If you don't do the work again, we will take the title away from your grandson. There are many people who would be happy to see someone else doing the work."

"I am an old woman," Chimate said, repeating words I had heard her say before. "I have been ill. Woi! How my head hurts me at times!" She rubbed a finger back and forth above her eyebrows. "I told Wombara, 'It is time for you to do the work. It is your title, the title which King Mijola left to my husband, Masa, Masa left to Amano, and Amano left to you. Your name is written in the government books, and it is time for you to do the work.' But Wombara became angry and did a foolish thing. He pointed out the elders who lead our assemblies and said, 'Take the halakas.' Because of this, everyone is angry."

"The governor can write a new name in the books," the policeman said, as he poured himself more liquor from the bottle on the table.

"It is *our* title," Chimate cried, sitting up very straight. "Wombara is young but he will learn how to do the work in time. I will help him."

"We want you, not Wombara, to supervise the tax collection," the policeman warned Chimate. "You'll have to go to Malo soon for a meeting with the district governor and the tax collector."

The town of Malo was a day's journey away in the lowland. "I'll go," Chimate assured him. "And you can release Wombara. The Dita people will bring the bamboo to Gulta for the police station."

The hailstorm had stopped. Air flowed in the door, crisp and humid. Chimate sighed and rubbed her forehead. The two policemen stood up and said good-bye. Hailstones crunched under their boots as they walked away.

Two years later while interviewing Chimate in Addis Abeba, I asked her if she thought that Wombara would ever become a good balabat.

"When Wombara worked two years ago, he got angry very quickly," she said. "Such anger isn't appropriate. Now he's slower to anger than the other boys. He will be capable of doing the work in the future. He doesn't get angry the way the other boys do. Unless he's been drinking he behaves very well; when he drinks, he quarrels with people. If he doesn't go and drink with the other boys, he is okay."

"What would you have done in Wombara's place when the policemen came to arrest him?"

She replied firmly, "If a policeman commands me to go to the police station, I will go. I will say, 'Okay.' I will not ask him to take other people of

Dita in my place. I don't want the halakas of our country to be put in jail instead of me. If the policeman arrests me and I don't want to go to the police station, I will bribe him and he will go back without me. Wombara doesn't know how to do this.

"If the people give me money, I buy drinks for the policemen, get them drunk, and fool them. They go back to the police station without taking anyone with them. After that, I make sure that the people do what the policemen have asked, taking the people with me. 'Come along and build the house!' I will tell the two chikashums who work under me. They will see that the people in their districts cut bamboo, carry it to Gulta, and build a new police station."

"No wonder," I said, "the people and the police wanted you to continue your work." We smiled at one another and turned to another topic.

As we talked about her life, Chimate was frank about a time ten years earlier when her political influence had been waning, not waxing. Her relationship with the district governor had been one of open antagonism. Her family temporarily lost the title of balabat, and for a year she was forbidden to do the work. It was Chimate, not her son Amano, who fought to get the title back. When Chimate told me the story of this period, it was interwoven with an even more painful story, that of Amano's death.

~

We lost our title because of a serious dispute involving Amano. One day Amano was drinking by the marketplace in the house of Kile's wife. She sells drinks there. While he was drinking, three other men—Kile, Nuguse, and Unka—were quarreling. Kile's wife took Kile's side and insulted Unka. She said, "If there was a fight, Unka, you wouldn't be able to stop it!"

At that time, Unka was one of Amano's seven retainers. "Oh, couldn't I stop people from fighting?" he asked.

"No, you couldn't," said Kile's wife.

Later that day, Nuguse and Unka took Kile's cow, which was tied near Amano's house, and killed her in Amano's false banana garden by his house. At the time I was supervising work on a road. Working way up there on the hillside, I heard a scream, "Woo-woo-woo!" from Kile's wife. I was with the district governor. The cry came from near Amano's house. Three times she screamed out "Woo-oo-oo!"

I was afraid that something very bad had happened or that someone had died. I mounted my mule, took my assistant Bodo with me, and rode to the place where she had been screaming. Before my arrival she had been chased away and had gone to another place to call our people to her. As she shouted, I came up to her.

"What has happened?"

"My cow was taken up there and killed, and Seyum's Mother tried to beat me and chased me away."

At that time Amano was married to Seyum's Mother. I arrived at Amano's house but Seyum's Mother barred the door in the fence and would not let me enter. I am the one who did the work of balabat. He had the title but stayed at home. She shut the door and sent me away.

"Run and bring Amano from Kile's Mother's house!" I told my assistant, Bodo. "Seyum's Mother didn't allow me to enter the house. Since she did that, call the district governor to come!"

I sent Bodo, saying, "Quickly!" But Bodo never went. He went home instead. He did me wrong. His excuse was, "The night was falling."

Kile and his wife went from house to house, crying out over what had happened. Kile's relatives also began shouting their witness the next day.*

"I never did anything like that," Amano said when accused of killing the cow. In order to settle the matter, I had sent Bodo to bring the governor quickly. At this time we had a district governor called Nuguse Abayneh who was a very bad man. I told him, "Amano didn't kill the cow; he wasn't even there while they were killing the cow. I sent a message to you to come and said that it was Amano's cow. Stop bothering him."

But the district governor had been bribed by our assistant, Bodo, and did nothing. I stood there in silence. He told me, "Don't help Amano."

"Woi! Why should I not help my son? I will pay for the cow."

"I won't accept such payment," said Nuguse Abayneh, and sent Amano to prison. Witnesses were brought who would say that they saw Amano cutting the neck of Kile's cow, even though Unka confessed in prison, "We killed the cow. Amano didn't see us doing it."

From there it went to Chencha court. The judge was an Amhara man named Tesemma, and I got from him an order that released Amano from jail.

"Pay for the cow," the judge told me.

*People actually walk through Dita shouting out their grievances as they go along the paths and cross the high pastures.

"Why should I pay?"

"A fifty-dollar fine and fifty dollars for the cow must be paid," he said.

"Okay!" I replied. "I'll pay for this cow I never saw." I paid one hundred dollars! I went home and stayed there. Because of having given false witness, the Dita people had many problems; gome was harming them. I kept quiet.

Nuguse Abayneh, the district governor, insulted me. "Give the work of balabat to your assistant."

"Woi! Give up the title?"

"Yes," he replied. "You and your son should not work as balabat. You should stay quietly at home."

"Woi!" I said, and went to Arbaminch to accuse the district governor in court. From there I brought a case against him to the Chencha court. After I had brought the accusation, he threatened, "Don't you dare try to accuse me again." He advised the chikashums against me, and they and my assistant Bodo went over to his side. I spent a year and six months fighting the case without reaching any agreement.

Nuguse Abayneh assigned the title of balabat to my assistant, and Bodo did the work for a year. Then he died. Our neighbors refused to visit him when he was sick and refused to mourn his death. I stopped him from working by going to Chencha and writing an application to the subprovincial governor there saying that the title belonged to me. The subprovincial governor wrote saying that the work of balabat was mine and not to give that work to Bodo.

Work was required in Arbaminch, in the lowland. Amano went with our people to supervise the building of a road and got sick there. He was sick for a year and then died. He was sick, he was sick, and the people refused to visit him. He was sick and the people refused him comfort. Even his brother, Mago, who later died, refused to comfort him. I asked myself, "Are they avoiding him because they think he killed one cow?" I answered myself, "Yes. God knows if he did it or not."

The Arbaminch governor sent a dresser (health care worker) to us to help cure Amano, for I wrote an application for help to him. I said that Amano got sick while working on the Arbaminch road. The people decided to beat the dresser with sticks because he had come to help Amano. I heard of this and sent the man back before dawn with a man called Mande. If the dresser had been killed, people would have said he died for coming to treat my son. I decided to fight with them if they came to my house. "I can hit people with sticks, too," I said.

While Amano was dying, he asked the people, "Are you listening to me?"

"Yes."

"Do you still believe that I killed the cow?"

"Yes."

"Then let your cows not give milk, let your ensete die, let your bodies be sick, let disease enter the country and never leave, let no male children like me be born ever again, and let the children living never grow!"

In our area people simply bury someone, but I am a Christian. My son was a Christian. Both of us were baptized in the Ethiopian Orthodox Church. He was buried with a church service by the Gulta priests in that town. Our Dita people didn't hold me when I was mourning his death.

After Amano died, we buried him properly. An Amhara man went to Gulta with the news of Amano's death and brought back the priests to accompany the funeral procession. All the people from the town came to the funeral except the district governor, Nuguse Abayneh. The policemen, the treasurer, the judge, and all the simple people came. We carried his body to Gulta. The people of Gulta wanted to bury him by themselves and stopped the Dita people from burying him. They said, "When we came from Gulta to the house of death, you were just sitting around silently and not crying out as you should have done. We won't let you bury him."

Six months after Amano's death, a man who had been a witness against Amano died. Isn't it gome to be a false witness, and can't gome kill you? Three months later Kile's brother-in-law, who had witnessed, also died. Of the three witnesses, only one is alive today. My son Mago died. Then the district governor Nuguse Abayneh died. Into the sky, into the sky they went. Nuguse had been mocking me about the death of my son.

My assistant Bodo, who wanted to take the title away, died. His relatives, Malka and Maganju, I avoided for five years. I decided not to drink water or to take food from their houses. I stopped taking fire from their houses; I started using matches. The only men who came to me during this time were Halaka Halke and Deneke.

The people of Ele brought their goats and buried dead mice outside my house.* They thought they could harm me in this way. I waited and wait-

---

*This is a form of sorcery.

ed, and from the houses of the people who had buried dead mice by my gate, seven people died.

~

"But after Amano died," Chimate concluded, "I didn't care much about my own life. What would it matter if I died, my son was dead!"

Chimate seemed to expect no reply to her outburst, and indeed I had no easy reply to make. My mind was racing, matching what Chimate had told me with what other people in Dita had said. Everyone else I knew still blamed Amano for the death of the cow, a fault Chimate had determined to ignore or minimize. I could see Chimate's dilemma. A woman active in a male sphere of politics, she could claim her position only through her son. If she were to join his critics, the title would surely be taken away.

What did Chimate really think, I wondered. Did she believe one thing and say another? Or was she so eager to vindicate Amano that she pushed any evidence of his guilt into a far corner of her mind? Certainly, she told the story carefully, admitting nothing, but adding, "God sees all. He alone knows if Amano did it or not."

Chimate had glossed over the ignominy of Amano's death and funeral. His body was carried to Gulta because the Dita people refused to bury him in the sacred grove of his clan. People also refused to mourn him, sitting silently in his house instead of going to the meadow used for funerals to run and cry out. The Dita people were executing a stern negative judgment.

Chimate, in turn, judged them. When she spoke of people dying, she asserted that their wrong behavior had killed them. The belief in gome is a convenient one, I thought to myself. The living can always point to the dead and say, "See, I was in the right. Gome killed my enemies, not me."

Chimate's story was not finished. As I listened, I admired her tenacity and sheer stubbornness in the years following Amano's death. The community had ostracized her, but she believed she was in the right and waited, unbending, for five years until they came to beg her forgiveness.

~

Amano and I were ostracized over the affair of the cow. All of Dita did not make us hilo, only the area in which we lived. Our own neighborhood was particularly strict. If someone is hilo, no one will help that person. If he needs fire, no one will give him fire. If his house is burning down, no one will bring false banana leaves to put out the fire. People try not to talk with someone who is hilo. And if he dies, no one will bury him. No one mourns. No one brings food to the bereaved relatives. No one blesses the dead person's name.

All of Dita can decide to ostracize someone. The elders who meet every market day in the marketplace make this decision. Or a part of Dita can make a person hilo. Why is someone ostracized? Because he or she refuses to listen to a judgment. A woman may refuse to pay a debt. A man may refuse to sell his land to a close relative, choosing instead to sell it to the person offering the highest price. When these problems are brought to the elders, they say, "Repay the debt!" or "Give the land to your relative!"

"No, I refuse."

"All right, we will make you hilo."

When a person who is ostracized repents, the problem is mediated. But that person must pay an extra fine to the elders.

Amano refused to confess that he killed the cow and was made hilo. I refused to stop helping my son. I refused to ostracize him. For this reason, the people of our neighborhood made me hilo, too.

I never went to the people and confessed that I was in the wrong. I waited and waited. I lived with my friends in Gulta. My enemies died, one by one. The people of Dita had many problems. Those who had made me hilo began to reconsider their decision.

Five years after the death of Amano, the people of Dita came to me and said that they were in the wrong. They said, "We will cultivate your land for you. We will rebuild your house when it gets old. We will repair your fences for you. We will repair your house. Forgive us!"

"All right. All right. What should I do? What could I be?"

"Be reconciled with us."

"All right. I forgive you."

"Untie us."

"I untie you."

Thus our quarrel ended. When an excuse is asked, you must always show forgiveness, or it is gome.

I lived in the town of Gulta for a long time. After Amano's death, I refused to go to Dita. But then I decided that I didn't want to sit in Gulta. I had no land there. If I sit in my house and am hungry for lack of food, what's the good of that? I don't have much money, and if I don't farm my land, I

waste my money buying food from the marketplace. By tilling my land, I'm
saving for my old age.

Amano received both the title of balabat and the title of king from his
father, Masa. The position of balabat was created when the Amharas came,
but the position of king has existed from the dawn of time. When my husband died, he said, "My father gave the title of king to me. I give my title to
my son, Amano." Masa died, and the people said, "Masa's older brother,
Tilinte, was cheated out of his title. Now we will make Tilinte king." I had
Masa's ring. They bought another ring and put it on Tilinte's finger. He used
that ring for two months and then died.

Would the people leave off? No. Again they made king a man whom my
husband's father had cursed. Didn't they go and give it to Woira? He died
too. Did they leave off? No, they made Bele the king. He died too. Didn't
Masa tell the people to make his son Amano the king? And didn't death use
up those false kings? Three men died, counting Bele.

The ring returned to our house, and when the people brought it, they
told me to guard it in a box in my house. They asked my pardon for having
given the ring to the wrong house. They paid me twenty Maria Theresa
thalers for their mistake. I cut cold grass, green grass, and put it under the
ring and put newly sprouted barley over the ring and kept this in a clean
box. The reason I put the ring between the grass and the barley was to cool
the gome. When it was cool, I agreed with the people.

But then they gave the ring to another man. You were present, Judy, at
his initiation. They've made Woira's son Wata the king now. He is not of
our house either. And have I told you his child just died? Right now the
people of Dita are getting used up by death.

Wata said to the people, "We haven't obeyed Leader Mijola's word and
Fitawari Masa's word. What are we to do?"

He has gone to the seer's house to find out what to do. Wata doesn't even
have a blind sheep! He has no cows. He walks alone. No one tills his land
for him. No one harvests his crops. When they were trying to make him the
king, he said, "The title doesn't belong to me. Leave off! It doesn't come to
me!" But they forced him to be king.

This is a serious gome for the people. Everyone is dying. From the two
houses of our lineage relatives, they have wronged our master, Masa. Now
four people have died from their houses. The people say, "We have gome!
Let's remove Wata from office!" The elders quietly talk to people in secret

in order to bring this about. We'll see what will happen and what they are going to do. If my son Atumo behaves well, he will get the title. He would be the sacrificer for all Dita. He's the one to do it, isn't he?

~

And so Chimate, indefatigable, continued her campaign.

13   Arson

She ran out of the house carrying a few clothes.
Everything else burned. Her paper money burned, her
coins melted.

~

"Judy, can you do anything for my daughter?" I was asked one morning by Sando, the young man who had carried my possessions from Dorze. He gestured toward his one blind eye. "I lost this eye when I was a child, and now she's losing her eye, too."

His daughter Afalo was about the same age as the little girl living with us. Her left eye was inflamed and oozing pus. On both temples were round scabs, marking places a local healer had burned her recently.

"I don't know how to treat her, Sando," I replied. "I'll give you money and you can visit the doctors in Chencha."

Sando hesitated, looking very nervous. "I don't know how to go to the hospital. I'm afraid."

"I can go with him, Judy," Gida offered. "We can spend the night in Dorze with my father and return the next day."

"Do you want to go today?" I asked Sando.

"No. I have to finish the gome first. At my father's house the neighbors are going to mediate between my wife and me." Sando evidently thought that his disagreements with his wife Borde might be causing his daughter's illness.

"Borde wants to divorce him," Nigatu said in a loud voice. "I don't see why. Every time Borde tells him to do something, Sando jumps!"

"You keep quiet!" Sando snapped at Nigatu. He stood up and left, thanking me. Gida, Nigatu, and I looked knowingly at one another. Borde was famous for her petulant ill humor and the way she dominated Sando. She was a small woman who seemed always to be smoldering over a grievance, her lips pressed tightly together.

"Sando's parents don't want Borde to leave Sando," Nigatu confided. "Ever since she married him, their land has given very good crops and their animals have multiplied. She brings them good fortune. Now they are telling Borde and Sando, 'The child is sick because of gome. The two of you must finish your quarrels. Then she will get well.'"

Two days later, Sando and Borde brought Afalo to the house while we were eating breakfast. "Sando says we have to go to Chencha, Judy," Borde began. "Are the doctors there *ferenji* like you?"

"Yes, a man and his wife from a foreign country called Bulgaria work there with the Ethiopians," I replied.

"Oh, well, if they're like you, I suppose I'll go. But who is going to carry Afalo all the way? Whose back is going to break? Not Sando's!" Borde sounded the same as ever. "Sando wants his wages from you when we get back. We have to buy a sheep and give it to Sando's father to finish the gome." She glared at Sando, as if their past quarrels were entirely his fault.

Gida grimaced in my direction before joining the happy party leaving for Chencha. When they returned the following afternoon, however, Borde was in a good mood. She had experienced something new, and she spent several hours sitting in the cookhouse telling about the hospital and the doctors. Sando reappeared; he had gone home, expecting her to follow. He looked diffident and rather afraid of Borde, but he gathered his courage and shouted, "Won't I ever get my supper?" The shout came out in a squeaky falsetto, and I had to stare very hard at the ground to keep from laughing. Grumbling, Borde took her time but did pick up Afalo, join Sando, and go home.

It was now almost the end of February. The rain that the month should have brought to the highland had not fallen. The highland people, though they did not know it, were suffering the first of several difficult years during which the dry season would stretch out much longer than normal. Every year the rain would finally fall in May or June and save them. At the same time, in northern Ethiopia a terrible drought would be killing crops, animals, and people, acting as one of the catalysts for the revolution that was to come in just three years.

Every day it grew harder to find fodder for the Dita animals, and every day the barley threshing was postponed. The clay threshing floors were useless until they had been thoroughly moistened. In the meantime, grain needed for daily consumption was shelled by hand.

The houses were dry and extremely inflammable. Built of bamboo and thatched with straw, a house once it caught fire disappeared in a few minutes. Reports of fires in Dorze, which was even more parched than Dita, reached us. Then one night the three houses of Bele's Mother, the woman who had jokingly offered to adopt me, burned down.

"She was asleep all alone in her compound when the sound of the fire woke her," Halaka Halke told us over morning coffee. "She ran out of the house carrying a few clothes. Everything else burned. Her paper money burned, her coins melted. She went to the tanners who live nearby. Of course, she couldn't sleep in their house—tanners are impure because of their work—but she borrowed a sheepskin and slept on it by the ashes until dawn."

"An enemy must have set the fire!" Chimate exclaimed.

"Yes, how can a fire start by accident during the night?" Balaye's Mother added. "People cover their fires at night and leave a few coals to start the fire in the morning. They blow out their lamps. How can a fire start by accident?"

"Bele's Mother had been sheltering a young woman who ran away from her husband," Halaka Halke continued.

"The young man came last week on market day while Bele's Mother was selling liquor and asked for his wife. He was told, 'I don't know where she is,' but all the time the young woman was hiding in another house in the compound. The husband left, saying 'If you help my wife run away from me, I'll make you suffer! Watch out for midnight!' "

"Perhaps he did it," Chimate replied. "We'll never know, but God knows." She handed her empty coffee cup to Balaye's Mother and turned to me. "Judy, let's go and mourn with her this afternoon. You should take her a gift to help her out."

"What should I give her?" I asked.

"Give her one of your coffee cups," she suggested, and I nodded agreement. "I'll take her some barley."

Gida and I left to visit the five sample households we would be questioning that day. As we rounded a corner in the path, I glanced at the hillside to the east. I stopped, crying, "Gida, look, a fire!"

Three-quarters of the way up the opposite hillside a house was burning. The fire appeared no larger than a match flame. People were running toward the area from all directions, some cutting bamboo poles, some twenty-foot-long false banana leaves; these they were bringing to the burning house and throwing on the flames. Another house stood to the left of the fire. People were pulling the thatch from the roof of this house. No sound reached us, but everyone must have been shouting for more help, for I could see distant figures walking along the paths suddenly begin to run toward the fire.

Within five minutes the fire had burned itself out. The second house stood intact, protected by people's quick action. Now people were leaving, fanning out in all directions from the spot. We learned later from Sando, whose father lived on that hillside, that a cooking fire had gotten out of control in a newly constructed house.

Chimate rode her mule that afternoon, for she was planning to continue her journey to an area of Dita where she would spend a week supervising the widening of a road. She had visited Bele's Mother and was gone before I reached the spot on foot. On the scorched earth stood a rickety old house that neighbors had found and carried to Bele's Mother. Slumped to one side, it was gray with age, but it would shelter her while she supervised the building of a new compound.

Gamo Highland houses were often moved from place to place. Sometimes an old house was used to replace one destroyed by fire, but even within a compound the house for the sheep might be moved in order to plant false banana plants in the richly manured area. When building a new compound or expanding an old one, a house might be moved to the area.

To carry a house, the thatch on the roof is removed in order to decrease the weight. The bamboo basketry walls, which are embedded in the earth, are cut off at ground level. Men encircle the house on the outside and stand along the inside wall, lifting the house with their bare hands and carrying it to its new location.

Inside the house that had been moved to Bele's Mother's compound, I joined a line of men and women kneeling in front of Bele's Mother. I hit my chest in the traditional gesture of mourning, saying, "*Tasa, tasa,* let this grief be mine."

Moving from person to person, Bele's Mother lifted each of us, murmuring, "No, this grief is mine to carry." I gave her the coffee cup. Thanking me, she set it down beside a plate, another coffee cup, and several small baskets of grain that others had brought to her.

"I don't have any coffee for you," Bele's Mother told me. "I don't have a griddle for roasting coffee. I don't have a coffee pot. I'm poor now! The fire ate all my money, all my possessions!" Her voice was rising and she seemed capable of talking on and on, growing more hysterical as she talked. Two men entered and interrupted her, channeling her emotion again into the cries and countercries of mourning.

The next day brought news of another fire—one that had occurred during the night. Five houses had burned down this time; people and animals had escaped unhurt. Again arson was suspected, and again the community immediately rallied to help the victims. This time I saw the house being carried to the site of the fire. Across the valley on the opposite hillside, a house with tiny legs was bobbing along a path. It lurched, it shuddered, it paused, it continued. It made a short upward climb past a grove of false banana plants. Trembling, it stopped, dropping to the ground, rotated a quarter turn in a puff of dust, and was still.

News of two more fires reached me during the following week. The rains did not come. Children herding sheep played hide and seek around the unthreshed barley stacked in the fields. Nigatu and Wara's Mother spent hours chopping false banana leaves into animal fodder.

Then one evening Gida told me, "A man has just escaped from prison in Chencha."

"Oh, yes?" I said inattentively, tearing off a piece of injera bread and dipping it into a lentil sauce.

"People say he's coming to Dita."

"Really?"

"Chimate had him put in jail for burning down houses and setting fire to people's barley stacks. Now he's saying he'll burn down her house in revenge!"

Trying to calm my suddenly racing heart, I said, "Well, she's not even here now. She's in Malo working on tax collection. She went there after they finished the road."

"Why should that stop him? He wants to destroy her property," Gida replied. "I think Dita is a terrible place! Burning down houses! In Dorze, houses burn down by accident. People don't set fires!"

Gida and I began a discussion that grew increasingly paranoid. Balaye's Mother joined in and grew frightened as well. We ended the evening in a panic, pulling all the boxes or bags containing our possessions out of the back storage area and positioning them right inside the door.

"There's just enough here to be moved in a hurry. This way we can save something if he comes tonight," Gida said darkly. "Keep your shoes and your flashlight right by your bed, Judy!"

Of course, we hardly slept all night. Gida got up intermittently and went outside, prowling around the compound, hitting walls and fences with a heavy stick, and feeling effective. Every small sound startled me. In the morning we rather shamefacedly hurried to put all the items back in hiding before we opened the door, so that no visitors could see what we had been doing.

"Let's ask Wilomo for advice," I suggested. Wilomo lived downhill and to the right of Chimate, several fields over. He had recently begun working with us daily, recalling local history and answering questions about customs and events I had observed.

Wilomo laughed when we asked him if Chimate's compound might be set on fire by the escaped prisoner. "No, no, he's a close relative of hers," Wilomo told us. "He wouldn't harm her. Don't worry, nothing will happen."

I tried to accept Wilomo's assurances, suppressing the thought that Chimate's very closest relatives, her grandsons, seemed quite willing to do her harm from time to time. We left the boxes in their place every night after that, even if we did sleep uneasily. When Chimate returned from Malo, she laughed very hard when I told her of our night of panic. "Don't worry," she said, "the man has been caught and is in prison again."

No more houses burned down before I left Dita at the end of March. Upset by the arson that had occurred, the Dita people held a meeting near Chimate's compound and decided to notify the government and ask for help. I could not imagine how outside officials could solve this kind of problem; it was a measure of the local desperation that such a solution was suggested. To my eye, the house burnings illustrated both bright and dark aspects of Dita—the willingness to mobilize quickly in aid of a neighbor in distress and the willingness to strike out in violence against that same neighbor.

14   Spirit Possession

*I know many men who beat their wives to stop them
from going to the cult leader's house, but sometimes
the wives divorce their husbands and keep on going!*

～

Balaye's Mother leaned forward confidentially. "Amano was Chimate's favorite son," she told me, "and he was a very nice young man, but he liked
women too much. I told you how he kept confessing adultery with this and
that woman when he was dying of a fever. And his wives! He would take
one wife for a short time, and then she would leave him.

"Of course, his mother didn't get along well with his wives. They would
quarrel and quarrel. Chimate likes to stay in charge of things. What young
wife likes a mother-in-law with a strong mind? It grew difficult for Chimate
to live in the same house with Amano, so she moved to the town of Gulta.
There in Gulta she was sick, very sick. She lay in bed without moving for
two months. One day, blood came from her mouth.

"I knew that spirits must be harming her. I asked her, 'Have you traveled to Addis Abeba?' 'Yes, I've been there.' 'If you go there, you can get the
chale sickness while crossing the Awash River,' I told her. She asked, 'If you
simply walk over it on foot, you can get this disease?' 'Yes,' I told her. I
showed her how to buy beads to make necklaces, and I showed her the chale
ceremonies to control the spirits that were harming her."

"What is chale? Is it like ayana?" I asked. I knew that ayana spirits were
thought to possess a person, riding that person as a horseman rides a horse.

"No, no! In chale the spirits have not come out. We don't know their
names, and they don't make us dance." Balaye's Mother too had her chale
necklaces and ceremony. "I'm afraid of people with ayana," she said with a
grimace.

I was about to tell her about my own encounter with ayana in Dorze, when a man I had been hoping to interview arrived and the conversation stopped. My experience in Dorze had been somewhat frightening. I had arranged to spend the night at the monthly meeting of an ayana cult group. The leader of the cult, himself possessed by many spirits, owned one little house isolated from its neighbors and located down a path by a stream. My Dorze friends feared him, and indeed he did seem strange. His face was unusually animated, especially his eyes. He had a way of fixing a stare upon you like a beam of light.

At dusk I went to his house. Indoors by the fire lay a large drum, its head tightening in the heat. The man's wife sat on a cushion at the back of the room. She patted the drum head from time to time and adjusted its distance from the fire. Behind her, a bamboo partition hid a second room. A leather and lashed-wood chair stood in the entrance to that room. It loomed above the cushions circling the fire.

Women began to enter, each giving the leader's wife money to pay for the coffee she was brewing. They intended to stay the night, drinking coffee, talking, going into trances, dancing, and conferring with their leader until dawn. This man had initiated each woman, inducting her into a trance for the first time and identifying which spirit possessed her by watching the way she moved. I knew that for the Gamo Highlanders, ayana was a twentieth-century disease, a way of understanding mental and physical illness taught to them by the northern Ethiopians who came to rule and live among them.

Ayana affliction is known in other parts of Ethiopia, Africa, and the Arab world as *zar*.* In this region, women form the majority of those possessed by these spirits. Some observers have suggested that this form of illness is partly caused by, and may help compensate for, status deprivation—that is, the subordinate role forced upon women in these cultures. In the anecdotes Chimate told about ayana, it is clear that husbands and sons resisted their wives' and mothers' involvement in the cult. During meetings of the cult group, women may take on different roles and behaviors—smoking and drinking in Islamic areas, for example. The family of a woman afflicted by spirit possession is often asked to stage special ceremonies for her, buy her new clothing, and feed her particular foods.

---

*The term "ayana" is taken from the Oromo (Chimate calls it Galla) language and refers to the central religious and political institutions of these people, as described by Morton in "Mystical Advocates." The term as adopted by the Gamo Highlanders refers to a spirit possession cult. See Appendix 3 for references on spirit possession.

Other documented functions of the zar cult not related to status deprivation include coping with mental illness, helping women master if not eliminate everyday problems, allowing women in towns to form associations with one another not based on kinship, expressing religious sentiments, and providing satisfying aesthetic experiences. Although spirit possession usually upholds the status quo, with cult members obtaining concessions from people in authority rather than directly challenging their prerogatives, at times spirit possession cults can become vehicles for mobilizing social protest.

The ayana leader entered and sat on the chair. A bright, multicolored scarf covered part of his forehead and was knotted back over his hair at the nape of his neck. He shared coffee with us and then began to sway from side to side. The spirits were beginning to possess him. He moved his chair into a back room, allowing a colored cloth to fall across the entrance to the room and sitting behind the cloth. His wife began to beat the drum—a deep strangled sound.

A voice began to speak from behind the cloth. It was a growling harsh voice, meant to frighten. The voice used a secret language. The woman beating the drum translated for the rest. The voice greeted the women and answered their questions.

One young woman fell to her knees by the fire. The drumbeat continued. She pulled her shawl over her head and face like a translucent winding sheet. Her hands touched the floor limply. She began to sway, twisting her head sharply upward and letting it roll back. Observing her movements, the leader had decided which spirit was riding her. He had instructed her how to propitiate this particular spirit. Perhaps the spirit had threatened to kill her unless she gave it a new dress or slaughtered a sheep for it or fed it butter porridge every week.

As the young woman melted to the floor in a faint, a man entered the house. I recognized him as Ufo, a moody young tanner who carved beautiful designs on drinking gourds.

From behind the cloth came a shout. The spirits were angry. Ufo had not come to the meetings for months. Now his ayana troubled him and he wanted to return. The rasping voice grew more and more vehement. A fine, it seemed, was being demanded, a fine of fifty Ethiopian dollars.

The tanner protested. He didn't have that much money. It would be very hard to borrow fifty dollars. The woman with the drum, which had silenced, translated the argument back and forth.

A sharp knocking sound came from behind the cloth. The leader's normal voice was heard. "Hello! Hello! Can I come in? What's the matter? Can I be of help?" He was speaking the normal Dorze dialect.

The matter was explained, and behind the cloth a new argument began. The leader's voice alternated with the growling voice. Both spoke in the argot of the cult.

"Ufo?" said the ayana leader.

"Yes, my master," cried the kneeling Ufo, bowing his head low to the floor.

"I have talked with the spirits." The leader was speaking intelligibly again. "They are willing to accept a fine of ten dollars. Bring it to our next meeting." The leader's voice disappeared and the spirits again used the leader to speak their messages.

To the slow drumbeat, Ufo was ridden by his ayana. He remained on his knees in one place, but his body arched back in terrible spasms and pitched from side to side. Then he too fainted.

As Ufo revived and took a seat on a cushion, the colored cloth rustled and the leader stepped out. He said nothing. In his right hand he held a walking staff taller than himself. Everyone except me stood up, and I saw that they had taken up similar staffs. These they held in their right hands, planting the tips on the earthen floor. They formed a circle around the fire, darkening the room as they blocked the only source of light. They began to sway, shaking their shoulders up and down. "Huh-huh-huh! Huh-huh-huh!" they rasped, a hoarse animal-like sound.

I jerked back involuntarily as the group stopped swaying and began to jump up and down, continuing their rhythmic cries. All around the walls, shadows hopped up, down, up, down between bristling spikes. The walls were crushing in on me, crushing me toward this sinister heartbeat, toward the little flames licking at the center.

I was at the door. I was outside the door, up the path, across the bridge. I said to myself in brisk professional tones as I walked the road home, "Hyperventilation. They're going into a trance together by hyperventilating."

Then I was home, and the little flames paled and faded away in the light of our hissing pressure lamp.

I was able to laugh at my fear—I had probably been on the verge of a trance myself—when I told my story to Chimate, but she said emphatically, "I don't like ayana. The spirits ride the person, they hit the person! Men have good reason to be afraid when their wives visit the leader's house. The ayana leader sleeps with the women who come to him! I know many men who beat their wives to stop them from going to the cult leader's house, but sometimes the wives divorce their husbands and keep on going!"

"What about the women who lead groups?" I asked.

"They're not as bad as the men. In fact, once a woman who had ayana gave me a prediction."

At that time, the woman was just beginning to have ayana. My son Amano was in Jimma, north of Dita, as a student. The time when the outlaws ruled the countryside began. "My son won't be able to return to Dita," I was thinking as I walked to market with Halaka Halke. We were crossing the river by the market and saw a woman washing tubers in the stream.

"Hee! Hee! Hee!" she laughed as she looked up at me. I don't say hello to ayana people but just walk on. I'm afraid of them. "What is it, my mistress? Hee! Hee! Hee!" she said. "Please listen to me!" She was standing in the river.

Halaka Halke said, "We won't make fun of you. Speak!"

"Take your mule right now and go to Chencha town and you will meet your son."

My son had been in Jimma for a year. "My son has been away for a year. Just where should I travel? The countryside is full of fighting." This was the time of the outlaws. The Italians had encouraged the villages to turn against each other and there was a lot of fighting. "Where shall I find my son? The foreigners took him to Jimma to study. Just where shall I get him?"

"Go home now. When you get home, take a mule and go, and you will meet your son."

I went home and put the saddle on the mule and went on the lower road with Halaka Halke. Galloping, galloping, galloping we went. "The outlaws rob people near Gulta," we said and took the road through Dokama. Hurrying, hurrying through the center, we got to Dorze and went through there to Chencha.

"Now whose house should we go to?" I asked myself. "The outlaws steal from people. Where did I use to go in the past? Fitawari Kircho is in Chencha. I'll go to his house."

We took the path to his house and went in. We found Fitawari Kircho and Amano there. I shouted with joy when I saw him!

Yes, after I had been without Amano for a year, I was going to market when the woman told me to turn back and find Amano. And I went home, went to Chencha, and met Amano. Halaka Halke and I know about this. The woman is now dead. I gave her nothing; from our house gifts are not given to ayana people. From our house it is forbidden to give anything to the maro seers or the ayana. And on her part, she didn't want anything from me.

Whenever diseases entered the community, she told the people, "Kill this kind of sheep, kill that kind of sheep."* She was strong. She would tell people in which years to expect diseases. "Go to so-and-so's house, it's burning. Go to so-and-so's house, there's a fire near it," she would say.

Her brother chased her away from his house. "She is good for our community," people said. "Where is she to live?" They gave her an empty house near Kuntsa's house. For three years she lived there. People blessed her and liked her. She didn't know how to tell lies. She spoke truthfully and people respected her. Everyone respected her. The elders and the halakas respected her very much. There was no one respected as much as she was! When she died, everyone mourned bitterly for her.

In the past, no one had ayana. Now people wear a *harambee*, a colored scarf, and say that they have ayana. Some say they have it, but it's not true. I don't know who brought the ayana to Dita. "I have ayana," people say. They start burning incense, they start dancing the dance of ayana. "I have ayana and cannot go to funerals," they say, and sit at home putting the scarf around their heads. "The ayana hits me," they say. I don't like to visit houses where people are possessed by ayana. They don't even take off the scarf when they mourn. They say, "I have ayana!"

Men have good reason to be afraid when their wives begin to visit the ayana leader's house. In Dita there was a man with ayana, a strong man. He was strong, good, and rich, but after he got ayana he never went out of his house. He just stayed home. Once a woman asked her husband, "Take me to his house." The woman begged, begged, begged her husband, and finally he let her go to the ayana man's house. She stayed there and then had a child. She nursed it. She had been with the ayana man a long time.

"I'm a little better, but I don't want to go home," she said. "I won't go.

---

*Note how the introduction of the spirit possession cult into the Gamo Highland allowed some women to perform functions traditionally performed by men, such as telling people what kinds of sacrifices to make.

I'm better here." Her husband was angry and took her home by force. "I'm sick," she said.

"I cannot be walking back and forth, up and down hill," her husband said. "Let him come and build a house here." The husband went to the man and said, "Come!" And the ayana man came. The ayana man had taken the woman as his own wife. The man didn't know this; he went about his work. His eldest son got sick and died. The younger son also died. The man was walking everywhere trying to discover what was wrong. He was killing many sheep to finish the gome. The he died too. Next she became sick and confessed, "I had intercourse with the ayana man."

"So you confess after the death of three people—your husband and your children! You didn't confess while your children were dying!" the people said, and refused to help her. "Let the disease finish her," they said. We wouldn't complete the ceremonies to absolve her. Ever since that time, our people haven't liked the ayana people. The ayana men are wordo, untrustworthy. You won't catch me saying they are tsilo, upright people.

The local customs affect people with ayana. They cannot just ignore the rules of gome. This woman brought an outsider into her husband's house and had intercourse with him. Her husband was killed. The children were killed. The woman confessed in order that she would get well, and then died. From that time onward no one has liked ayana. If the ayana person is a man, women's husbands keep them from visiting him. Ayana men are troublemakers.

～

"I know many things about people who have ayana," Chimate commented, "but I'm afraid of most of them. I will never go to the cult leader's house to spend the night there, drinking coffee and dancing. I kill a sheep every year for the chale spirits and sit quietly in my house."

In her role as acting balabat, Chimate was independent, decisive, and constantly busy. Her son and grandsons were unpredictable and sometimes violent, and the position she occupied was frequently the focus of controversy. The chale ceremony gave her an opportunity to depend upon others for attention and comfort. Once a year she had to sit still and live simply for most of a week, the object of others' help.

～

At one time, I was very sick. My hands weren't able to work. My feet would not walk. I told people, "I don't know what is the matter with me." Balaye's Mother and Zawde's Mother—they were working for me then—explained that the sickness had caught me when I crossed the Awash River on my way to Addis Abeba. It just caught me. It catches people without their even knowing it.

"What can I do?" I asked.

"We'll do the chale ceremony."

"Okay!" I agreed. "What shall I do?"

"Quickly, buy the necklaces. Buy the beads."

"I'll buy chale beads," I said, and sent the money. Green, black, white, and mixed colors I bought.

Then they said, "Buy large beads to mix with the small ones."

What does one do when putting on the necklaces once a year? For the feast of chale we work together—myself, the neighbors, and Balaye's Mother. June, June, June, every year I prepare the feast. Just as June begins, all the Amhara people make this ceremony. The local people do it in our New Year, Maskal.

I must buy a red female sheep and keep it in the house for a whole year. If I don't buy a sheep and keep it in my house until the day for sacrificing it, won't I become sick? I won't be able to walk. If the sheep dies during the year, I quickly buy another. Every year, every year, I kill a sheep. Year after year we pay taxes, don't we?

With chale, the spirits have not come out. They sit inside without disturbing me if I perform the ceremony every year. I call the women around. They grind barley for porridge, keeping the chickens and other livestock out of the way. I put on a special shawl, with many colors in its border. I wear it overnight, with the necklaces.

The women put a full pot of water on the fire, ululating, "Li-li-li-li-li!" It is necessary to cry out like that while putting the pot on the fire. I put the beads around my neck. They take water from the pot and put it in a second, small pot. I was told that the green beads needed their own separate pot for porridge, and the women cover the pots and put them to one side.

The women take two pots in which they have made beer and put one on each side of me, this side, that side. Then they take twenty-two coffee beans whose skin has not been removed and put them in a small pot on the fire. Butter, then, butter is put in with the coffee. Unhulled coffee with butter boiling, boiling, boiling, boiling!

In this hand I pick up six cooked coffee beans, six in that hand, and I swallow them. I immerse the tips of some stalks of grass in the butter that was cooked with the coffee, and I stroke the necklaces with them. I say, "Eat, eat, eat, eat!" while smearing the beads, and I also smear butter on my ears. I do this many times. Then I sit quietly like a new bride.

The women take the porridge and mix it with butter. One of them puts porridge in my right and left hands, two sticky balls of porridge, and I begin to eat it. When I finish, I am given two glasses of beer. I hold one in each hand. From the right-hand glass I take beer and spit it toward the door of the house and then toward the door of the bedroom. It's a rule that I must spit out the beer before I swallow any of it. Unless I do that, no one could eat or drink. Then everyone else present is allowed to eat and drink. I have to eat from the porridge, I have to drink first, because it is my chale.

I put butter—a whole bundle!—on the heads of the people present. After the butter is put on their heads, they sit a while, then leave. On the next morning, they make more porridge and we eat it, adding it to the porridge left from the day before. The women wash everything on the third day, including the porridge pot, and throw away the grass that has been covering the floor.

On the third day, my son Atumo kills the sheep. The bones of this sheep are not given to the dogs. All the bad parts are kept in the house and buried. Then on the fourth day, all the neighbors come and eat the meat. I invite the people living close to me. "Now *athathe* is being done," I say. Athathe is the name of the feast.

People drink a lot of beer at my feast and eat a lot. Butter is put on their heads just as at other important occasions like marriage. Two days after the feast I can live a normal life again. Until then, I just sit around, and I have to sleep on the grass on the floor.

When I die, the chale will go to Atumo. He is my only living son. He will do the ceremony every year, but he won't put the beads over his neck. He will just sit in his house and put them on his knees.

People from Dita have had ayana for a long time. Now they are starting to have chale. It has caught my grandson's mother and also my daughter Alimetu. They caught it from Addis Abeba.

~

In her account Chimate stresses her adherence to Amhara custom as opposed to local custom, for she performs the chale ceremony in June, although local people perform similar propitiatory sacrifices for ayana in September or October. No matter when the ceremonies were performed, they offered women the same opportunity to become the focus of household attention and to give feasts on their own behalf. For Chimate, the chale ceremony also provided a break from her very busy life and leadership role. Being possessed by ayana spirits did just the opposite for many other women. With their periodic visits to the cult leader's house, these women were increasing their social contacts and independence.

An Ambivalent Friendship

My mule is much sicker than Nigatu.

⌇

Two days after Seyum slept with Tije in the cowshed, Chimate brought her cow and sheep to her new compound. She put them in the cookhouse, moving her bed into the back room of the reception house parallel to mine. In the cookhouse now lived Paranko, a plump teenaged girl who was Tije's replacement, Wara's Mother, and Chimate's granddaughters, Nigatu and Katse.

Paranko was very affectionate with Katse, calling her "Little Broom," teasing her and chasing her about. When I tried to be playful with the little girl, Chimate and Gida scolded me for behaving inappropriately. As an older member of the household, I was supposed to train Katse to be obedient and deferential. "Don't let her sit in your lap, you'll spoil her. She'll expect us to do that all the time!" they warned me. Katse was expected to remain quietly in the background. She could not ask for food while the adults ate. At the end of the meal, someone would call her and put roasted grain into her cupped hands as she stood there, head bowed. For a two-year-old this was hard discipline, the training needed to be part of a society that respected age.

I was thirty-three years younger than Chimate, and in normal highland etiquette I owed her the same obedience and deference Katse owed me. I addressed Chimate as *inteni,* "you," while she used the more familiar *neni,* "thou," with me. From the time of my first visit, I had approached Chimate not as a dependent but as an autonomous person, because at first she had been my hostess and I her guest. Eventually we came to lead parallel lives, each the mistress of a little household within a household.

Two chains of command within one compound was abnormal for Dita. Wara's Mother, Nigatu, and Paranko worked for Chimate, Gida and Balaye's Mother for me. Sando tilled his one small field nearby and worked off and on for both Chimate and me. Halaka Halke built houses and fences for Chimate and came daily to discuss Dita history with me.

One day Gosho, one of Chimate's younger grandsons, was sitting with me in the reception house. When we were alone together, we tacitly broke the rules. He would gather courage and chatter at me like a little bird. I couldn't understand half of what he was saying but I listened as he sat by the fire, talking away.

I gave Gosho a small cardboard box that had contained flashlight batteries. He was playing with it, opening and closing it, putting things inside and taking them out, when Chimate came into the room. She sat down and said, "Gosho, come here." He went to her. "What's that you have?" she asked him.

"A box. Judy gave it to me."

"Give it to me." Sadly, Gosho handed it to her. "I need it to give to the shepherd boy who works for me," she said flatly, putting the box away.

Gosho sat down in a corner and began to cry silently. I was furious and probably looked it, although I said nothing. From Chimate's point of view, my gift must have seemed erratic and irrational, not applied where it would do the most good but subject to the whims of the day. "Judy gives this interesting and unusual object to the first child she finds," I can imagine Chimate thinking, "not to the child who works for us." In addition, by giving the gift myself, I was undermining Chimate's position as household head.

Earlier in my stay, Chimate had bent my gift giving to her purposes without my realizing it. My object was to introduce myself to the Dita community, particularly the district in which Chimate lived, and to gain goodwill and cooperation. Chimate's object was to enhance her own local influence and to bring about change in Dita.

I tried in Dita to repeat things I had done in Dorze, where I had headed my own household. I was not yet aware of just how different my position in Dita was, as a member of Chimate's household, and also how different the Dita people were. In Dorze I had gone to the assembly of elders, contributing money that the elders said they would use in building a new church. Whether or not they actually used it for the church, I never knew. In Dita I suggested doing the same thing.

Chimate objected to my plan. "If you give the money to the elders, who knows how they will use it? Why don't you come down to see our new church with me? We can ask the people building the church what is needed, and you can buy it for them."

I thought that was a fine idea. I visited the church, met Sola Kata, and offered to buy the wood. Chimate even saw to it that I went to Chencha with the men and bought the wood for the doors myself—a measure of her suspicion that the others might not use the money as intended.

I did not publicize my own deed by going to the assembly of elders and telling them about it. I followed my natural shyness about making speeches to the Dita assembly and remained silent. If I had wanted to establish myself as a person separate from Chimate, I should have gone directly to the assembly and given them money to use for any purpose they chose, as I had done in Dorze.

Later I realized that the Ethiopian Orthodox Christian Church meant far less to the people of Dita than it meant to the people of Dorze. Those who did want the church, like Chimate, regarded themselves as more progressive than their neighbors.

My second attempted gift was a feast. Upon completion of my new house in Dorze I had given a large feast, inviting many people. We had slaughtered an ox for the occasion, and afterward I had been dubbed "Giver of Meat."

I proposed that I give a feast in Dita. "What a good idea!" Chimate responded. "Yes, *we'll* give a feast." Each of us bought a sheep, I bought grain for baking injera bread, and she brewed beer.

Chimate insisted on guiding Gida when he invited people to the feast, and she made a lot of invitations herself. Neither Gida nor I knew people well enough to realize that Chimate was inviting important people from all over Dita at the expense of her immediate neighbors. She was using the feast to cement her ties with her particular Dita faction.

The feast was regarded as Chimate's feast and not mine. This distressed me until I learned that she had offended her neighbors by not inviting all of them. I was happy not to be blamed, as I was concentrating upon interviews with people in that district. I had been naive to think that Chimate would have allowed me to set myself up as a rival by giving a feast of my own while living in her household.

After the incident between Wombara and the police, Chimate began working as the balabat again. She was away a third of the time supervising work on a road that was being opened between Chencha and Dita and doing government business in the town of Malo. I had to deal with the ordinary matters of daily life alone and take responsibility into my own hands. I began to buy food for the whole household from the market, supplementing the barley, milk, and false banana products that Chimate provided with meat, butter, maize, eggs, and potatoes. I bought gifts for the people working in the household. I took an old pair of flannel pajamas, cut it up, and sewed a dress for Katse. Katse actually kissed my feet in thanks. It was a strange feeling, watching a little girl kiss my square-toed hiking boots.

A critical voice was whispering in my mind as I made that dress. I admit I was thinking, "Isn't Chimate rich enough to clothe Katse in something other than that little shawl she wears? Chimate has plenty of clothing herself."

There was a certain competitive flavor to my musings. "I take better care of my dependents than she does of hers," was my repressed thought. I ignored the fact that I, immeasurably wealthy by Dita standards, would stay only a short time, while Chimate housed, fed, and protected people for years on end.

Even deeper beneath the surface of my thoughts was the question, "How well would Chimate take care of me if I were ever fully dependent on her?" I seemed to find an answer in Chimate's reaction to Nigatu's illness, an answer that was not reassuring.

Nigatu had begun to go to the ayana spirit possession house, not for an overnight session but to drink coffee during the day. Her ayana had not "come out" or manifested itself clearly yet, and the cult leader did not know which spirit was possessing her. Her visits to the ayana house took place surreptitiously, when Chimate was away.

Nigatu had been coughing a lot. She spent days lying quietly in a corner, too weak to work. I asked her in concern, "Is this the first time you've been sick?"

"Oh, no, My Mother," she replied, listless and clinging. "I've been sick for a year. It's my lungs."

"Has anyone ever tried to get medicine for you?"

"Do you have something for me, Judy?"

"No, I don't. Would you be willing to visit the doctors in Chencha?" I asked.

"I can't walk all the way to the hospital. I'm not strong enough for that," she replied.

"Could you ride a mule?"

"I guess so."

"Would you go with me to Chencha?"

"Oh, yes, yes," she said, ducking her head in agreement and thanks.

Chimate was not eager to send Nigatu anywhere for treatment. I had simply given money to other people and they had walked to the hospital. Chimate had not been involved. Nigatu was in Chimate's charge, and Chimate refused to help me take Nigatu to the doctors. "She's not very sick," she said when I asked her about Nigatu.

I recoiled from Chimate's cool dismissal of Nigatu's pain. Chimate complained copiously about her own ailments, I noticed. I doubted that Chimate would refuse if I offered to take *her* to a doctor. A certain emotional wariness began to distance me from Chimate.

Chimate and I were reaching a point found in any close relationship, a time of heightened awareness of flaws in the other person, a time of disillusionment and readjustment. From her point of view, I must have seemed unpredictable, occasionally ill-advised, and competitive. In a long-term relationship, these new facets can be incorporated slowly as intimacy ebbs and flows. But Chimate and I lived within a time limit. I was going to leave her soon. For both of us, it was best not to grow overly attached to one another. I felt an underlying guilt about abandoning my highland friends who cared for me as well as relief at the prospect of going home. I am sure that they felt both anger at being abandoned and relief at being rid of a puzzling stranger. Chimate and I found partial catharsis over more superficial matters that angered both of us at the end.

Chimate did turn to me in need just ten days before I left Dita. It was a market day, and as I was walking to the marketplace I met Chimate returning home. She looked very upset. "Come back to the house as soon as you can!" she begged me.

"I will," I promised. I stayed for half an hour at the market, then left. When I reached Chimate, she was sitting in the reception house talking with two women. The rapidness of her speech and the agitation in her voice surprised me.

Chimate took my arm and pulled me down to sit beside her. "It's terrible, terrible," she began. She held onto my arm tightly. "Kebede hit Galante in the face! She sells him liquor, and he owes her two dollars. She asked him for the money today. When he refused to pay her, she started shouting at him, and he hit her and ran away. She fell down. Blood came from her mouth and her nose. We stayed with her until she stopped bleeding; then she went home, and I came here." Chimate covered her face with one hand.

"Stay here with me the rest of the day, Judy," she finished.

I assured her that I would.

"I raised Kebede, just as I raised Amano's children. He has spent more time with me than with his father Atumo. I sent him to school, I bought him clothes. . . ."

I said nothing. I had had my own troubles with Kebede and did not care much for him. Over the preceding year he had written out false records of local events and had stolen the saddle and bridle from my horse and sold them. I did not know why Chimate continued to depend on him, using him for errands, letting him stay with her periodically. I agreed with Alimetu, Chimate's daughter who lived in Dorze, that Chimate should cut herself loose from Kebede.

Whatever irritation Chimate might have felt toward me at times, I was an island in the rough seas of her grandsons' tempers. I may have been critical of Chimate, but I did not attack her or steal from her. I had no desire to take her land and houses for myself. Now, in a moment or crisis, she allowed herself to lean on me briefly before continuing her independent course.

A week later when Alimetu came for a visit, her distaste for Kebede was obvious. Alimetu was a tall woman with a heavy jaw and a direct gaze. Her husband was one of Dorze's richest and most powerful men, but her life with him was shadowed by the fact that she had no children.

Alimetu and I were sitting in the reception house when Kebede burst in. He had paid his debt to the liquor seller and had begged Chimate's forgiveness. He came and went as usual, noisy and abrasive.

Alimetu looked up at Kebede, smiling a sardonic little smile. "Hello," she said.

"Hello, hello!" he exclaimed loudly. He put down his walking stick and took off his cape. Alimetu watched him expectantly. He approached her, bending to offer the necessary respectful kiss. Alimetu's smile deepened on her lips and began flickering in the depths of her eyes. She sat very still. Kebede bent lower and lower. Alimetu did nothing to stop him. When he almost reached her feet, he choked out, "Well, aren't you going to stop me?"

"Aren't you going to kiss me?" she countered as he hovered above her feet. Then, her teasing finished for the moment, she reached down and lifted Kebede's face to her level and kissed him on both cheeks. She held his chin for a moment and looked into his eyes. "Yes, hello, Kebede," she said, and let him go.

The day after Alimetu's arrival, a guest of mine joined the household, a friend and colleague named Dan Sperber. Dan is a French anthropologist. He had been working in Dorze for the past two years, concentrating on the study of gome. We had talked of making a grand tour of the various Gamo-speaking communities of Ethiopia. By now that tour had been narrowed to a three-day trip to one community farther west, Bonke.

I was much more cautious this time than I had been in January 1970. Dan and I both had letters to the Bonke balabat, but I still asked Chimate to help us. She dictated to Gida a letter of introduction and signed it with her thumbprint.

The letter did us very little good when we reached Bonke. The balabat was absent, his wife was ill, and his servants were afraid to help us. Once again someone came forth and rescued us at nightfall—a man who proved to be a talkative and generous host. When I sneezed, he taught us a new blessing for the occasion that made us all laugh. "Kill an elephant!" he said. We spent two nights with the man, visiting the Bonke market, exploring Bonke, and leaving on the third day.

When we returned from Bonke it was late afternoon. I spent the rest of the afternoon giving away the things I had decided to leave behind in Dita and packing the rest for the trip to Dorze. I gave about half of the items to Chimate and divided the rest among the other members of the household. I also gave small sums of money to the people who had worked for me.

In the evening we had a party. I bought bottles of liquor and invited Chimate's household, her grandsons, Sando who worked as a carrier for me, two men who had gone with Dan and me to Bonke, Halaka Halke, and a man named Wilomo who had worked on Dita history with me. They all came except Halaka Halke; two other men, Unka and his brother Kircho, showed up as well.

We sat around the fire, drinking and talking. I told Dan that I planned to take the longer road to Chencha the next day and hoped he would be willing to take the shorter road with the carriers to Dorze. I explained that Chimate had agreed to send Nigatu to the Chencha hospital for treatment, lending Nigatu a mule to ride.

Innocently turning to Chimate, I said, "I'm glad Nigatu is going with us tomorrow."

"Going with you tomorrow?" Chimate asked, her face hardening. "Now just how is she going to make the trip? She can't walk that far!"

"You said you'd lend her your mule!" I cried.

"Well, I'm not going to lend her my mule," she said.

"What! Why not?"

"My mule," Chimate said with a cold, final tone in her voice, "is much sicker than Nigatu."

My whole body reacted to Chimate's words. I felt as if all my skin were shrinking, tightening around every bone. Staring into the fire, I too burned. I believed that Nigatu, with her sharp tongue and firm mothering of Katse, was in real danger. Now I could do nothing to help her.

Dan took it upon himself to talk me out of my mood. This was, after all, my last night in Dita. He pointed out that I couldn't expect Chimate to have my faith in Western medicine. "What if Nigatu does need hospitalization for tuberculosis?" he asked. "Can she survive the emotional isolation of a long stay in the hospital in Chencha? Who would be able to visit her and feed her?" And so on. I began arguing with Dan and the first bitter rush of feeling subsided. I was able to look about the room again, smile at my friends, urge people to drink up the harake.

Wombara started strumming on the lyre just as he had done my first night in Dita. The young men began to dance. Wilomo, thoroughly drunk, mumbled sentimental good-byes. Seyum, Kebede, Gida, and Sando danced. Then Unka, with a flashing gap-toothed smile, took the floor.

Unka's dancing was exceptional, both controlled and fiery. Bending forward from the waist, almond-shaped eyes narrowed, head poised, he beat out small fine rhythms with his feet. He remained in one corner of the room, his feet scarcely disturbing the grass strewn on the floor. Then with a cry of "Aiee!" he picked up a bamboo splint. Leaping, posturing, his face lively with pleasure and self-mockery, he charged at us, whirled, stamped, and charged again until his brother Kircho, too excited to sit quietly, cut in, took the splint away, and began his own dance.

I ignored Chimate through all of this, although I was aware that she sat to my right, on the far side of the fire from the dancers. Kircho danced, then gave his place to Dan.

Dan, bearded, dressed in canvas boots, khaki jacket and pants, his straight brown hair falling into his eyes, began a deliberate parody of Dita dancing. Where others stamped, he hopped. The bamboo splint oscillated randomly in the air as he advanced in seeming menace, eyes narrowed, teeth showing. Everyone was laughing. He whirled, limbs flailing like a marionette almost out of control.

Chimate was laughing as I had never seen her before, great spontaneous gusts of laughter. Swept along in the current of laughter, I caught Chimate's eye and laughed with her. Sando's voice reached me, "Oh, oh, my intestines are being cooked!"

Dan obliged his audience with spectacularly uncoordinated leaps and lunges. He too was laughing by now. Chimate and I looked at one another again. "I can't remember when I've laughed so much!" she gasped. "Very good, very good," she said to Dan, who was sitting down, panting and looking quite pleased with himself.

I felt more comfortable with Chimate for the rest of the evening. We spent the night in our parallel beds, sleeping in the second room. In the morning, Wara's Mother prepared my favorite highland food, barley porridge with butter and bitter spice powder.

Paranko, the new servant girl, came up to Dan and me as we were eating. She told me, looking quite disappointed, that she wouldn't be able to help carry my things to Dorze. I was surprised; she had been looking forward to the trip, boasting about how she would spend a night in my house before returning to Dita.

"Wara's Mother isn't going either. Chimate has decided to move some of her things to Gulta and we have to go with her."

There was no reason why Chimate had to make that trip on that particular day. I knew this was a deliberate withdrawal of help, and I was angry. I hastily found Sando, who hurried off to see if Wilomo would rent us two packhorses. Chimate was in the back room of the reception house. I saw that she was removing false banana pulp from the large storage bin buried in the floor, wrapping it with leaves. I made no comment as I moved my own things out of the room.

We had quite a time on our hike to Dorze with the packhorses. None of us knew how to load them properly, and we had to retie the loads more than once.

I thanked Chimate properly for her hospitality when I left, forcing myself to smile. She was busy with her packing and spared me little attention. Nigatu, Balaye's Mother, Paranko, and Katse followed me through the door in the compound fence and watched us from the lookout point as we scrambled downhill, calling out, "Have a good journey!" Wilomo came running up and accompanied us part of the way out of Dita, turning back at the river.

Wading through the cold, rushing water, I thought of Chimate. My anger seemed as hard and indissoluble as the pebbles beneath my feet. Good-bye, Chimate, good-bye, I said in my heart. I never expected to see her again.

16   Reconciliation

But you do have friends here in Dita! I'm your
relative here. We lived together, we had good times
together.

~

Reconciliation can take a turn that is almost comic, proceeding by indirection and by half-truths underlain by deeper but unvoiced truths. So it was for Chimate and me. In September 1971, six months after I had left Ethiopia, I returned for a one-month visit to the country and spent two days in Dita. The trip was sponsored by *National Geographic,* which was planning to publish an article I had written about the Dorze weavers.* The editors of the magazine had asked me to travel to Ethiopia with one of their photographers in order to introduce him to the Dorze community.

When I reached Dorze, I learned what I had done earlier in Dita to provoke Chimate's anger. A Dorze friend told me, "Chimate's daughter Alimetu is married to my neighbor. When Chimate visited her daughter, Chimate told me, 'Judy gave Balaye's Mother a blanket but she didn't give me a blanket. When Judy left Dita, she gave money to other people but not to me. She lived in my house, but she helped other people, she didn't help me.' "

"But that's not true!" I cried. "I gave her a sweater before I even came to Dita! I lent her money, five times as much money as I gave anyone else, and canceled the loan! I gave her half of my things when I left Dita and divided the rest among everyone else! It's true I didn't give her a blanket. She had plenty of blankets; Balaye's Mother had nothing."

"Well, she tells people, 'Judy caused me a lot of trouble, and she didn't treat me properly.' She is very angry with you."

My assistant Gida, who had been listening, said, "And how well has she

*See Olmstead, "Ethiopia's Artful Weavers."

treated Judy? She has been seen wearing Judy's missing sweater, the one that was stolen just before we left Dita. Maybe she didn't steal it herself, but she kept it when she caught the thief!"

Changing the subject, I said, "Gida, would you like to visit Dita again? I'm here to work in Dorze, but I'd like to spend a few days in Dita." I thought to myself, It's strange, but now that I know what is on Chimate's mind, it will be easier to see her again.

"We can ask her for the sweater back and see what she says!" Gida replied.

"No, I don't want to mention anything about what she did to me or I to her," I said. "I'd rather ignore that now."

"Well, we should keep our plans a secret. Chimate is in Dita now. If she finds out we are coming, maybe she will leave."

Several days later I was climbing the steep path to Chimate's compound, loose earth sliding under my feet. I ducked to enter the door in the fence and passed first the storehouse and then the cookhouse. There was Chimate, stooping as she came out of the reception house, an expression of surprise on her face. "Judy!" she cried.

We kissed one another on the cheek. She looked at me and smiled. "Katse came running into the house, calling 'Judy is coming! Judy is coming!' I didn't believe her, but she was right." Chimate glanced with affection toward the reception house, where Katse stood just inside the door, peering out shyly.

We walked into the reception house. Everything looked familiar, the grass covering half the floor, the bare clay by the fire pit, the low cushions and the rawhide chairs, the woven bench curving along the wall. Katse sidled up to me and I kissed her. Chimate's two servants, Paranko and Wara's Mother, entered, bringing the flat iron plate for roasting coffee, the wooden mortar and pestle, and the coffeepot.

"I've brought you something," I said to Chimate. I got out shoes and a bag of coffee beans. She seemed pleased. I gave scarves to the other women in the household and a small cotton cape to Katse.

Nigatu was even thinner than before. Her flowered dress hung loosely from bony shoulders. "How are you feeling?" I asked after kissing her.

"I'm able to work, but I cough a lot," she told me. "I've been going to the ayana house."

Chimate looked up as we were drinking coffee and said casually, "You know, I had a lot of trouble on your behalf. In the district capital, Malo, they asked me, 'Did the foreign woman have permission to work in Dita? Did she have official papers?' They called me into the government offices again and again to explain. I lost ten days there!"

"I'm very sorry," I said, and began apologizing profusely for the inconvenience she had suffered. As I spoke I saw that Chimate's grandson Seyum had come into the room as I was talking. He stood by the door, his hand over his mouth, his eyes gleaming. Later in the day I understood that gleam. He and I were returning from a visit to Chimate's friend Halaka Halke, who had been very sick in my absence. I said to Seyum, "I'm sorry I caused Chimate so much trouble in Malo."

This time Seyum's laughter spilled out freely. "Oh, Judy, it's not true!" he gasped. "Our Mother just made that up to make you feel bad!"

Well, Chimate has gotten an apology from me, I thought wryly, even if it's for something that never happened.

That evening Chimate quietly spun cotton, her left hand rising and falling as she drew out the thread and wrapped it around the spindle. "I'm going to a funeral tomorrow morning," she told me. "I'd advise you not to go. People don't remember you, and your presence will distract them."

I agreed. Gida and I spent the next morning at a friend's house. When we got back to Chimate's compound, Chimate was sitting in the reception house with King Wata, the young man whose initiation as king of Dita I had attended several years before. With them was a man I knew only slightly, Halaka Keso. Feisty and talkative at all times, Halaka Keso reminded me of a hornet that afternoon. To my polite hello, he replied, "Why have you been walking about among my sheep? Do you have permission from the government to be here?"

"Yes, has the government given you permission to come here?" King Wata said in a challenging voice, a tiny smile on his lips.

I admitted that I didn't have a letter with me, ending, "Did I bring a new letter every time I went away from Dita and returned again when I was staying here before?"

Halaka Keso said, "You should leave. You're not supposed to be here. We don't like you walking through our fields and through our animals!"

"You don't have permission to take photographs here!" Wata added.

"So you want me to go away," I said slowly, gazing very hard into Wata's eyes. Wata, I knew, was more sophisticated than most Dita men. He had once worked as a weaver in Addis Abeba.

Wata returned my gaze coldly. "Yes, go away!"

"And never come back?"

"Yes, yes, very good."

I looked at Chimate, wondering how much she had done to create this confrontation. Her face was calm and deliberately masked, as if she were the mediator in a dispute. Probably she had been talking against me all morning at the funeral, I decided. I could imagine her describing my arrival, complaining about my lack of permission to work in Dita, commenting on the nuisance we were causing as we walked around Dita. Now Wata and Halaka Keso were sitting in her house, convenient mouthpieces, harassing me as she sat back and watched. She could have stopped them had she so chosen; of that I was certain.

Gida broke in, almost shouting at Wata, "We don't have to listen to you! You aren't the balabat of Dita, you aren't even a chikashum! You don't know anything about letters and permission! We don't need letters!"

Wata pulled his cape over his mouth. I was convinced he did it to hide a delighted grin. Leaning back against the wall, he was silent. Halaka Keso took his place, saying loudly, "Let me see your letters of permission! Let me see them!"

I sat in silence, looking slowly from one person to the next, planning what I would say. I caught and held Wata's eyes. "Do you know what the Dorze people say about the Dita people?" I began. He did not reply. "The Dorze people say"—and here I started to speak the literal truth—"that the Dita people are ignorant and dirty. 'Why would you want to live in Dita, Judy?' they asked me when I moved here. 'The Dita people aren't civilized. They're only *gamo.*'" Gamo, in this context, meant "slaves," a deadly insult.

I paused. No one spoke. I rushed on, embroidering the truth this time as I talked. "When I came to Dorze again and said I wanted to come back to Dita, people told me, 'Why do you want to visit Dita? Stay here in Dorze, Judy. You have only a few weeks to spend with us.' But I told them, 'I have friends in Dita. I want to see them again.' I came back to Dita, even though my Dorze friends thought I was foolish to travel here."

Wata sat stiffly, no longer smiling but using his cape as a barrier between my words and himself. He knew quite well what I was talking about. He had seen for himself in Dorze and in Addis Abeba how the Dorze people felt themselves superior to everyone else in the Gamo Highland.

"I came back," I continued, "and look how I'm being treated! Maybe the Dorze people know better, maybe I should have followed their advice! Maybe in Dita, past friendships mean nothing!"

This was too much for Chimate. "But you do have friends here in Dita, Judy!" she protested. "I'm your relative here. We lived together, we had good times together. What about Halaka Halke? He left his sickbed this morning and walked all the way here to find you, but you already left! You do have friends here."

I was touched by what she told me of Halaka Halke and pleased to have roused her at last. I also felt amused. Having, in all likelihood, set the others against me, Chimate was almost defending me now.

Halaka Keso continued his attack. I had not expected him to be moved by my speech. "If you don't have a letter of permission, leave! You don't belong here!"

"We're leaving tomorrow," I told him crisply. "We're returning to our friends in Dorze. You can't force us to leave any sooner."

"Good! Go, go!" he shouted.

"Judy, you have friends here. Don't forget that!" Chimate cried.

I stared over at Wata again, and he stared back, saying nothing. I felt triumphant. Maybe I'm learning how to play the game in Dita, I thought. It's fun to be so dramatic!

Gida, however, was very upset. "We won't ever return to Dita," he said harshly. "We'll never come back! So this is the way the Dita people behave! This is the way they treat their guests!" He stamped out the door, heading for a friend's house. "You won't see me in Dita again!" he called over his shoulder.

The next morning Halaka Halke came by again, balancing himself carefully on his walking stick as he followed a terraced field above the compound. Descending slowly from field to field, he reached the door in the fence and entered the compound. He drank coffee with us and said goodbye. "When will you return to Dita?" he asked me.

"I don't know," I said truthfully. "When God wills it." Gida said nothing, but his eyes narrowed and he pressed his lips together tightly. I could see he was still angry.

This time Chimate followed us through the fence as we departed. "May God protect you," she called after us from the lookout point. At a curve in the path I looked back one last time and saw Chimate outlined against the fields, tall in her gray dress, black scarf, and white shawl. Nigatu had emerged from the compound and was driving a red female sheep and lamb downhill to a spot where they would be picketed for the day. "Good-bye," I called again, but neither one of them heard me.

17   Chimate's Expanding Political Career

*I've become relatives with our local governor and his
wife. He's the head of our* mahaber *association, too.*

∾

The rainy season had begun in the Gamo Highland. The road connecting
highland and lowland was dotted with miniature ponds, places where a
truck or bus had foundered in the mud and had been shoveled free again.
In the highland, the heavy morning fog thinned by noon and drifted in
wisps across the landscape for the rest of the day. Men tilled the fields barefoot and bare chested, dampness gathering on their skins, their shorts, and
on the cotton capes they had discarded at field's edge. Under gray clouds
the hills glowed with two saturated colors, red-brown and a green that was
almost chartreuse.

I had returned to Ethiopia in late June 1973 to gather Chimate's autobiography and to obtain additional demographic information in Dita for my
doctoral dissertation. Over the preceding two years I was not able to turn
away from Chimate with finality. She and I both ventured beyond the domestic sphere into a world not controlled by our own sex, and this is lonely. I found myself thinking and talking about Chimate. How had she created a place for herself in local politics? How difficult had it been for her? I
needed to hear her voice among the voices of history, and I wanted to record
that voice so others could hear her as well.

My plan was to live for a few weeks in Dita and then to take Chimate with
me to Addis Abeba for six weeks. Gida had discussed my plan with her
during his Easter vacation from school, and she had agreed. I knew that if
we were to attempt to work in Dita, she would never find the time to sit for
hours talking with me. Only by taking her away from the constant demands
of Dita politics could I hope to work with her.

I found Chimate's career in full swing when I reached Dita. Gone were the attempts to hurry Wombara into the role of balabat; gone were Chimate's doubts about continuing the work. Wombara was married and had become an industrious young husband, tilling the fields beside his house like any other Dita farmer. He occasionally helped mediate quarrels, but that was all.

Chimate was doing quite well in factional politics. No longer was the district administered from a distant lowland town. Instead, a new town, Wulo Kore, had been built in the highland near Dita. Chimate had made herself a household in Wulo Kore and spent much of her time there. In the give-and-take of daily life she formed close relationships with local officials, keeping track of what was happening elsewhere in the province.

Wulo Kore was located on a wide shelf of land poised between mountaintop and mountain slope. The little village was bare of trees, windswept and austere. A rambling bamboo fence enclosed a grassy area in which a few tin-roofed houses stood, their unplastered walls made of bamboo poles embedded in the ground and lashed together. This was the government compound. Sparsely scattered tin-roofed and traditional thatched houses dotted the hillside below.

Chimate now owned a prestigious tin-roofed house, although she used it only during the daytime. She was really more comfortable in the two traditional houses squatting in the back, a reception house and a cookhouse. Part of the tin-roofed house she rented out to a young trader named Tafesse, thus helping to establish the very first store in the Dita area. Like other new towns and villages throughout Ethiopia, Wulo Kore was outside the sphere of local rules of property holding. In building houses there Chimate was taking advantage of this fact. All over Ethiopia women had been doing the same—establishing stores, bars, and small hotels.

The total inventory of Tafesse's store included a few spices, safety pins, bars of soap, packets of detergent, hair grease, ballpoint pens, sugar, spaghetti, thread, matches, aspirin, knives, metal plates, notebooks, sheets of paper, packets of tea, bottles of locally distilled liquor, and bread imported from Chencha. For ten cents Tafesse sold a glass of tea with a chunk of bread, refusing to sell one without the other and measuring out the sugar for the tea very carefully.

When I first reached Wulo Kore, I waited for Chimate in Tafesse's store. I chose a chair near a charcoal brazier whose glowing coals kept a teakettle boiling. A teenaged boy entered, carrying a small bundle and dressed in ragged shorts and a dirty cape. With an air of self-importance he sat down and ordered bread with tea, slapping down his ten-cent piece. His eyes bright and excited, his body stiffly poised with his bare feet flat on the floor, he sipped his tea and ate the bread slowly. "Give me another!" he called to Tafesse in a commanding tone, finding a second coin in his pocket and offering it abruptly.

Soon after he left, I was embracing Chimate, kissing her on both cheeks and being kissed in return. She looked as alert and lively as ever. "I'm working on the tax collection," she confided as we sat down. "Next month, in July, all the year's taxes must be paid." Chimate turned to Tafesse. "Give us bread and tea," she demanded, holding out two coins.

In the course of the following conversation I learned that Wombara, Kebede, and Seyum had all married. Nigatu had been very ill for a year but was now much better. The young servant girl had married a lowland man, borne him a child, and died of malaria soon afterward. "I really liked her," Chimate said sadly. Another girl from Chimate's apparently inexhaustible supply of goddaughters had taken the girl's place as Chimate's servant, joining Wara's Mother. My cook of two years before, Balaye's Mother, was living quietly in the town of Gulta.

Seyum's career as a seducer of women, which had started with Tije in the cowshed, now seemed assured. "He sleeps with the wives of the officials here when their husbands are away," Chimate told me in a worried voice. "I wish I could stop him, but I can't. I keep telling him to be careful."

On her part, Chimate wanted to learn how much money I earned in my new job as an instructor of anthropology at the University of Massachusetts campus in Boston and how much my plane ticket to Ethiopia had cost. During the following days she used this information often with the government officials and people living in Wulo Kore, emphasizing that this rich American friend had paid an enormous sum of money just to come and see her.

I was eager to give Chimate some unusual news. "In just three days, on Saturday, we will see something very interesting here in Dita," I began. "The moon is going to cover the sun for a few minutes." I held my hands up in the air, moving my right hand slowly until it covered my left hand, then moving my right hand away. "The moon will cover the sun, and everything will grow dark. Then the sun will shine again."

Chimate's thoughtful frown lasted only a moment. Then she smiled in recognition. "Yes, I have seen that!" she exclaimed. "Sixteen years ago, I left my home in the morning to go to a funeral. Suddenly it became dark as night. The sun was covered over! I was so frightened I turned back and ran home. I stayed in my house for two days before I dared to come out again!"

A short man with a round face who wore a suit, hat, and coat came into the store. "This is the district governor!" Chimate told me in a stage whisper. After she introduced us, he and Chimate asked me questions about my journey and my work in America. A young girl brought us a tray of injera bread with a sauce made from potatoes.

After the meal, Chimate and the district governor withdrew behind a partition and had a long, quiet conference. Chimate obviously liked him. He came from the Gofa region of Gamo Gofa Province and spoke a dialect closely related to the Gamo language that Chimate used. This meant that she could converse with him directly, influencing him more thoroughly than previous governors who spoke Amharic.

When the district governor left, Chimate confided, "I've become relatives with our local governor and his wife. He's the head of our *mahaber* association, too." This was a group who regarded themselves as bound by a special tie of friendship. Although such groups were common in Dorze, this was among the first to be organized in the Dita area. The groups met once a month on a specific holy day to eat special consecrated bread, drink the local grain beer, and spend a pleasant afternoon socializing. "I'll take you to the governor's home some day. But now," Chimate was standing as she spoke, "come with me. I'm going to pay my taxes."

Confidently, Chimate led the way to one of the houses in the government compound. A low partition the height of the tax collector's desk separated him from the front of the room, but when he saw us he invited us to join him and found two chairs. He wore a suit, a white scarf twisted several times around his neck, and very pointed shoes.

"Here are the records of the taxes our family pays," Chimate said, pulling documents from her sash. She put her hand inside the neckline of her dress, drawing out a pouch, and carefully counted out the money she owed. Then she asked about two other people's tax debts. The tax collector found the records and told her that one of them had not paid taxes for three years, the other for five years. "They will pay you this year," she assured him. "There's no need to put them in jail."

When I had a chance to introduce the topic in the evening, I said lightly to Chimate, "Why not travel to Addis Abeba with me and visit a doctor there?" Although she was feeling well, she had had serious problems with her health during the past year.

"I can't come to Addis, I'm afraid of the bus," she replied.

"You rode in a bus before. You can do it again."

"Isn't there a woga, a traditional rule, against old people going to Addis?"

"Old people ride there all the time."

"All right, I'll smear color in my hair to turn it black again and I'll walk around the city with you," Chimate said with an arch smile, linking her arm through mine as if going for a stroll.

Supervising tax collection was one of Chimate's major responsibilities. Many people from Dita came to Chimate with questions about their taxes in the following days. I heard her advise one man, "Make sure that your neighbors borrow money and come here to pay their taxes. As for the new houses they've built, who knows about them? They're taxed only in terms of their fathers' houses by which they are registered."

A highland ritual leader came to Chimate in agitation after talking with the tax collector. His hair, which he as a priest could never cut, hung in coils to his shoulders. "The tax collector says I must pay for last year as well as this year!" he told Chimate.

"Did you pay your taxes last year?"

"Yes, I gave my money to my chikashum who works under you."

"Did you get a receipt from him?"

"What's a receipt?"

"A receipt is a piece of paper with writing on it. It says that you have paid your taxes for such and such a year."

"But I have paid my taxes!"

"Without a receipt, you'll have to pay again. No one will believe that you have already paid."

"I have paid. I gave the money to my chikashum!"

"I believe you, but you must pay again. Get a receipt this time and guard it carefully," said Chimate, trying to end the discussion. The man was not convinced. He continued to argue with her for some time, and she continued to answer him patiently.

Chimate was enjoying herself, repetitive questions or not. She moved briskly, she spoke with authority. A parliamentary election was in progress and Chimate was busy campaigning for one of the candidates who would be elected to represent not only the district of which Dita was a part but the whole subprovince. After giving advice about taxes, Chimate would walk over to the wall of Tafesse's store where the pictures of the candidates were posted. "See this man?" she would say, pointing to one of the pictures. "He's a good man. I know him. Vote for him!"

This candidate, Mesfin, was linked to Chimate by fictive kinship ties. He was the godfather of Chimate's grandson Kebede. A man of the Amhara ethnic group born in northern Ethiopia, he had worked as a schoolteacher in the highland for many years. His symbol on the campaign posters was an ox. His portrait and symbol would be posted above his box in the voting area, where illiterate voters could drop their ballots.

The provincial governor wanted Mesfin to be elected, and Chimate had joined his faction. Only one person of the opposing faction spoke out to me while I was in Wulo Kore. He was willing to talk only because he was giving me a lift in a government Landrover and could not be overheard. An agricultural extension officer, he knew some of my Dorze friends who were critical of Haile Selassie's regime.

The man began by telling me how much he hated the way Ethiopia was being governed. "Our country is just sleeping compared with the rest of Africa," he said. He talked of abuses he had seen in Gamo Gofa Province. "The provincial governor keeps taking land for himself and his friends from people in the lowland. He took the tax money collected to build a road here in the highland. He built a road in the lowland instead! That road went straight to the coffee area where northern Ethiopians like him own land." He paused and looked at me suspiciously. "I don't tell people here what I'm thinking," he said in a warning tone. "I'm stuck here for life. You'll be leaving here in a few months, so I can be open with you."

"I know about that road," I said. "My Dorze friends are very angry about it. They took a case against the provincial governor to the courts and appealed it all the way up to the emperor. They wanted the emperor to remove the governor, but all he did was promise to reprimand him."

"Well, if our candidate for parliament wins, he'll oppose the governor," the man said. "In Dorze, people care about this, but out in Dita people know nothing. They will just do what their balabat recommends. All the balabats and government officials from the highland were called to Arbaminch [the provincial capital] by the governor. He warned them to campaign for

Mesfin. They asked for favors in return; Chimate, I've heard, asked for a piece of land, and he agreed."

I spent three days in Wulo Kore with Chimate before traveling to her compound in the center of Dita on Saturday. I wanted to attend the market and witness people's reactions to the solar eclipse. We were north of the area of total eclipse, however, and the day was so cloudy that no one seemed to notice the slight darkening of the sky.

When I returned to Wulo Kore, I found that the eclipse had been more visible there. Chimate added my prediction of the eclipse to her speech about me, which also had come to include a humorous description of my sleeping bag, a lightweight, down-filled mummy case. She would mime my actions as I climbed into the bag and pulled the hood over my head, saying, "She goes down inside it and pulls it up around her face. What a nice kind of clothing to wear at night!"

Staying with Chimate was an elderly man whom she introduced to me as her brother. "He still lives in Tsela, where I was born. He has come here to pay his taxes," she explained. "He has a weak heart and is ill. He can't eat rich foods with butter and milk in them. He can't eat anything with red pepper in it, and he can't drink tea or coffee or liquor. That's what the doctors told him." She spoke as if all these restrictions conferred a special distinction on her brother. He smiled austerely, his thin hands crossed on his lap.

At bedtime the three of us shared the same room. The old man's heart was troubling him. Chimate gave him the bed closest to the fire pit. He lay there moaning as she built up a large fire, using wood rather than bamboo, although wood was very hard to come by.

"Lie on your side, facing the fire," she told him crisply. She pulled the blankets off his shoulders and down to his waist, exposing his bare chest to the heat. On the other side of the bed she placed the curved bottom of a broken pot and heaped coals into it. From time to time she turned her brother over. She kept the fire burning high, and the old man's dark skin reflected the wavering red and gold flames.

Chimate's manner was confident and alert. She showed neither an excessive tenderness nor a forced cheerfulness. Trying to occupy her brother's attention, she told him stories about events in Dita, her voice animated and incisive. She sat up all night with him while I slept fitfully on the opposite side of the room. In the morning he felt better and went off to see the tax collector about his taxes.

A Granddaughter's Dreams

If I marry an Addis boy,
I'll make delicious coffee!
I'll wear nice clothes!
I'll get beautiful clothes
From a rich husband!

While waiting for Chimate to join me in her Dita household, I had an opportunity to observe her grandchildren running the household. They were enjoying a moment as teenagers without an authority figure near, sharing their dreams, and trying on the role of mediator themselves. Immature though they might be, this generation of Chimate's family would soon be among the carriers of Chimate's dreams in Dita society.

It was early afternoon. In Chimate's Dita compound, Nigatu and Yetse the servant girl, faces shining with excitement, were putting on their best clothes. Over her ordinary workday dress Nigatu pulled a short-sleeved, gaudy nylon dress printed with pink roses and green leaves. Yetse donned a white cotton dress with a wide patterned border at the hemline. Taking turns, they tied flowered scarves on their heads, one girl holding up a small mirror while the other meticulously adjusted the folds of her scarf and the line with which it curved across her forehead.

Next came the matter of draping the transparent cotton shawls with colored borders around their shoulders. Eight feet long, these shawls could be arranged in many ways. Each girl helped the other fold and wrap her shawl, hoping that the result reflected the latest Addis Abeba fashion. Finally, the two pushed their feet into black imitation leather shoes with small heels.

"Take our picture, Judy!" they demanded.

"Where are you going?" I asked as I got my camera.

"To our girlfriend's new home. We'll walk in the procession with her when she comes out of her bridegroom's house for the first time, and then we'll return to the house with her for a feast," Nigatu told me.

Smiling with anticipation, Yetse added, "We'll probably be out all night. We'll eat a lot and drink a lot!"

The girls posed for the camera. As I took the picture, Wombara came into the compound. Grasping Nigatu around the waist, he caught her off balance and swept her off her feet. He held her skirt tightly wrapped around her legs and folded her over to show her backside. "What's this, Judy?" he shouted. "What's this? Something bad!"

Two more of Chimate's grandsons, Kebede and Seyum, had entered the compound, too. As Wombara put Nigatu down, a general free-for-all of bawdy joking, jostling, pulled clothing, and chasing began. The five managed to stand still for another portrait. Gida, who had joined me two days earlier when his school closed for the summer, joined them for a final set of pictures.

Chimate was still in Wulo Kore but planned to visit central Dita soon. Not only had she built a new compound in Wulo Kore, she had added new houses to her Dita compound. Where there had been three houses, there were now five. After Nigatu, Yetse, and the three young cousins had left for the ceremony, Gida went indoors to read a book I had given him, and I pulled a cushion outside and sat against one of the new houses.

The older servant woman, Wara's Mother, had been milking Chimate's two cows in the cookhouse. She herded them outdoors, taking them downhill for water and a few hours of grazing. Fat rain-bearing clouds blew along the valley, small patches of sunlight scurrying after them across the landscape. I looked around Chimate's compound, remembering how Halaka Halke had worked on the houses and the fence and how Chimate's son Atumo had slaughtered a ram, sprinkling its blood over each door to bless the compound for use. Now the ram's horns hung over the entrance in the fence, as gray as the weathered bamboo to which they were attached.

Herding their sheep and cattle, children on the hillside above whistled shrilly and cried, "Get going! Get going!" Men below clustered in a group, nailing a coffin together. Dita was suffering from an epidemic, and many people were dying. Staccato hammer taps mingled with the screaming of a neighbor's baby. In a bamboo grove a flock of small birds twittered, a light constant sound like raindrops falling.

Katse, now a lively four-year-old, ran into the compound with her play-mate. The little girls tumbled around in front of the cookhouse, squealing and giggling. Katse found the rind of a small green lime. She showed it to the other girl and then put both hands behind her back. Bringing out one closed fist, she opened it. Her hand was empty. "I don't have it!" she cried.

"Neither do I!" cried her friend.

Katse brought out the other fist, exclaiming as her fingers uncurled, "Here it is!"

"Here it is!" chirped the other girl. As they continued to play with the lime rind, Amsale, another of Chimate's grandsons, went into the cook-house to look for eggs. His two hens came exploding from the cookhouse door, followed by Chimate's two roosters and a laughing Amsale. Lighting on the rim of a large clay pot standing under the eaves of the cookhouse, the red and gold rooster shook his feathers and began to crow. Amsale snatched up the lime rind and ran across the compound, expecting the two girls to pursue him. Instead, Katse's friend took a used battery from her pocket—I recognized it as one of mine—and rolled it toward Katse, start-ing a new game.

A woman I had never seen before entered the compound, stooping very low so that the bundle of grass she carried on her back would clear the door. She walked toward me, and suddenly she was on her knees kissing my feet. Startled, I lifted her and kissed her cheeks. She went into the reception house, dropped her bundle, and left. I saw that she had brought the tough long-stemmed grass used for covering the floor.

I called for Amsale, a ten-year-old grandson who was living in the house-hold and helping Nigatu with the work.

"Yes?"

"Who was that woman?"

"A tanner woman. The tanners bring grass to us," he explained. "They do it to honor Our Mother. We pay nothing, but other households have to give them a basket of grain every year."

The next person to arrive that afternoon was a big man wearing a cro-cheted pillbox cap. Bujito was a weaver who had made an old-fashioned arrangement with Chimate. He lived and ate in Chimate's household, set-ting up his loom there to weave a cape from the cotton thread Chimate and Nigatu had spun. When the work was finished, he would receive a small fee. Fifty years earlier, this type of arrangement had been common, with itinerant Dorze weavers traveling throughout the southern half of Ethiopia from household to household. Now most weavers worked in their own homes, selling their work to middlemen who resold the cloth.

Nigatu and Yetse loved to tease large, slow-moving Bujito. They would provoke him into exchanges of insults, each side trying to top one another's comment. "Go to your father's funeral!" they would cry. "Give birth to stones!" he would retort.

The following day, when Yetse had recovered from her night at the new bride's coming-out ceremony, she persuaded Bujito to leave his loom and help her dig potatoes. Bujito put the two-pronged hoe over his shoulder, Amsale joined him, and they went with Yetse to the potato field beside the compound.

Soon Yetse came stamping into the reception house, shouting, "He insulted me! Bujito insulted me!" Bujito and Amsale came crowding in after her, shouting too. Nigatu and Gida set themselves up as mediators, learning this role through practice in household quarrels just as Chimate must have done as a teenaged girl. Amsale became the witness. Under questioning, the story came out.

The quarrel had started with Yetse's refusal to step out of the way as Bujito turned over the soil with the hoe. Bujito had reminded her, "Your brother killed a man!" referring not to a deliberate killing but to an accident.

"Your mother slept with her neighbor!" was Yetse's retort, and the exchange of insults began. After a time, Bujito wandered off, spoke to a shepherd boy, and returned. The boy came up to Yetse, saying before running away, "My penis isn't big enough for you! Use Bujito's!"

Bujito, after careful persuasion from Nigatu and Gida, finally admitted that he was in the wrong and apologized to Yetse. Gida said privately to me, "Bujito plays around with the girls like that. They don't respect him. They provoke him and get him into trouble."

In the evening, there was barely enough wood for a fire to boil the potatoes for supper, and none to heat the room after the meal. "I'll find more wood," Bujito volunteered, and left. He did not return that night. I sat in the cold reception house, my sleeping bag pulled around me, trying to forget how chilled I felt. Nigatu and Yetse sat side by side on the floor, their backs against a partition, their legs stretching straight in front of them. "Why don't you sing some songs?" I suggested.

"Will you take out your machine and tape them?" they asked.

"Of course. After you sing, you can listen to yourselves," I agreed.

Clapping their hands in separate, complementary rhythms, the two sang, sometimes in unison, sometimes taking separate parts. My favorite song described a girl named Tume and her feelings about marrying boys from various highland communities and from Addis Abeba. The pull of modernization on Nigatu and Yetse was evident; the boys from Addis were clearly preferred. The two girls had been pleading with me for several days, "Judy, when you go to Addis Abeba, can we come, too?" That decision, I always replied, would rest with Chimate.

Yetse improvised the lines of the song as she went along, with Nigatu clapping and interjecting a brief one-note "Eh!" every few words. They started with the chorus. "Eh, Tume!" sang Yetse.

"Eh!" replied Nigatu, using a slight vibrato.

"Eh, Tume!"

"Eh!" repeated Nigatu. Both girls broke into a moment of complicated hand clapping and then Yetse began her first verse. These were her words, without the interjections and without the chorus:

> Now the boys can marry.
> They think of work.
> Dita boys learn to trade.
> Dita boys ignore farming.
>
> I won't marry a Dita boy!
> I don't like eating smelly tripe!
>
> To go to Addis
> The road passes Dorze, Wolamo, and Sidamo.
> With the telephone
> I can call Kambata!
>
> I won't marry someone from Dita!
> Dita stinks!
>
> If I can drink good coffee,
> I'll marry a Zad'a boy;
> But I don't like working hard,
> And they make their wives carry things on their backs!
>
> If I marry a Doko boy,

He'll make me a beast of burden!
His people don't step off the road to shit!

If I marry a Dorze boy,
He'll make me carry things, too,
But the Dorze town is nice.
Boys wear shoes there!
In the market, where people gather,
You can hear the bus horn shouting!

I won't refuse an Addis boy!
I won't refuse tasty injera bread!
If I marry an Addis boy,
I'll make delicious coffee!
I'll wear nice clothes!
I'll get beautiful clothes
From a rich husband!

But I won't sit at home alone,
Guarding his house!
And I don't want him beating me!
I won't refuse an Addis boy,
But one thing I don't like:
Addis boys stay out all night
And don't come home till dawn!

When Nigatu and Yetse had listened to the tape, we all went to bed. I woke the next morning to the sound of falling rain and stepped outside. Our compound seemed to have been cut adrift from earth and to be sailing through a cloud, sailing so slowly that instead of parting the cloud it dissolved into it. With a comfortable sense of isolation, I went back to bed, sleeping late with the others.

The rain had stopped by the time we had eaten breakfast. Seyum and Sando, the young man who carried my things between Dita and Dorze, arrived. They were going to help Gida and me gather additional information on Dita demography from households I had not contacted two years before. Sando was to work with Gida, Seyum with me.

Slipping along the paths, Seyum and I visited twenty-three households, asking questions about who was living in each household, their ages, and the birth history of each woman in the household. One man invited us to share his lunch of steamed potatoes and cabbage. While the food cooked, the man stood on a ladder changing the thatch on the roof of his house. As he pulled away the mossy, rotting thatch before replacing it with fresh straw, toads and grubs fell to the ground.

As we ate, the man asked me the same questions I encountered in almost every household. "Are you married? No? Don't you want children?"

When we had finished for the day and were sitting with Gida and Sando in Chimate's compound, Bujito came back. "I spent the night in Addis Abeba," he told us humorously. He had a large tree branch with him, which he and Sando began to chop into firewood. Prudently, no one asked Bujito where he had gotten the wood.

Nigatu and Yetse sat in a corner of the reception house, laughing and whispering. Katse had an enormous wooden comb and was trying to comb her hair with it. Sando, tired of chopping wood, came in and went over to Nigatu. He plucked at the black tights she was wearing that day and the two started to wrestle.

Suddenly Amsale was at the door. "Our Mother is coming!" he exclaimed, a nervous expression on his face. The young people quieted immediately. The older servant woman, Wara's Mother, hurried into the room. Addressing Yetse and Katse, she said crossly, "You don't help me with anything! You let me do all the work!"

The two girls got up, joining Wara's Mother and Amsale in the tasks of straightening the house, lighting a fire in the reception house for coffee, and preparing food in the cookhouse. I found this burst of activity quite comic. "We have a proverb in our country about this," I told Seyum. "We say, 'When the cat's away, the mice will play!'"

Seyum laughed in recognition. "That's true, Judy," he agreed.

When Chimate had arrived and was going about the house like any householder after an absence, finding fault everywhere, Seyum said with a giggle that bubbled up like a small, clear spring, "Oh, that Judy, she knows what's going on here. She said to me, 'When the cat's away, the mice will play!'"

Chimate, seeing the humor in the situation, laughed and paused for coffee. As she sat drinking from her special cup painted with a spray of leaves, a loud noise was heard from the cookhouse. "What!" Chimate exclaimed angrily. "The mule is kicking the side of the house! My house will fall down! Why haven't you done anything about it?"

Nigatu said quickly, "It's the first time it has happened." This was a patent lie; I had heard the mule kicking every day.

Chimate was soon roaming the compound again, poking into every corner. Nigatu, Yetse, and Amsale were sneaking around the household, trying simultaneously to listen to Chimate respectfully and to disappear. I felt sorry for them, and the next time Chimate walked through the room, I invited her to listen to the songs I had recorded in Dita.

Chimate sat down. I played the songs Yetse and Nigatu had sung, then the songs from an evening party. Chimate relaxed and was genial for most of the evening, but the last sound I remember hearing as I fell asleep that night was the sound of Amsale sobbing loudly in the cookhouse over a final reprimand.

19   Chimate in Addis Abeba

"Where will we write this book?"
"Here in Addis Abeba."
"Are you going to write about me?"
"Yes."

∽

"Weaving! Weaving! 'I'll go to Addis Abeba, I'll wear shoes, I'll wear clothes, good clothes,' say the boys. Even the girls don't want to stay in Dita!" exclaimed Chimate, perhaps thinking of Yetse's song. "The boys say, 'I'll go to Addis and learn how to weave.' They don't stay in Dita. As for me, I don't like weaving. If every man were a weaver, everyone would be lazy. Men go to prostitutes in Addis Abeba, and they want to sleep with other men's wives. When they're not weaving, they want to steal things!

"Instead of this, learning in the school is a good thing. If boys were educated in Dita, they would do more farming, and Dita would be filled with money. Even if Ethiopians stopped being weavers, the foreign countries are filled with clothes. Why don't we buy those and wear them?

"I've been sending one of my granddaughters, Nigatu's sister, to school in Chencha. A few other Dita families do the same thing, but most Dita children never go to school. I have worked for many years to bring a school to Dita, and just this year we have opened a primary school. One hundred and fifteen students are attending the school. All look at their paper and can write their names on it! All are learning to read, they started right after Easter!"

The young people overhearing this discussion sat in skeptical and forbearing silence. Nigatu and Yetse still hoped to accompany Chimate to Addis Abeba. As for Sando, who had begun cultivating a dependent client relationship with Chimate shortly before I first met her, his dreams had changed radically since I had taken him for medical care to Addis Abeba. He was doing his best to learn weaving so he could return to the city again. "What is there to see in Dita?" Sando would ask me. "What is there to do in Dita?"

Like many others who introduce social change, Chimate was finding that the school had unintended consequences that were the opposite of what she had hoped. She told me wryly, "And now that school is out, what happens? The students' parents send them to Addis to weave! Weaving, now! There are many, many, many Dita people in Addis, more than four hundred, more than necessary. The land in Dita just sits here uncultivated. Just how many men have become impoverished through weaving?"

Chimate was experiencing on a small scale what was true for the whole of Ethiopia. The program of modernization initiated by Emperor Haile Selassie included the creation of primary and secondary schools, the establishment of Haile Selassie I University in Addis Abeba, and the sending of promising students abroad for further education. It was this educated group that was persistent in criticizing the pace of change as too slow. During the late 1960s, for example, the university students created one of the strongest student movements in Africa. As for the military, the lower ranking officers who had been educated abroad would eventually play important roles in the Ethiopian revolution.

For the time being, Chimate was pleased with the changes that had come to Dita through the establishment of the district capital nearby. Dita now had access to a school, a store, and an agricultural extension office through which Chimate and others planned to buy fertilizer for their fields. Chimate's friendship with the district governor gave her a strong voice in local politics.

Chimate's candidate for parliament, the man with the ox on his campaign poster, won the election. He and the provincial governor now owed Chimate political debts. Through them she could hope to gain a link to provincial and national political factions that could further enhance her political role.

Chimate, who was enjoying local politics, was not eager to travel to Addis Abeba with me. Gida finally had a private talk with her one morning while Seyum and I were interviewing Dita households. When we returned for lunch, I could see Gida and Chimate walking together high on the hillside above Chimate's compound, following the edge of a terraced field. When they came back, it was my turn to walk with Gida out of hearing of the household.

"Well?" I asked.

"Chimate says that she'll go to Addis Abeba when the tax collection is over and the government pays her for the work. She doesn't want us to tell anyone that she's going to work for you. We're going to take her to the doctor, aren't we?" I nodded, and he continued, "That's what she's going to tell people. She says she wants to ask permission from the district governor for going."

"Again? She's already asked him once."

"Yes, maybe she thinks he'll say no this time," Gida said pessimistically.

Gida and I took it upon ourselves to write a letter to the district governor and secured his assent. I decided to travel on to Addis Abeba alone, in part to work on a questionnaire among the Dorze weavers, in part to entice Chimate to join me.

Addis Abeba occupies a series of hills resting on a high plateau thousands of feet above sea level. Eucalyptus trees grow everywhere. In the poor quarters of the city, people cook their meals over blue, smoky fires of eucalyptus leaves and wood and build their homes from eucalyptus poles plastered with mud and straw and roofed with tin. Through the eucalyptus groves and broad muddy lanes of Addis Abeba, asphalt boulevards bordered by wide cement sidewalks thread their way, stringing together clumps of modern buildings like so many beads.

I moved into a house along Churchill Road, which I shared with various itinerant Peace Corps volunteers, renting a room occupied during the school year by a British schoolteacher. A pair of Ethiopian students lived unobtrusively in the rear portion of the house. Half an acre of grass and eucalyptus trees surrounded the square, Italian-built house. A fence made of corrugated tin enclosed the whole area. A guard and his family lived on the premises. As in similar households throughout the city, his principal job was opening the main gate to visitors and keeping an eye on the compound after dark.

This household was typical of moderately well-to-do Ethiopians and of foreigners living in Addis Abeba. Here I waited for Chimate. On a Friday afternoon at the very end of July, Gida came to the door.

"Welcome, Gida!" I cried. "Did you bring Chimate with you?"

"Yes, she is here in Addis," he replied. "The district governor has come to Addis, too." Gida looked tired and irritable.

"How was the journey?" I asked.

"Chimate was terrified!" Gida burst out, with the kind of disgust only adolescents seem to muster. "She sat next to me, and all the time she kept holding onto me and moaning!"

Impatiently, I waited to visit Chimate the next day, but when Gida arrived he told me that she wanted to be alone for several days to settle into the household of her younger daughter, who lived in Addis. On the third day he went to find her but returned alone. "She's too busy to go with you to the doctor, Judy," he reported. "She must mourn with all the people she knows whose relatives have died, and many people are bringing cases to her to mediate. She's waiting for the district governor to come see her, too."

The next day Gida and I went to the house of Chimate's daughter Almaz, waited for Chimate, and returned without seeing her. The following morning we tried again. A taxi, one of the blue and white Fiats shared by passengers going in the same direction—they cost only a quarter—dropped us at one end of a wide dirt road. As we walked along, we saw women selling vegetables and spices by the side of the road. A leper lying on a mat begged money from us. With a warning honk of its horn, a green Volkswagen swept by. We crossed a bridge, turned left, walked up a stony path between a row of houses, and entered a house whose door stood open. Its brown earthen walls had been covered inside with newspapers, and its floor was made of coarsely woven bamboo.

The young woman who hurried into the room was Almaz. She greeted me shyly. "Our Mother is out," she said. "Why don't you stay here and wait for her?" She pushed a charcoal brazier, which had been smoldering in a corner, toward us and fanned the coals.

Yetse entered the room. "Hello, Judy!" she said, coming to kiss me and to be kissed in return. She put a pot of lentils on the brazier and began to stir them.

"So you did come to Addis Abeba," I observed.

"Nigatu had to stay in Dita, but I've come here to help Our Mother!" she said, smiling. "I like Addis very, very much."

"Our Mother doesn't like Addis," Almaz informed me, "but all the Dita people are treating her very well. They're giving her new clothing to wear and money to spend."

Kassa, Almaz's husband, went to find Chimate. I felt frustrated and tense, wondering if I was ever going to see Chimate again, and was unable to summon any small talk as we waited.

But at last Chimate arrived. She bustled through the door, magnificent in a white dress and black coat, both gifts from the Dita people living in Addis Abeba. She handed Almaz money to buy us each a bottle of beer and sat down smiling, ready to tell us a story.

"This city is a terrible place!" she began. "You know our neighbor from Dita, the woman called Karetse. She came to Addis a little before I did. She went out to buy cotton in the market one day, but on her way home she got lost. She asked a Dita man to help her. 'Of course I can take you back to your husband's home,' he told her. 'Just follow me.' She followed him through the streets, and he brought her to a strange door. 'Come in,' he said.

" 'This isn't my home!' she cried. 'Of course not,' he said, 'I just want to drink some coffee before we continue.' So she went inside, and when he had her in a room, he locked the door. She screamed but no one came. He spent the night there with her. He slept with her! He kept his promise to bring her home, but he did it early the next morning."

"Her husband won't bring her to the city again!" exclaimed Kassa. He was a short man whose suit, tan raincoat, pointed leather shoes, and narrow-brimmed hat bespoke his success as a weaver.

"Would you like to visit my house before we go to the clinic?" I asked Chimate. I admit that I was childishly eager to show Chimate a bit of my own culture, a house with wooden floors, large glass windows, and a fireplace. After having been Chimate's guest for so long, I wanted to impress her with the existence of my own independent world.

"Can we walk to your house?" Chimate queried anxiously. Almaz and her husband exchanged glances. They knew how afraid Chimate was of taxicabs.

"No, we can't," I said, "it's too far."

During the ride, Chimate kept her eyes shut and held my arm tightly. When we got out she steadied herself, then picked her way carefully through the puddles in the path leading to the door in the compound fence. Almaz and Kassa had accompanied us, ostensibly out of solicitude for Chimate but in reality, I suspect, out of curiosity about my house and about the doctor's office.

As the household cook made coffee, Chimate, Almaz, and Kassa sat on the edge of the living room sofa. All three were somewhat reserved, obviously wishing to observe their surroundings but also concerned about maintaining their dignity. Chimate remarked on the woolen throw rugs and the large dining table with six chairs planted around it. Kassa began leafing through a magazine. Almaz sat with the alert stiffness of someone who wants to look everywhere without turning her head too much.

Chimate spotted something on the mantelpiece over the fireplace. She looked very hard at it and started to laugh. She pointed it out to the others, who frowned and squinted at the object and then laughed too, Almaz covering her mouth with her hand. "Is that from America?" Chimate asked me.

The item in question was a crudely carved statue of a naked man. A foot tall, it was scarcely more than a round post with large circles of bone stuck on for eyes and bone slivers like piano keys pushed under the upper lip for teeth. Above the statue's barbaric face, a phallic ornament sprouted from the forehead, and from the loins hung a huge phallus.

"No, it's not from America. It's from Konso in Ethiopia," I replied. "This is for foreigners to buy. The Konso people make big ones," I indicated the height of four feet, "to put on the grave of a man who has killed an enemy in battle."

"I know Konso," Chimate said. "It's in the lowland, two days' journey from Dita. We buy these from them." She pointed to the phallic ornament. Made of brass and tied to the forehead with a headband, the ornament was part of the initiation attire when a man took the title of halaka. Chimate looked at the statue in disapproval. "No one but a child is seen naked in Dita," she said.

The statue remained the focus of amused interest as we drank our coffee. Then we took a taxi to the airport, where the Ethiopian doctor recommended to me worked in a clinic. Together Chimate, Almaz, and I went in to see him. Chimate was dignified, composed, and unafraid as he examined her. Then Almaz asked if the doctor could examine her, too. Far more nervous than her mother, she kept exclaiming, "I hope he won't want to cut me open! I won't let him cut me open! I don't want any injections either!"

The doctor prescribed some medicines and told me he wanted to see Chimate again. He explained where I could reach him the next day. As we emerged from the clinic, I asked the others if they would like to watch the airplanes land. Eagerly, everyone agreed. We went to a snack bar with an observation balcony and ordered a meal.

Kassa began explaining airplanes to Chimate. "I've seen them!" she interrupted him. "Three times a week an airplane comes to Arbaminch from here. Judy rides in airplanes, but as for me, I'll never step in one. Flying up there in the clouds! I'd be frightened!"

As we ate, we saw one small plane land and one large jet take off. No other flights were scheduled for many hours. Chimate had a wonderful time, exclaiming and gesturing, and was disappointed when we had to leave.

During the taxi ride to my house, Chimate kept her eyes open and sat up very straight. "You see," she said with a shaky laugh, "I'm used to it now." I hurried out to a pharmacy when we reached the house, and Gida began to play tapes he had made of men singing as they cultivated a field in Dita. When I returned, everyone was smiling and moving in time to the singing. Kassa was shaking an imaginary spear in his hand and looked as if he wanted to dance. "Play those songs again!" he commanded Gida as the tape ended.

Carrying the medicines with them, Chimate, Almaz, and Kassa finally left. I asked them, "Can Gida come and get Chimate tomorrow? The doctor wants to see her again."

"Yes, of course," they agreed, but on the next day Gida came to me alone. "Chimate is spending the day with the district governor," he told me gloomily. "When will we be able to work with her?"

Chimate did in fact arrive the following day. After the visit to the doctor, we returned to my house. Gida, talking loudly over the sound of rain on the tin roof, began, "Now I'm going to tell you about the book."

To this cryptic statement, Chimate sensibly replied, "What book?"

"The book Judy is going to make from what you tell her," explained Gida.

"Will it be a textbook for students?" Chimate asked. Her main contact with books had been with the schoolbooks of her grandsons and granddaughter.

"Anyone will be able to read it," Gida answered. "She will write it from the history you know."

"Where will we write this book?"

"Here in Addis Abeba."

"Are you going to write about me?"

"Yes," Gida replied. "After the book is written, Judy will go to her own country. There are people there who make books. When the book is published, if people buy it money will go to you, to Judy, to me, and to the publisher. Now if we work well, we might get a lot of money!"

"Let's start working today!" Chimate exclaimed. "I'm glad I didn't bring anyone here with me! I'm glad I came alone with Gida. No one else should come with me here. When I come here I'll say that I am going to the doctor."

I was amused by Chimate's response. "Will the governor create problems for you?" I asked her.

"The governor is telling me to hire men to till my land," Chimate replied. "It's the time to do that. He is going back to Dita on Monday, and he told me to go with him. You should go to the governor and give him some reason why I can't return with him. He can explain that I will come later. I'll stay here, but I don't like living with my daughter's husband."

"I cannot guarantee that I will make a book from what we do here," I told Chimate truthfully. "I will pay you for every day of work, just as I pay Gida."

"Very good," said Chimate. Our conversation turned to other topics. I found myself talking about the way people in Dita had been asking me if I was married. "In my country," I told Chimate, "not every woman wants to marry. Women can work and support themselves without husbands."

"Don't you want to have children?" Chimate asked in surprise.

"Only some of us do. Even then women may leave the children home and go to work. Sometimes our husbands help us. I know one family in which the woman takes care of the children half of the time, and her husband takes care of them half the time."

"You take turns with the children!"

"Some of us do. Some of us share the work in the household, too," I replied. "My sister is married. She doesn't have any children yet; she hopes to have some one day. She takes turns with her husband. One day she cooks the food, the next day he cooks the food."

"Men cook food?" Chimate asked skeptically.

"Both my sister and her husband have their work to do outside the home," I explained. "They share the work inside the home."

"Men don't work in our houses!" Chimate said emphatically. "What a man brings home, a woman cooks. She stays home and guards the house. While a man works, the woman stays home and eats what he produces. Women spin the cotton, have it woven, and wear it as buluko and gabi capes." Chimate paused, considering what I had told her. Thoughtfully, she continued, "In your country everyone must be educated. It's good for a husband and wife to help one another. But if you ever marry, your husband wouldn't allow you to return to Ethiopia!"

"If he wouldn't come with me, I'd come alone!" I cried. "If he was free to come, I'm sure he'd come with me."

Chimate inquired with a smile, "Are you going to go home, enter your husband's house as a bride, and return to us?"

"I don't know. *Ts'os eres,* God knows!"

Pleased, Chimate exclaimed, "By now, you even know how to call God's name!"

"I don't know if I'll have a child or not," I continued. "There would be a lot of work involved." Chimate began to laugh. "A woman has to watch over her baby most of the day and feed and clothe and educate it. It takes many years."

Chimate said with a sweeping gesture, as if she were calling the world to witness, "She says she doesn't want a baby. A man wants one right away!"

"There aren't any servants in my country to help with the work," I said. "The parents of a child have to look after it. Usually the mother does most of the work."

"Does the mother look after the child by herself?" Chimate asked. She began laughing again. "You don't want to have to deal with this problem!"

"Yes, I don't want to be bothered," I agreed.

"Carrying a baby is hard work," Chimate said. "For ten months we carry our babies on our backs. When a baby cries, mothers take care of it, or else they think its neck will break."

"Did anyone help you look after your babies?" I asked Chimate.

"I don't know how to carry babies on my back after giving birth," Chimate admitted. "I didn't even breastfeed my own children. Two people helped me. One was an old woman. One came in the morning, one in the evening and spent the night sleeping with the baby. When my eldest son Amano was born, I did carry him some but didn't nurse him."

"All women are not the same," I said. "There are women who enjoy taking care of babies and women who don't enjoy taking care of them."

Chimate hastened to inform me that her behavior toward her babies was not her free choice. "In order to have many babies, my husband didn't let me sleep with my babies and nurse them. I'm not like other women. I was well liked by my husband." She smiled, thinking of the past. "Yes, an old woman slept with the baby, and a young girl carried the baby during the day. The young girl was the age of my granddaughter Nigatu. In the past, the slaves did this work. The old woman fed the baby when it was hungry, and in the evening she would wash the baby and grease it and take it to bed with her. I gave her a buluko cloth. I didn't sleep with the babies."

"It seems to me that Nigatu likes babies," I said.

"Yes, she likes caring for them," Chimate agreed. "Her mother didn't raise her; an Amhara woman fed and washed and raised Seyum and Nigatu and Genet, not their mother."

I changed the topic slightly. "Right now we think in our country that women who want to have babies should have them and those who don't want to have babies should do something else."

"There are many babies!" Chimate commented. "What's the use of having so many babies? There isn't much food these days, and if there are many babies born, what's going to happen?"

"Maybe people here want to have many children because they know that many will die when they are young," I said. "If you knew that all of your children would live, would you want to have a lot of children?"

Chimate replied realistically, "There are many people who want more than nine children."

"But if this happens, won't the land for each one be very small?"

Contradicting what she had said earlier, Chimate replied, "They can buy land if they earn money. Today my son Atumo has ten boys and a girl. Right now his wife Tulje is pregnant. Each one of the children will have its own chances in life. Some will be weavers, some servants, whatever they want. It's their own luck. Why get rid of children if God gives them to us? There are many people who have more children than Atumo. If a husband doesn't have sexual intercourse with his wife, she will criticize him to her neighbors. 'My husband hasn't slept with me for two or three months! He ignores me!' she will tell them."

Continuing the topic of unwanted children, I said, "In our country if we don't want another child, we can take medicines."

"That's gome here," Chimate replied. "The district governor's wife has had babies, babies, babies. She has begun to have very difficult deliveries. He has said to me, 'We have enough children. What shall we do?'"

"Also in our country, if a woman becomes pregnant before she is married, she may get rid of the baby," I told Chimate.

"We have this custom, too," she said. "When women have been stolen from the road by a man and broken and have become pregnant, there are old people who give them medicine to get rid of the baby. Women in the past would leave an illegitimate baby in the forest because it was gome to keep such a baby. There is a special forest for that. Hiding the child, the woman would take it when no one could see her and would leave it in the forest."

"You've heard of the Borana people, haven't you?" I asked. "They live farther south from you in Ethiopia, near the country of Somalia. Among the Borana people, the husband and wife marry for a lifetime but each one can have as many lovers as desired. Any child to whom a woman gives birth is counted as her husband's child."

"This Borana custom is bad!" Chimate exclaimed. "Every woman is any man's wife. Every man is any woman's husband. That's bad! But one man in our country can marry three wives. That's not good, I don't like it. Once my husband had two wives, but I didn't like it. There was always trouble. I didn't like it. There are some women who go crazy because they hate each other so much. Kassa has two wives, Almaz and another woman. The other woman is the mother of the boy who lives with Almaz now. That woman went crazy, and when Kassa took her to the hospital, the doctors told him she was sick because of her hatred for his other wife. But she refused treatment and came home.

"When my husband, his other wife, and I were living together," Chimate admitted, "I started hitting her when he wasn't home. I don't like it when a man has more than one wife. Men like it. 'Hashu, marry! Hashu, marry!' the other men say. As for me, when my husband was away, I hit the other wife. I don't like that custom!"

I was surprised and a little shocked by what Chimate had just told me, but I didn't have to make any reply. She launched into a story—one of her stories that I call a moral tale. The story underlined a point she had just made and showed the folly of the behavior she condemned.

∼

During the reign of King Mijola, a man called Kile married two wives and kept them in the same house. When Kile was living with his two wives, the first one hadn't given birth, and that is why he wanted to have a second wife. Rich, rich, rich he was and brave, too. He was my husband's relative.

After he married his second wife he spent night after night with her. He never came to his first wife. He didn't come to her for many days and she was very angry. She took a large knife and heated, heated, heated it in the fire and went to the place where they were living. She fed them supper and they ate it. The knife kept heating; she gave them a full gourd of beer with honey in it. They thought she was showing her approval of the marriage. Thinking she liked the second wife, they went to bed.

She came in with the heated knife. First, she thrust it into her husband's stomach and turned it around and around, then into the woman's stomach and stirred it around as if cooking. Again she stabbed the woman. The woman had caught hold of her wrist while she was stabbing her husband.

The first wife watched, watched, watched the two; the second wife moved around before she died. The husband didn't move at all. At last, the first wife killed herself. All three died. To this day, no one takes anything from that land. It has been marked off. The place where the house stood has been marked clearly. People don't walk over it. If they have to relieve themselves, they don't do it there. No one cultivates the land. It's blood-soaked land. Killing three people on that piece of land, she left off. Women were cruel in the past. In the past, they didn't put up with bad treatment. Three died by one hand.

～

Chimate looked out the window. The rain had stopped. "I think I had better go now," she said. "Almaz wants you to come to our house for a meal tomorrow. Can you come for lunch?"

"Of course. Thank you very much," I said, as she and Gida left.

20 *The Prince*

The book tells the truth!

∾

Finding Chimate and working with her on a specific day continued to be difficult. Even in Addis Abeba, the Dita people made many demands on her time. Gida would go to get her in the morning, escorting her to the house where I was living if she was free to work. Each trip was explained as a visit to the doctor. I suspect that Chimate insisted that no one know of our work together in order to maintain her own prestige. Far better that I seem to be helping her, waiting upon her daily, than that she be known to be working for me.

On the days Chimate could not come, Gida and I worked frantically, transcribing the tapes of our interviews. Apart from the interviews, Chimate and I made three bona fide trips to the doctor and shared many meals in my household and hers. Once a German anthropologist, himself working with a balabat from a community two hundred miles south of Dita, invited Chimate, Gida, and me to lunch and engaged her in a discussion of marriage customs. She was intrigued by his arrangement with his wife, whereby one of them did fieldwork in the south while the other cared for their children in Addis Abeba. On another occasion, an Ethiopian journalist invited us to lunch and came away praising Chimate's poise and beauty. "She is a real aristocrat!" he exclaimed.

Chimate continued to find amusement in my way of life. One day, spaghetti caught her attention. She valiantly tried to eat some, laughing at herself as she pursued it around her plate with an unfamiliar fork. "So this is what Tafesse sells in his store!" she said. "I'm never going to buy any!"

On a Sunday afternoon late in August, I gave a feast for Chimate, Kassa, Almaz, Gida, the students living in the house with me, and several young men from Dorze. The tapes of Dita music were played and people danced. Then Chimate asked, "Can't you show us some American dancing, Judy?"

I put an Aretha Franklin record on the record player, and several of the young men and I danced. The students were proficient dancers who went to the discotheques when they could afford it. We had a good time dancing, and Chimate, Kassa, and Almaz had a good time watching us and whispering among themselves, observers from the sidelines just as I had often been in Dita.

My interviews with Chimate focused on her life and Dita history, but occasionally I introduced other topics. One day I tried to discuss further with Chimate American women's changing conceptions of their domestic role. She was not very interested. Her brief comments about women's roles were fatalistic. Had she not married a king, she felt that her life would have been like that of most highland women. She did not like many of the women's tasks, but she would have done them. The idea of social change, of transforming Dita society so that any man or woman could choose from a variety of possible activities, had no place in her mind. She was bored by the discussion and cheered up only when we started to read Machiavelli to her.

We spent two days translating portions of my paperback copy of *The Prince* for Chimate. She listened with the excitement of one who sees familiar events being put into a larger, more general framework. "Yes, that's true!" she often exclaimed. She was impressed by the fact that the words of Machiavelli had survived in books for hundreds of years.

The situation described in *The Prince* was quite intelligible to Chimate. Machiavelli gives advice to a ruler who takes over a throne not hereditarily his and to a ruler who incorporates new territories into his kingdom. The southern half of Ethiopia had been incorporated into the empire within living memory. Dita had changed from an independent kingdom into a minor segment of the empire in 1897. Chimate could recognize in Machiavelli's descriptions some of the tactics used to govern her own people.

When we read the portion describing how a prince may try to colonize an area in order to make it more secure politically, Chimate said thoughtfully, "Yes, the prince sends a lot of people in. He sends a lot of people in. Yes, I've seen it. A long, long, long time ago Fitawari Sono took our title and sent a lot of Dorze people into Dita, to keep the Dita people from rebelling against him. That was while the Italians ruled."

The discussion in *The Prince* of rebellions against a prince and their prevention had an immediate relevance for the reign of Haile Selassie. Chimate assented vigorously, "The book tells the truth! If a king hears that the people are going to rebel against him, he tells the police to catch the leaders and put them in jail, doesn't he? But sometimes the people rebel successfully. Then there's no king to put them in jail. It's best for a king to move slowly and to cooperate with his people, then won't he sit in safety? And the people who rebelled against the king, they make a new king. Don't they fear the old king?"

Obviously thinking of her first husband, Fitawari Masa, she continued, "But the best is the king whose people have ruled since the dawn of time. That kind of king won't be unfair to his people!"

Chimate still seemed deeply attached to her memories of Masa. No other man lived up to her idealized images of him. She had been very young when she married Masa and relatively young when he died. As an independent older woman, she preferred to remain unmarried and to work as Dita's balabat.

On quite another topic, I tried to draw Chimate out on the question of what she thought of me, but she was guarded and diplomatic. She was not about to discuss our past conflicts. Instead, this is what she said.

～

When you first came to Dita, Judy, people liked you because you brought the photo of Amano. Everyone heard that you brought the photo and liked you. But didn't another white woman come with you to Dita? She came and walked everywhere and came to my house through the flocks. "That foreigner, what was she going to do with our animals?" Halaka Keso and King Wata were saying. "This woman has brought harm to us. Why did Judy bring her? What does she plan to do to us? That person will do us no good."

Other people said nothing. These two men said, "Six, seven times she wandered through our animals, writing something. She was walking slowly."

Because you brought the photo, they didn't say you were bad. "She brought our master's records. She brought our master's photo," they said. "Chimate's foreigner, Chimate's child," they said. They didn't say anything bad about you. They liked you for bringing the photo. Nuguse cried when he saw the picture. His sister, when she saw the picture, cried and cried and cried.

The thin white woman was walking slowly over the hills. "What did she want to bury among our animals? What did she want to bury among our houses? Why does she write?" people said. Because of this people were angry, angry with her.

The people were also saying, "Judy brought the photo." This Judy, Judy! People are happy. Dita people aren't too afraid of you. But some of the old people fear you. The young people don't fear you at all; all the young people like you.

~

The woman Chimate referred to is a slender, redheaded Englishwoman named Caroline who visited me in Dita for a few days in 1971. Caroline spent one long morning walking alone in Dita. But I had spent many long mornings walking through the Dita farmland, pausing to gather information for a map. Surely most of the wrath of the Dita farmers was directed against me, not Caroline.

When I returned to Dita in September 1971 for a brief visit, Chimate seemed to be inflaming suspicion against me. After our reconciliation I can imagine her doing just the opposite, attributing every inconvenient action of mine to Caroline. I can hear her saying, "Oh, no, that wasn't Judy you saw. It was someone else, the thin white woman. People bless Judy. She brought Amano's picture."

Chimate enjoyed our discussions, but she was anxious to return to Dita. She worried about her houses and her fields. She dreamed one night that the fields had not been planted and that she was starving. Gida told me soon afterward that Chimate had been to see a fortune-teller.

"What kind? The kind who looks at coffee grounds?" I asked.

"No, the kind who opens a book," he said.

"So Chimate is working on a book with us and has gone to someone who sees the future in books!"

"Yes. He told her that in order to live long, she shouldn't leave Dita during the two-month fast before Easter, and she should be careful about crossing rivers then. He told her what kinds of sheep to buy every year and how to sacrifice them for her good health. He warned her against walking outdoors when it's raining, too," Gida concluded.

Thus, Chimate prepared to leave Addis Abeba, fortified by both modern and traditional medical advice. When at the end of August I prepared to return to my teaching job and Chimate to return to Dita, Gida took me to say good-bye to her. "Chimate hasn't been feeling well," Gida told me, "and she has moved into the house of another relative. He's a dresser in a hospital, and he's been giving her injections."

It had rained the night before. Wind shook the leaves of a eucalyptus tree, spattering us with a second, false rain as we walked along. We crossed an open meadow where a cow and a calf were grazing on the muddy grass. A weaver walked back and forth between two wooden pegs he had driven into the ground, preparing the warp thread for his loom. The thin white filaments hung suspended a few inches above the mud.

Chimate's bed stood near a loom. Instead of getting up she invited us into the room. We crowded into a corner and stood there talking with her. "I'll be going to Dita in two days," she told us. "I'll take the bus that goes to Dorze and ride my mule from there to Dita." Cheerfully she exhibited a bruise on her arm where she had had her latest injection. "I'm feeling better now," she said.

"And I'll be leaving tomorrow," I told her. We chatted for a while about her farmland and the planting to be done, the district governor ("I'm sorry you didn't become his relative!" Chimate exclaimed), and my teaching job. We planned to exchange messages through the letters Gida and I would write to each other.

"Return soon to Ethiopia!" she said, smiling.

"I'll try," I replied, returning her smile. We embraced warmly and wished one another a safe journey.

Gida's first letter from Dorze, written in late September, told me that he had visited Dita. He wrote, "Chimate told me to say to you, 'I have been feeling much better since I saw the doctor in Addis Abeba. When are you coming back to Dita?'"

Part Three

The Title Is Abolished

Revolution

*Chimate has been in jail for a long time. Her son
Atumo and her grandsons Wombara, Seyum, and
Kebede are all in prison. They did bad things to their
country.*

∽

A Dorze friend's letter reached me in February 1975. "You wanted to know about the revolution," he began. "The people were exploited by balabats and chikashums. Now no balabat or chikashum is in power. They were chased by the people. In Dorze the leading exploiters have gone down the ladder, rolling on dirty ground, and still have no one to lift them."

Gida had been more guarded. "During the revolution in Arbaminch," he had written six months earlier, "three people died. Two of them were students of the Arbaminch secondary school. I can't write more about it until peace comes."

During my years in Ethiopia I had talked with many people who were unhappy with their government. The covert wish of many Dita citizens was to return to local autonomy, turning their backs on Ethiopia and recapturing a glorious past. In Dorze, the dream was different. People believed in the emperor but wanted to replace his representatives, particularly the provincial governor. The Dorze men and women were learning to speak the national language, Amharic, changing their names to Amharic names, buying manufactured clothing, listening to radios in the bars, and traveling back and forth to Addis Abeba. Rather than leaving the Ethiopian Empire, they wanted a better place in it.

Then there were those who were critical of what the empire had to offer. Some, like the agricultural extension agent, chafed at the slow pace of modernization—the illiteracy that exceeded 95 percent, the lack of roads and hospitals, the economy dominated by peasant farming with its hand labor and ox-drawn plows. Others, primarily the university students and intellectuals I met in Addis Abeba, hoped for a social transformation. They wanted not only to modernize Ethiopia but to change inequities in the distribution of land, wealth, and political power.

The origins of revolution lay in the structure of the Ethiopian state, which had become an increasingly ineffective instrument for acknowledging and resolving political differences and demands. Haile Selassie had shown extraordinary success in the role of emperor. In the words of the political scientist Christopher Clapham:

> This was an essentially household system of government, in which the emphasis on personal leadership in Ethiopian political culture was brought to its peak, providing a skilled emperor with limitless opportunities for the manipulation of the personal relationships through which political power was exercised. This was an activity at which Haile Selassie was unsurpassed, as his presence at the centre of power for nearly sixty years . . . help[s] to indicate. Far from autocratic in the actual exercise of power, he was a cautious ruler whose skill lay in the management of factions and individuals in a manner which promoted their dependence on himself, while maintaining his own freedom of action. . . . [The] effect was to suck decision-making into the court. Decisions of the most trivial kind had to come to the emperor for formal approval. . . . [It] became impossible for any politician to build up any personal political base, or indeed any personal reputation, beyond that provided by the emperor. . . . There were . . . severe limitations in what a system of this kind could do. It was eminently adapted to manipulating individuals, once these could be identified. . . . It was on the other hand entirely incapable of dealing with any social movement or grouping which went beyond the scale of a small court faction.*

As an example of centralized decision making that reached all the way into Dita, recall the first story Chimate told me about Sola Kata's murder of Goncho. The case was appealed all the way to Haile Selassie, who pardoned Sola.

Ironically, Emperor Haile Selassie created two new political constituencies that became progressively alienated from his regime as well as instrumental in its downfall—the intellectual elite and the military. When it came,

---

*My discussion of the revolution draws heavily on Clapham, *Transformation and Continuity in Revolutionary Ethiopia*. The quote is from pages 32–33.

the revolution was urban rather than rural in origin, only subsequently spreading to the countryside.

Two factors, drought and inflation, played important roles in converting discontent into revolution. I had seen a minor drought in the Gamo Highland in 1971, with the dry season stretching on much longer than usual. In Dita the threshing of grain was delayed and the search for animal fodder grew intense; Dorze, located at a lower altitude, suffered more, with pastures drying up and animals dying from hunger. During the next four years the problem recurred, but every year the rain eventually fell.

Not so in northern Ethiopia. There the drought was so severe that by 1973 a major famine was in progress in Wollo, a famine equaling in intensity the well-publicized famine in the southern Sahara that was occurring at the same time. The Ethiopian government concealed the seriousness of the situation, exporting grain and doubling its foreign exchange reserves while its own people starved. In late 1973 when the government was forced to admit the problem, international relief measures were not particularly welcomed and were ineffectively utilized. Continuing into 1974, the drought and famine spread south and eventually killed an estimated 100,000 people. The rural people affected by the drought did not rise up against the government, but for urban Ethiopians, the widespread human suffering and death glaringly underlined government corruption and inefficiency.

At the same time, oil prices increased fourfold, putting inflationary pressure on the Ethiopian economy. Taxi drivers went on strike to protest high gasoline prices. Buses were stoned by urban people protesting increased fares. Teachers went on strike for higher wages, as did dockworkers, railway personnel, and a fledgling labor organization called the Confederation of Ethiopian Labor Unions. Student demonstrations, begun in 1973 to call attention to the famine, continued. Most important, the military and police refused to intervene and suppress these strikes and demonstrations.

Revolt started within the armed forces in January 1974, when army officers at a base in southern Ethiopia refused enlisted men access to the officers' well when the enlisted men's well ran dry. A month later, the mutiny there was followed by one in the northern city of Asmara. Enlisted men seized control of the city and demanded higher wages, forcing Haile Selassie's cabinet to resign. The lower echelons of the air force and the navy rallied to the support of the army dissidents. An air force helicopter hovered above Addis Abeba and dropped leaflets encouraging the police to join their military counterparts. The Ethiopian Armed Forces Coordinating Committee, or Derg, was established, its members having no rank higher than major.

By late June 1974 the rebel armed forces occupied Addis Abeba and the *derg*, or committee, took over effective command of the country, although it moved slowly to abolish existing forms of government. On September 12, the derg placed the emperor under arrest. That evening he was forced to watch a program being broadcast over Ethiopian television, a harrowing documentary in which the gruesome effects of the famine were sharply contrasted with the lifestyle of the emperor. Still in confinement, he died eleven months later at the age of eighty-three.

Plans for the nationalization of land were formulated during the final months of 1974 and culminated in the proclamation of March 4, 1975, which removed all rural lands from private ownership. A family was allowed to use, but not own, up to twenty-five acres of land. Peasant associations were created to administer access to land and to serve as focal points for education, economic trade, and local peacekeeping. By the time of the proclamation, banks, insurance companies, and businesses had already been nationalized. Urban property, aircraft companies, and private schools were to follow. Urban associations were created as administrative counterparts of the peasant associations.

Fierce internal power struggles within the derg began soon after it was created. Extreme violence was used, with one faction purging other factions by killing their leaders. By the time I visited Ethiopia in March 1977, Colonel Mengistu Haile Mariam had emerged as the leader of the derg. Some of the strongest challenges to the derg, however, came not from within but from leftist students and intellectuals who objected to the primary role of the military in the revolution. Acts of terrorism against the regime alternated with periods of retaliation during which people were shot or imprisoned.

The southern half of Ethiopia welcomed the revolution. By March 1974, during the period of slowly crystallizing rebellion, there were demonstrations in the south, one of them in Arbaminch where students clashed with police. The conquest of the south had occurred within living memory, when indigenous groups saw their land given away to northern Ethiopians. In some regions vast estates had passed into the hands of the local elite and the northerners. This pattern was broken temporarily by the Italians, and in some places, such as the Gamo Highland, it was never fully restored. In economically attractive areas like the Gamo Gofa lowland, with its potential for growing coffee and cotton, land had passed once again into the hands of outsiders after the Italians left. These landlords then converted local people into their tenants and paid laborers. In the Arbaminch area, news of the revolution was followed by the killing of a few northern settlers—the large landowners were already gone—and the quick exodus of the rest.

Dan Sperber lived in Dorze in the Gamo Highland during the latter half of 1974 and reported a period of euphoria and optimism. Newly elected officials actually came to Dorze and talked with the people instead of staying in their offices in the town of Chencha. The younger people challenged the rules of seniority that had regulated Dorze politics, claiming a more important role for themselves. Ideas about women, tanners, and potters being allowed to participate in the political assemblies and to own land were being introduced.

Three years later the reports I received were more cautious. The local assemblies now included the full range of Dorze citizens but could be called only by a government official. The price of food and land had increased dramatically. Most local neighborhoods in the highland now had jails on the meadows once used for public assembly. The mood was one of caution, of watching and waiting to see if the hopes for economic prosperity and full political participation raised by the revolution would be fulfilled.

What had become of Chimate in this period of social change and political turmoil? At first, after my summer with her in 1973, I had had regular news of her. I sent my greetings with every letter I wrote to Gida, and when he happened to visit her he repeated what I had said and forwarded her greetings to me. A letter of February 1974 foreshadowed the criticisms that would later be directed against Chimate's family. Gida told how Chimate's grandson Seyum had kidnapped and raped his ex-wife after meeting her on a Dita path. Gida concluded, "The balabat's relatives believe that they have the power to do everything they want. It is too bad." Again in August, Gida wrote of Seyum, "He killed Chimate's mule with a spear. I was very sorry when I heard it. Also, Chimate's brother is dead. I will go to her in order to mourn and say tasa."

Chimate continued to play an important role in Dita politics as the revolution gathered momentum. In June 1974, a Dorze man and teacher who ardently supported the revolution wrote me about the Dita people's aborted attempt to wage war on the Doko people:

The Dita people rose up to fight against the Doko. Why? It is very traditional and superstitious. You know about the drought in Ethiopia. When the rain stopped the Dita people faced great problems. Being so conservative and traditional they thought that the drought came as a punishment for not fighting against the Doko people. The people requested Chimate Chumbalo to allow them to fight against the Doko people. She replied that she could not give permission herself and advised them to wait patiently until she asked the governor. Mokonnen Dori was the governor in those days. Chimate, who I claim is a very smart lady, made a nice decision. She told Mokonnen the evil problem and requested him to send some policemen to arrest those who initiated the matter. Mokonnen did exactly what she said. So the leaders of the rebellion were taken to the court in Chencha and it is said that things are looking better. Do you see how risky it is? The conditions in Gamo Gofa are still unsettled.

Eight months later Chimate's position had changed. Gida wrote in February 1975:

> I went to the balabat of Dita to tell her your warmest greetings and that you were sorry about her brother's death.
> Now the balabat is going to court because she is accused by Sola Kata of being the friend of the district governor of Dita, Balanbaras Demse. He is in jail now because he took bribes from people. A few days ago I met the balabat of Dita in Chencha while she was searching for an advocate. She will be set free if she has done no wrong to the people of Dita and Sola Kata.

As I read this I remembered that the first story Gida and I had heard Chimate tell was about Sola Kata, and I wondered why he had become her accuser.

It was during this period that the balabats were stripped of their power, and a completely new structure of administration, utilizing the peasant associations, was put in place. A year later I learned what had happened to Chimate. A letter from Gida casually mentioned, "Chimate has been in jail for a long time. Her son Atumo and her grandsons Wombara, Seyum, and Kebede are all in prison. They did bad things to their country."

By this time, I knew that I would be returning to Ethiopia. I wondered whether it would be safe to visit her in jail and felt sorrow and repugnance at the idea of seeing her in such a setting. But in October 1976, Gida wrote that Chimate had been freed and was living in Addis Abeba.

I returned to Ethiopia for a short visit in late March 1977, arriving just one month after President Jimmy Carter had announced that the United

States would discontinue military aid to Ethiopia in the coming fiscal year because of alleged human rights violations. Anti-American feeling was high and would culminate a month after my visit in the ouster of the American military mission and four other American agencies.

I was standing diffidently in a crowded, dark airport room waiting for my luggage when an Ethiopian angel of doom bore down upon me. She announced that she worked for the Ethiopian Tourist Organization. "This isn't the best time for tourists in Ethiopia, but the ETO wants to help you all it can," she said. Dropping her voice, she spoke vehemently. "These past three weeks have been the worst we've seen so far in Addis Abeba. You're American? Be careful. The newspapers and the radio have been full of reports of CIA agents. You may be suspected."

Feeling uneasy, I checked through customs and took a taxi to a hotel. Addis Abeba was still a beautiful city, with wide eucalyptus-lined streets on the outskirts and interesting modern architecture downtown. People walked quietly along the sidewalks; women were wearing the dazzling white dresses and colored scarves I remembered so well.

I settled into my hotel and was on my way by midmorning, waiting on a curb for a taxi to carry me to the Institute of Ethiopian Studies. As I tried to hail a cab, the taxi drivers paused, asked ridiculously high prices, and drove on. Did I imagine reserve and hostility on their part, or did it actually exist? Someone took me at last. On the steps of the institute, a guard armed with a submachine gun was not eager to let me in. Upstairs the museum was locked behind a sign reading "Closed Indefinitely." No one seemed to be around. At the end of a corridor, I discovered two secretaries at work and collected the letters addressed to me.

I next visited a place where I hoped to find my Dorze friends. This was a piecework factory where in 1971 over twenty men had sat at their looms making a fine grade of cloth. I walked up a steep cobbled path to the low wooden building. Most of the windows were shuttered. Only five weavers worked at looms inside, huddled into one corner of the building. Everyone remembered me and shook hands. I went to the front room, the store where the cloth was sold, with Halaka Bezabeh. He had been just Ato ("Mister") Bezabeh in 1973, taking the title of halaka in the following year. He told us that he was the last man to hold that office in his district. Along with other traditional forms of leadership, the position of halaka had been abolished in Dorze and in the other Gamo Highland communities.

Halaka Bezabeh said that he didn't know if all the changes in Dorze were for good or for bad. "We shall see what happens in the future," he said. He promised to tell a particular friend of mine, Asfa, where to find me that evening. No, he said when I asked him, he knew nothing about the Dita people and their former leaders.

I ended the afternoon by talking with an American friend of mine who lived and worked in Addis Abeba. I sat in his home, where he could speak openly. "Last night is the first night in two weeks in which we didn't hear guns and mortars all night," he said. "It's been sounding like a city under military siege. Many people have died, forty-seven students have been shot at a mass meeting at the university alone, and in the city over two thousand people have been shot in the past week."

He explained that the weeks before my arrival had been part of a campaign to stamp out counterrevolutionary elements. House-to-house searches were authorized and, along with guns and ammunition, typewriters were a major target of the searches. Opposition literature could presumably be written with the typewriters. Some of the shooting and searching was done by the army, but the rest was done by the police. Addis Abeba had been divided into some three hundred associations, each with its leaders and armed militia, each with the power to declare some of its own members enemies of the people.

"The military council has called an end to the shooting," he continued. "The curfew has been changed from 8:00 P.M. to midnight and lasts until 5:00 A.M. If things are quiet tonight, the worst is probably over." And indeed, that evening I heard no gunfire. It resumed the next night after curfew, but my friend told us, "This is nothing. Just a few scattered shots."

I went back to the hotel before dark. Asfa came to see me that night at the hotel, and I asked for his help. Several days later, he arrived in the morning. "I've found someone who knows where Chimate is," Asfa said. "When do you want to see her? I can take you to him before I go to work and he can take you to Chimate, if you wish."

We took a taxi to the spot where Asfa said we would find his friend. Deneke was an older Dorze man who seemed busy and important. He took charge, and Asfa left for work. We began to walk through the residential section of town along the broad clay streets. Deneke met various Dorze men along the way, and they greeted us. A truck unloaded mineral water in front of a small bar. Deneke and I discussed the relative merits of Ethiopian and imported thread for weaving. A woman spread grain on a mat to dry in the sun. On we walked, stirring up a small ripple of reaction as we passed and frightening a few children, who ran away when they saw my white face. No one questioned us, and I saw no one carrying a gun. People seemed as aloof and as surreptitiously curious as ever.

After twenty minutes we came to a wooden door among many other wooden doors in a row of identical mud-plastered, tin-roofed houses. A man standing outside recognized me, and he let us in.

Chimate was in a back room. "She is sick," I was told. "She has been in bed for a long time." I hurried into the room indicated, a room scarcely larger than the bed on which Chimate sat, wrapped in a thick, white bulu-ko cloth. In the confusion of our greetings, extra chairs were found and carried to the foot of the bed.

I kept saying, "Tasa," to Chimate, commiserating with her on her illness and her difficulties. She replied "*Aiko dena*, it's nothing." Her voice wavered, but she was certainly the same person as before. She was ill and discour-aged, but the very vehemence with which she managed to communicate her feelings bespoke her tenacity for life.

Soon she was demanding that something be brought us to drink. Then, leaving her tired body behind, she began to sparkle a bit. Her voice grew louder and firmer as she told a long story to Deneke, a story about conflicts in Dita after the revolution. She talked rapidly and I could catch only phras-es. Her luminous smile began to appear.

She turned to me. "I haven't seen you for four years. I'm an old woman now."

"Your face looks the same to me," I said truthfully. "You're thinner than before, but I don't see any more white hairs on your head."

I asked after her family. One of her daughters was still married, the oth-er divorced. Her son Atumo now lived in Addis, as did his son Kebede. "I haven't seen Kebede for over a year," she said, not seeming to regret that fact.

Two of her granddaughters were married. Nigatu, the elder of Amano's daughters, had married a teacher. As for Genet, she wasn't too young to be married, "She's as tall as you are, Judy." I remembered her as the round lit-tle schoolgirl staying for a few days in my Dorze house in 1970, pert and cheerful as a sparrow.

Of her grandson Seyum, Chimate said, "He is in Dita," but others pro-tested, "No one knows where he is." Her eldest grandson, Wombara, the one registered as balabat in Dita in the past, "is poor and lives in Dita. He's working hard. He farms along with the farmers' association."

Sando, the young man who had worked for me, had achieved his ambition. He was living in Addis Abeba, city of his dreams, weaving alongside his brother. His wife had died, leaving behind their two children, whom his parents were raising.

"Is Halaka Halke still alive?" I asked.

"Oh, yes, he's alive. He was in prison for a while. He paid a hundred dollar fine to the community."

I couldn't bring myself to question her about her imprisonment. Obviously she still had enemies whose anger she feared, for she was living quietly and keeping out of sight.

We sat and sat. We had accepted an offer of coffee, and it took almost an hour to buy, roast, pound, and brew the beans. On one subject everyone agreed most emphatically. The revolution was *machasar lo'ok,* "good for women." Women in Dita and Dorze now owned land, took part in public meetings, and carried arms as part of the local militia.

As I left Chimate, I promised to visit her again. I told her that I would return after visiting the Gamo Highland.

That evening Ethiopian Airlines called. The next day's flight to Arbaminch had been canceled. I booked a Sunday reservation. I noticed that I had a low fever. I went to bed, and after curfew the shooting began, intermittent bursts of sound like distant firecrackers in the early morning hours.

When you return, you will mourn at my funeral.

∼

I never flew to Arbaminch. By Saturday night I was too ill with influenza to make the journey. Although the plane did leave on Sunday, I might have waited a long time for a return flight. I was warned by a friend who had just arrived from the south, "Planes don't land at Arbaminch for weeks at a time."

I told this friend about my visit with Chimate, and said, "I'm nervous about going to see her again. I've asked Asfa if it might be possible to bring her here to visit me tomorrow. There's been more anti-American propaganda over the weekend. A speech made over the radio said things like 'Don't be tempted by a few tourist dollars to overturn the revolution.'"

I admitted to having moments of utter paranoia. I knew I was in an irrational mood at times, just as when in a lonely apartment I would believe that every branch tapping against the window was a burglar breaking in. I felt that I was in danger and that I might put my Dorze and Dita friends in danger.

"They're not killing foreigners, they're killing each other," my friend pointed out. "By arming the militia and giving power to poor people, a whole political class will be eliminated. The killing isn't random, though of course there are excesses. Compared to most revolutions, a remarkably small number of people have died."

"In theory, it's comforting to know all that," I said, "but I'm still nervous when it's happening around me, and two thousand died in the past week."

"It's more than that, even the official counts are higher than that," he interjected. "It's not an easy time to be here, I admit."

Tuesday morning Asfa came to see me, saying, "I asked Deneke about bringing Chimate here to the hotel. She's too ill, and she can't walk."

"She can't walk!" And then I wondered to myself whether the cause was physical or psychological. Years before when in considerable conflict with her son, she also couldn't walk. At that time she had begun her propitiation of the chale spirits.

Asfa continued, "If the people in the house hadn't seen you they would have kept Deneke out. They guard her very carefully, but they knew she would want to see you."

"Tomorrow is a holiday," I said. "I'm feeling better and could visit her. Could you and Deneke meet me here so we can take a taxi to the area where she lives? I'm leaving Ethiopia the day after tomorrow, and I'd like to see her again."

Asfa agreed, and the next morning the three of us set forth in the quiet town. It was the thirty-sixth anniversary of the day the Italians had left Ethiopia. Truckloads of people from the countryside were arriving for the celebration at Revolution Square, and the townspeople were walking along the avenue near the hotel that led to the square. Only a few souvenir vendors wandered along the shuttered storefronts, crowding around me until I got into the taxi.

At Chimate's door I told Asfa and Deneke, "I'd like to see her alone." They sat in the outer room while I went in, saying, "*Saro, saro,* hello, hello."

Chimate was lying on her bed, head on a pillow. She stirred, looking up at me. "*Saro, saro,*" she replied as she pushed herself up into a seated position. Her movements were stiff and jerky.

My back to the door, I stepped up to Chimate's bed. I reached under my clothing and brought out a roll of Ethiopian currency, purchased with a five-hundred-dollar advance I had received from a publisher buying the first option on our book. She silently took the money and hid it under her bed-clothes. I spoke softly, "Here is more payment for the book we worked on."

We smiled at one another as I stepped back and spoke loudly. "I didn't go to Arbaminch," I said. "I was sick and stayed in a hotel. I felt better today, so I came here to see you."

"I thought you were visiting Dorze by now," she said. "I expected to see you next week. I'm sick, sick. Yesterday a man came and gave me an injection." She showed me a large subcutaneous lump on her forearm.

"Aren't you going to visit the hospital? Won't people take you there?" I urged.

"We'll go tomorrow," she promised.

"I wish I could take you myself, but tomorrow I'm leaving Ethiopia. This isn't a good time for foreigners to visit. I really hope that some day we can return and see you again."

"When you return, you will mourn at my funeral," Chimate said bitterly.

"That's not true!" I cried. "You have lived through difficult times before."

"I'm much older now," she replied.

"Will you be mediated with Dita?" I asked.

"I don't know. They asked seven hundred dollars from me as a fine. I could offer only two hundred dollars."

Seven hundred dollars! I knew what that meant. The Dita people couldn't refuse to pardon someone who sincerely asked their pardon; that would be gome. But they could set the fine impossibly high and keep her from completing the mediation. I was relieved to know that with the money I'd given her, she could pay the fine.

What were the specific charges against Chimate? Again, I had no desire to harass her with questions, and I had no opportunity to question anyone else from Dita. I recognized Sola Kata, her primary accuser, as the man from the story she had told me seven years earlier, the man who had shot a policeman. After having been jailed for twenty years by the former government, did he hate everyone associated with it, even though Chimate had helped him at a crucial moment? Did he resent Chimate's role in jailing other members of his family who had killed people? Was he committed to social change or just taking an opportunity to express old grudges?

But there I stopped myself. The early impetus of any revolution, surely, was partly derived from a desire to settle old scores, not from visions of a new social order. Next should come the task of reeducation. When the Chinese Communists had consolidated their power, they had turned from bloodshed to education. Many people who had been stripped of their old privileges were encouraged to take part in a new kind of society, rather than be discarded.

This process had not yet begun in Ethiopia, where the basic questions of political power had not been settled. The very territorial boundaries of the empire were unclear, with a conflict with Somalia to the south and a war of secession in the Eritrean area in the north. The bloodshed continued and the outcome was far from obvious.

The convulsions of social conflict in Ethiopia made sentimentality out of place. Chimate and I were separated now and could meet only briefly.

We might never have news of one another again. We said a warm good-bye and she huddled down upon her bed to rest. "Go to the hospital!" I urged her once more. "They can help you!"

"Yes, yes," she automatically agreed with me, but I had no faith that she would go.

As Asfa, Deneke, and I left the house, I sensed a bleak, stern expression on my face. I was almost frowning and my mouth was tightly closed. I felt no impulse for tears. Tears would have been a kind of protest, and protest was a luxury. I walked the hard-baked mud street as I would have walked a beam balanced high over a ravine, concentrating on what did exist and not upon what might exist. I said good-bye to Asfa and Deneke, thanking them, and caught a cab.

The taxi glided slowly downhill to my hotel. The rally was over and one lane of the street was cordoned off. Hundreds of people were marching uphill, the men with sticks firmly planted on their shoulders like rifles. Wind caught at the flags, straightening and crumpling the red, green, and yellow stripes. I got out and watched for a moment. Knots of people in the procession were singing. The midday sun burned down impartially as I turned and went inside.

Postscript: October 1995

In the years following my 1977 visit, I have seen Chimate's life much as I saw the sky in Dita during the rainy season—in scattered patches of pale blue among drifting, looming, obscuring clouds. Few letters have reached me from my three Dorze correspondents—no one in Dita has been able to write to me—and the letters have seldom held news of Chimate. These young men were finding their places in the revolution, seeking education, marrying, and looking for jobs. The drama of their lives might carry them to Russia or Turkey but not to Dita.

Letters exchanged in both directions were filled with caution about openly discussing the circumstances of a former balabat now declared an enemy of the regime. The dried husks of etiquette were what remained of the personal exchanges between Chimate and me. I sent her messages that I was doing well, and she sent me the same messages months later. It was from Turkey in early 1982 that I received an extended account of what had happened to Chimate. She had returned to Dita and was living quietly. As my friend wrote:

> After the revolution, everything that belonged to Chimate was taken over by the peasant association of Dita. Now everything is normal. The people have admitted her to live with them. The people themselves have built a new house for her on one of the lands she possessed formerly. Her house is not at the former place but somewhere on one of her lands. The people have also planted false banana plants around the house, as it should be. I can confidently state that she has the respect of the people to a good degree.
>
> People actually don't go to her for mediation. Disputes are seen and finished in the peasant association's office. This doesn't necessarily mean that the customs practiced by the people in the old days are prohibited or totally overthrown. Disputes among neighbors or even among unknown individuals are usually solved by the neighbors or other elders as in the old days. Under such circumstances, the balabat also has a good part of attention from

the people. Now-a-days she is not, in any case, a neglected individual. She
lives with her granddaughter Katse.

I heard nothing more of Chimate until a letter from Gida reached me
in December 1986. "I have given your greetings to all your Dorze and Dita
friends," he wrote. "I expect that you didn't hear that Chimate has died. She
died last year."

That is all I heard for many years. In the meantime, Mengistu Haile
Mariam's forces had been challenged and defeated in a series of battles in
1990–91. By May 1991, Mengistu had fled the country. Eritrea, whose free-
dom fighters had joined in battling Mengistu, seceded from Ethiopia in 1993.
The new socialist government of Ethiopia was reorganized along ethnic
lines, and the local political climate changed radically. In 1995 I learned from
Jacques Bureau, an anthropologist who worked in the Gamo Highland and
who heads a research institute in Addis Abeba, that the Gamo Highland
communities had reclaimed many of their former institutions. Once again,
communities were sacrificing for gome and electing halaka to head their
assemblies. At the same time, the gains achieved by potters, who had begun to own land, and by women and younger people, who had been more
active politically, had been erased.

In March 1995, Gida reestablished contact with me, saying that for three
years he had had no permanent address. I wrote back to him, explaining
that I was working on this book, and asked for further information about
Chimate and about Dita. He replied in August: "You know Sando, who carried our luggage from Dorze to Dita and from Dita to Dorze. I got information from him." Gida reported that one of Chimate's greatest ambitions
had been achieved—the return to her son of the second title her husband
Fitawari Masa had held: "You know her younger son Atumo. He became
Dana [that is, received the title of king or *ka'o*] in 1993. Due to the Ethiopian Marxist Revolution in our country the people of Dita gave the title Dana
to persons of other clans. This brought poverty, hunger, death, etc., in the
area. And now the people of Dita made Atumo Dana and now there is no
poverty, hunger, etc., in Dita. As a whole the society is [doing well] and
[people] respect Atumo and his relatives." And Chimate had received the
ultimate Gamo Highland mark of respect, the final measure of any highland person's life—an elaborate funeral: "There was a big funeral for Chimate like the balabats and the ka'os of the past received. The [Gamo High-

land] balabats, ka'os, and [prominent] persons of the neighboring and far areas came to her funeral."

Although criticized, repudiated, and jailed at the height of the revolution and living obscurely at the time of her death, Chimate had received the kind of funeral I had seen only once or twice, full of honors for a prominent, respected person. I can imagine the ostrich plumes on men's heads, the *dunguse* handwoven pants brightly striped in yellow, black, and red, the songs of praise and commemoration sung by masses of women and men marching round and round the sacred funeral meadow. I can see the line of her relatives, each accompanied by a neighbor, receiving every person present—the cries of mourning, the ash-smeared faces, hair being pulled, faces being scratched, and a young man falling to the ground, catching himself on his shoulders and hitting the ground with the full length of his body. I imagine this, I participate, and I say good-bye, Chimate. Good-bye.

Appendix 1

A Note on Pronunciation

All syllables are sounded in the local names and words used. There are no silent final vowels. Thus, Chimate = Chi-ma-tay, gome = go-may, and so on.

There are five vowels, pronounced roughly as follows:

a as in father
e as in may
i as in me
o as in mow
u as in new

The diacriticals for glottalized consonants are omitted from the text. The two terms most often used for which this is the case are *halak'a* and *ch'ima*.

A List of Major Characters

Alimetu	Chimate's eldest daughter, married to a Dorze man
Almaz	Chimate's other living daughter by her husband Masa, married to a Shame man and living in Addis Abeba
Amano	Chimate's eldest son, who died ca. 1962
Atumo	Chimate's only surviving son, living in Dita
Balaye's Mother	old woman of northern Ethiopian origin who worked as Judy Olmstead's cook in Dita
Chimate	acting balabat of Dita, born ca. 1910
Gida	student from Dorze, Judy Olmstead's assistant
Halaka Halke	titled elderly man, Chimate's neighbor, friend, and critic
Katse	Atumo's daughter, Chimate's granddaughter
Kebede	Atumo's eldest son, Chimate's grandson; lived and worked primarily with Chimate

Masa	Chimate's first husband, the king and balabat of Dita, who was executed by the Italian occupying forces, ca. 1939
Nigatu	Amano's eldest daughter, Chimate's granddaughter
Seyum	Amano's second son, Chimate's grandson
Unka	member of the same kin group as Chimate's grandsons, neighbor in Dita
Wara's Mother	woman servant of Chimate
Wata	king of Dita, initiated in 1970
Wombara	Amano's eldest son, Chimate's grandson, heir to title of balabat

A List of Place-names

Addis Abeba	capital city of Ethiopia
Arbaminch	capital town of Gamo Gofa Province, found in the lowland to the south of the Gamo Highland
Chencha	small Gamo Highland town, former capital of the province, a half-day walk from Dita, subprovincial capital
Gamo Gofa Province	province located in Ethiopia's northwest corner, named after its two major highland areas
Gamo Highland	highland area roughly ten miles long and five to ten miles wide located just north of the lowland provincial capital, Arbaminch, and 250 miles south of Addis Abeba
Dorze	a Gamo Highland community, known for its skillful weavers
Gulta	small Gamo Highland town, a four-hour walk from Dita
Malo	small lowland town north of the Gamo Highland; in 1970–71 it was the district capital, and its administrators were responsible to Chencha
Dita	farming community of the Gamo Highland; Chimate's adopted community
Wulo Kore	small village located in the Gamo Highland an hour's walk from Dita; by 1973, the district capital, replacing Malo

A Note on Military Titles

Both the Ethiopian emperor and the Italian governors of Ethiopia conferred military titles on local male leaders as a reward. Chimate's husband Masa became Fitawari Masa, for example. The titles were not purely honorary; these men were expected to support the government in times of warfare, and many earned their titles by participating in battle. In descending order, the military titles used by the empire were ras, liqamakwas, dejazmach, azmach, fitawari, grazmach, kenyazmach, balamberas, shi halaka, meta halaka, hamsa halaka, and asir halaka.

Inheritance of the Titles "Ka'o" and "Balabat": Dita Genealogy as of 1993

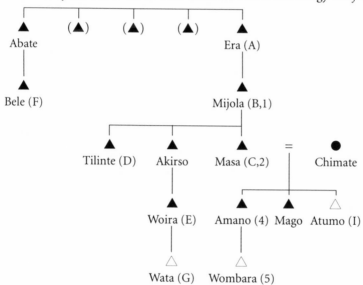

Holders of Ka'o or Dana Title:

A. Era
B. Mijola held this title at the time Dita was made part of the Ethiopian Empire in 1897.
C. Masa   D. Tilinte
E. Woira   F. Bele
G. Wata
H. At some time during the revolution of 1974 and continuing until 1993, the title was given to other Dita families.
I. Atumo was given the title in 1993.

Holders of Balabat Title:

1. Mijola received the title after Dita was incorporated into the empire in 1897.
2. Masa
3. During the Italian occupation, the title was held by a Dorze man.
4. Amano
5. Wombara (The title was abolished by the 1974 revolution.)

Note: All names are pseudonyms.

Appendix 2: Women as Political Leaders Not Visible in Written History

The intention of this appendix is to present an analysis of Chimate Chumbalo's political situation, explaining why a woman was a good candidate for the position of Dita's balabat. Similar political forces were at work nearby: in two other Gamo Highland communities, women worked as the balabat in the 1970s (Bureau 1978). More broadly, I will argue that other women may have played important, yet invisible roles in the political lives of communities that are incorporated into empires. In developing this argument, I will use the present tense for describing the structural niche I believe women occupied, and the past tense for describing Gamo Highland history.

From 1897 until the revolution in 1974, the Gamo Highland was part of an empire, either Ethiopian or, briefly, Italian (1935–41). Until the Italian occupation, the Ethiopian Empire supported its local administrators and soldiers stationed in the Gamo Highland by assigning them local families or gabbar who owed them labor and tribute. From each previously independent kingdom, a king was chosen to become the balabat, responsible for seeing that people paid the tribute they owed, organizing labor for public projects like road building, and taking a part in dispute settlement. Each balabat was assigned a number of families from his own community as his gabbar. The overall impact was to increase the king's power; previously, he had been the chief sacrificer for the good of his community, with few economic or political prerogatives (Abélès 1981).

The Italians deposed the balabats they found in place but chose new ones and continued to utilize them as political intermediaries. When Haile Selassie was restored to power in 1941, he began to support his government through taxes, not tribute. The position of balabat was retained, but now the balabat was asked to supervise tax collection and to urge people to vote for the party favored by the emperor. The functions of organizing corvée (unpaid labor) and taking an active role in dispute resolution remained. Chimate Chumbalo worked as balabat on behalf of her son and then her grandson from the early 1940s off and on until the 1974 revolution. For five years, just before and after her son's death, the workings of local politics put the position of balabat in other hands.

There are two elements in Chimate's rise to prominence that I believe may favor the emergence of women political leaders elsewhere. The first, meriting a brief discussion, has to do with Dita's relative isolation from broader political, economic, educational, and religious networks within the empire, in a context where men had an advantage in participating in these networks. The second, on which most of this essay will focus, has to do with the structural characteristics of the office of balabat—or indeed, any similar office in an imperial form of government.

It was in isolated Dita, not in Dorze with its migrant weavers and ties to the rest of the empire, that a woman worked as the balabat for thirty years. Only in an area where neither men nor women had much contact with the empire could a woman hope to compete effectively with men for the position of intermediary between her community and the government. In Dita, neither sex had acquired special skills that would give its members competitive advantage in dealing with the new rulers. For example, Chimate possessed more familiarity with the Amharic language than most Dita men and women, yet she could not read or write it, and she never spoke it. She understood others when they talked in Amharic, but she used a translator to convey her replies. This was an appropriate strategy for anyone who wished to re-tain a dignified image but who could not speak Amharic fluently. Amharic speak-ers in positions of power were particularly proud of their verbal skill and used fa-cility in the Amharic language as one means of judging and ranking people.

In Dorze, men as a group were at an advantage in dealing with the government because they were much more likely to learn Amharic than women. Dorze men traveled more widely and plied a craft that brought them a cash income larger than that women earned from occasional trading of agricultural products. Moreover, the few children sent to school were usually boys, not girls.* A man did the work of balabat in Dorze.

Dita's relative isolation from the Ethiopian Empire was one reason for Chimate's political prominence. Another reason why a woman was doing this work is found in the nature of the role of balabat. The balabat was used as an intermediary be-tween a local community and the government—a role at the bottom level of the administrative hierarchy.

During the creation of any new empire, one problem the new rulers face is how to incorporate the diverse people who have been conquered. At the outposts of the empire, the local people have little understanding of the new regime and, literally as well as figuratively, speak a different language. To teach all these new citizens a different mode of political action would be a very expensive and time-consuming task. Conversely, it would also be expensive to expect a large number of outside administrators to rule a recalcitrant group that can easily preserve many secrets from outsiders. The strategy of imperial rule often chosen is to coerce and attempt to co-opt a small number of local people, who will be asked to play a key role in governing their own communities.

---

*There is a well-documented trend of excluding women from acquiring crucial new skills and political resources during the process of incorporating local groups into larger political units and during the process of modernization (O'Barr 1984; Robertson and Berger 1986; Parpart and Staudt 1989; Awe, Geiger, Mba, Mbilinyi, Meena, and Strobel 1991).

This strategy is an ancient one. In relatively recent times, Machiavelli described it in *The Prince*, and Chimate recognized his description as apt for the Gamo Highland. If there are insufficient resources to administer the whole of the new empire directly, he said, appoint members of the local elite as your representatives. Choose the people's present king, give him privileges resembling your own, threaten him if necessary, and put the local political system to work for you. The legitimacy already acquired by that king will be transferred in part to you.

Machiavelli's description fits the position of balabat, which the Ethiopians used throughout the newly conquered southern half of the empire. It also fits the various positions through which the British governed their African colonies.* The person filling such a position is simultaneously relied upon and blamed by both the local group and the larger government.

The political role of intermediary is a particularly difficult one. The person chosen must be capable, in a sense, of walking through fire. On the one hand, this person symbolizes a hated new regime to his or her own people. The local community has not, in its own eyes, become a part of the empire. The role of intermediary always includes the supervision of tax collection, and taxes are paid in a spirit of bitterness. The memory of a politically independent past remains vivid, and local people resent the intermediary.

On the other hand, the community also uses the intermediary as a shield, a refuge, a source of information, and a possible sacrificial pawn to be offered the new administration. It is to the advantage of community members that the intermediary remains close to them. To perform various tasks for this person and give gifts might be considered an act of deference, but it is also a way of keeping the intermediary dependent on the community. The administrators of the government are, for other reasons, equally ambivalent about the intermediary. This person might be able to lead a revolt against the new regime, yet the intermediary would be ineffective if genuine ties to the local community did not exist. Thus, both the community members and the administrators have a complicated and paradoxical desire that the intermediary be simultaneously strong and weak—not too strong, yet not too weak.

---

*Fallers discusses this situation in "The Predicament of the Modern African Chief." Published in 1955, his essay recognizes that chiefs in Uganda were required to participate simultaneously in two political systems and conflicting sets of values—a modern administrative bureaucracy and kin-based societies. Fallers infers, possibly incorrectly, that the chiefs internalized both sets of values and experienced some degree of psychological tension in performing their roles.

Dennis describes a different situation in "The Oaxacan Village President as Political Middleman" (1991). He found that many men tried their best to avoid ever becoming president: "The Oaxacan village president . . . gains little power, and on the contrary must exhibit considerable dexterity in dealing with the contradictory expectations of fellow villagers and higher authorities. Men are reluctant to attempt the role; those who are successful at it must be able to preserve themselves as effective intermediaries, by arguing persuasively for actions acceptable to their superiors, by avoiding personal participation in violent incidents, and at times by temporarily abandoning their post to escape responsibility" (1991, 208). For other works discussing the role of political intermediary, see Appendix 3.

This dialectic between the needs of local people and the needs of local government creates a political role in which women as well as men may be used. Women are apt candidates for this type of work precisely because they do not tend, as a group, to wield political power within their own societies. Women in any patrilineal society, such as Dita, are familiar with the demands of the role of intermediary because it is a role that all of them must assume in their everyday lives.

When a society is organized largely by kinship ties, each kin group is a unit of economic cooperation and a focus of political power. Women in patrilineal societies are sent away from the kin group of their fathers and brothers into the kin group of their husbands. Relatively powerless when they arrive, they have responsibilities to both their new and old kin groups. They are simultaneously ambassadors and captives. They do not own resources directly, yet through bearing children they will contribute to their husband's kin group its most precious resource. The political and economic importance of that kin group is directly related to the number of men, women, and children who live in it.

A woman in perpetual suspension between the patrilineages of her husband and her father and brothers must learn how to manipulate events without directly imposing her authority. She must cultivate powers of persuasion, lacking direct access to basic resources such as land. She learns to study the character of the people around her, to observe relationships closely, and to amass information about kinship ties. These are skills that can be useful in any political situation of mediating between groups. In the ambiguous position of balabat, such skills can be used to translate externally imposed policy into terms local people can understand and accept and to communicate effectively with outside administrators.

As already stated, the intermediary between a local group and an empire should be simultaneously strong and weak. The skills women acquire in kinship-based societies can be turned to good use. Political astuteness based on the ability to influence others is required in full measure from anyone choosing the difficult role of intermediary. At the same time, women are in a vulnerable position and therefore can be less threatening than men. Consider Chimate's community, Dita. Land was owned by men. Men performed the rituals necessary to maintain health and prosperity, and only men might sit in large-scale political assemblies. As a member of a local ritual leader's family, Chimate was more favored than some women, but this advantage was tempered by a practice common among elite groups throughout the world. She was sent in marriage to a community so distant from her own home that her father's patrilineage had no representatives in Dita.* She

---

*The marriages among the sons and daughters of elite groups help to cement political and economic ties among such groups. This generally means that the women are sent long distances to the homes of their husbands, but the opposite may also be the case, as can be seen in the history of royalty in Europe. I have deliberately used the phrase "elite groups" because in the late nineteenth-century Gamo Highland, social classes seem not to have existed but there were nonetheless differences in access to key resources (Abélès 1981). In most cases, of course, the elite groups also were members of an upper class.

had to rely entirely on her husband's kin for support, unlike most Dita women, who could rely on their fathers, brothers, and patrilineal kinsmen and kinswomen.

I have hypothesized that Chimate's case may provide a model for a general process that brings women to positions of political prominence. Tracing these women in historical records, however, will prove difficult if Chimate's situation is typical. First, many of these positions may have been found primarily at the local level of administration, where little attention may have been focused by chroniclers and historians. Second, the activities of these women may be kept a secret from the central government in order to allow factional politics free play and in order to preserve the image of male-dominated rule. Third, nonliteracy is part of the remoteness that allows women to compete with men for the work of intermediary.

In states and empires with no electoral mechanism, such as Ethiopia, central imperial governments use a variety of means to guarantee the vulnerability of local-level administration. Chief among these is the simple tactic of frequently transferring officeholders from one place in the empire to another, making sure that an individual is not sent to govern his own ethnic group. The local intermediary like Chimate, however, has been given office within his or her home community and own ethnic group precisely because the new government wants to turn the local political system to advantage, using the existing system to help control the local people. To transfer this person would obviate the very reason for which he or she has been chosen.

Under these circumstances, the intermediary may well build up a significant amount of power, dominating the local community and influencing the local administrators who are constantly being changed. To guard against this, the local community and the local administrators may collude by altering the position of intermediary in significant ways. The original intermediary chosen has been that person who, to the best of the new administration's knowledge, actually held a position of political prominence in the kingdom or tribe.* In the Gamo Highland, this person was the king, who was appointed the balabat of his community.

One way to temper the influence of the intermediary is to keep him as the official intermediary while allowing someone else to do his actual work. This diminishes the importance of the intermediary, who is no longer supported by traditional legitimacy such as that accorded to a king in the Gamo Highland. In fact, women were being used as intermediaries in three separate communities in the Gamo Highland.† In Dita, Chimate was the acting balabat, while her son and then her grandson held the title of balabat. The provincial governor knew Chimate and dealt with her but felt no need to put a woman's name down as Dita's balabat in the records forwarded to the central government in Addis Abeba.

---

*Outside rulers who conquer a group whose traditional politics are egalitarian may choose as intermediary someone who has no traditional power base, in which case the local group can still rely on its traditional political system to provide checks upon the intermediary's political role.

†Bureau (1978) describes the relationship between the titles of balabat and king throughout the Gamo Highland as he observed it in the early 1970s, including the three instances in which women acted as balabats.

A second way to temper the influence of the intermediary is to make an official distinction between traditional and imperial authority, assigning the title of inter- mediary to someone other than the king. The local communities incorporated into the Ethiopian Empire were not the passive recipients of a new system of adminis- tration. They had acted to influence the local administrators and to regain some measure of control over their lives. Within the Gamo Highland, the workings of local factional politics had produced four separate patterns of accommodation. There were a few communities where king and balabat were the same person. In other places, the king held the title of balabat, but a so-called assistant did the work. Some communities had taken formal steps to appoint as balabat a person separate from the king. Dita typified the fourth pattern, with a separate king, a titled bala- bat, and an acting balabat. When the acting balabat was a woman and the official balabat was a man, the patriarchal bias of the local political system and of the na- tional political system was not directly challenged.

Dan Sperber has pointed out that the very choice of a woman is a third way to temper the influence of the intermediary. "Choosing a woman for this kind of role has a further advantage in case either party, the local people or the central power, is seriously unhappy with the intermediary. She will be easier to blame than either a local man eminent enough to have been accepted by the local people, or some- one whose criticism by the locals would have to be considered rebellious toward the central authority. If need be, a woman is easier to blame, and both parties can end up agreeing that it was her fault" (personal communication).

These structural solutions can be flexible, with a community's pattern changing over time. One way the local police threatened Chimate was by saying that they would see to it that her grandson was no longer the official balabat. The local community made similar threats at various times. The very fact that transfer of the responsibili- ties of balabat was possible gave a degree of flexibility to the workings of local fac- tional politics. These maneuvers were in large part invisible to the central government.

If the local and secret nature of the use of women was not enough to make his- torical reconstruction difficult, the nonliteracy of local communities like Dita com- pounds the problem. Chimate was able to compete effectively with men because no one in Dita was literate save a few scattered individuals. She transacted her business in a local language that had never been recorded. Thus, informal local documents, such as diaries and letters, are not available from which to trace her existence. Places where her name may appear include records of events in the courts—she often had to attend court sessions—and the local political correspondence within the province, if it has been preserved.

My hope in writing this account of Chimate's life is that others will be inspired to reexamine their assumptions about the role of women in expanding empires and to reconsider the available data. Particularly in the late nineteenth and twentieth cen- turies, the administrators of the European colonial empires kept detailed records of local contacts and events, and anthropologists made many studies within the colo- nial context. It is here that the discovery of parallel cases may most easily be made.

Appendix 3: Suggestions for Further Reading

This essay will give the reader some starting points for exploring topics relevant to Chimate Chumbalo's life history. The books and articles referenced here contain further bibliographies that can guide in-depth exploration of a particular topic. As time passes and this bibliographic review is less up-to-date, I recommend consulting two sources mentioned here: the journal *Signs* and the *Annual Review of Anthropology*. Both periodically publish updated review essays on key topics.

Ethiopian History

An excellent starting point for readers interested in Ethiopian history, and in Ethiopian society in general, is an essay by Donald Donham, "Old Abyssinia and the New Ethiopian Empire: Themes in Social History" (1986). Donham draws upon a broad range of studies in history, anthropology, economics, and ecology. After describing the empire, Donham narrows his focus to the southern area of Ethiopia, where Chimate lived, discussing the ways in which local people responded to the empire. Donham could be writing about Chimate when he asserts that "local histories were never simply determined by the centre. What happened was also influenced by the organization of local societies and cultures, even the presence of local personalities" (1986, 44).

The Gedeo people live directly across the Rift Valley to the east of Chimate's Gamo Highland. Their incorporation into the Ethiopian Empire is documented in detail by Charles W. McClellan (1988) and provides a useful comparison with the experiences of Chimate's people. He covers the period from 1895, when the armies of Menelik II conquered the area, until the 1935 Italian invasion. McClellan focuses on the economic and political relationships among the Gedeo people, the settlers who arrived from northern Ethiopia, and the governors representing the Ethiopian Empire.

Bahru Zewde's *History of Modern Ethiopia, 1855–1974* (1991) takes the country to the eve of the revolution. Bahru draws a comprehensive portrait based on both published sources and unpublished essays and theses on file at Addis Abeba University. An attractive feature of this history is the large number of photographs that have been included. The jacket shows a folk painting of the 1930 Battle of Anchem, in which Chimate Chumbalo's husband, Masa, participated.

A *History of Ethiopia* by Harold Marcus (1994) covers the broadest timespan of any history reviewed here, beginning in prehistoric times and continuing to 1991, after the Ethiopian revolution's failure. The photographs illustrating the book reflect the ethnic diversity of the country. Despite current pressures toward political fragmentation, Marcus believes that economic and geographic logic tie the region together. Throughout Ethiopia's long history, "notwithstanding the most extreme cases of secession and governmental weakness, the country reunited" (1994, 217).

In describing the context of Chimate's life, I have touched only briefly on a fascinating topic, the nature of Amhara social organization and the intricate dynamics of empire. Allan Hoben's (1973) description of a twentieth-century Amhara community explores the Amhara system of cognatic descent, access to land, and politics. For accounts of the lives of two emperors who shaped Ethiopia and some insight into how the system functioned, see Harold G. Marcus's biographies of Menelik II (1975) and Haile Selassie (1987).

Christopher Clapham's *Transformation and Continuity in Revolutionary Ethiopia* (1988) picks up where Bahru's history ends, discussing the first twelve years following the revolution. Clapham's thesis about the Ethiopian revolution is that it has succeeded "not despite but because of its inheritance from imperial Ethiopia" (1988, 14)—that is, the revolution was built upon the institutional structures of the empire. Clapham describes how Ethiopians live in one of Africa's poorest, yet most powerful states and ends his book expressing skepticism about the adequacy of a strong central political regime in fostering economic development.

The most recently published account of the revolution is by an Ethiopian scholar who draws extensively on sources written in Amharic, the national language. Andargachew Tiruneh's interpretation of the revolution is revealed in the title, *The Ethiopian Revolution, 1974–1987: A Transformation from an Aristocratic to a Totalitarian Autocracy* (1993). A postscript discusses the events leading to the collapse of Mengistu's regime in May 1991.

An important development since the publication of these histories has been the creation of an independent nation, Eritrea, in May 1993. This northernmost region of the former empire had been engaged in a war of secession since 1961. Bahru, Marcus, Clapham, and Andargachew Tiruneh each discuss the issue of Eritrea in detail, and their work provides a good context for understanding the eventual outcome.

Gamo Highland Ethnography

The book in which Chimate saw her son's picture is Helmut Straube's *Westkuschitische völker Süd-Äthiopiens* (1963), which is based upon his expeditions to southwestern Ethiopia in the 1950s. An expedition of geographers from Oxford University visited the Gamo Highland in the 1960s (Jackson, Mulvaney, Russell, and Forster 1969; Forster 1969; Jackson 1971). French anthropologist Dan Sperber and I both lived in the Gamo Highland from 1969 to 1971. Sperber's publications focus on politics, ritual, and symbolism (1975; 1977; 1980), mine upon economics and demographics (1972; 1973; 1974a; 1974b; 1975a; 1975b; 1976). The ethnomusicologist Bernard Lortat-Jacob visited the Dorze in the mid-1970s and produced an extensive commentary on the subject (1975) and a well-documented recording of Dorze music (1977). Dexter Burley provides a history of Dorze migration to Addis Abeba (1979), and Harald Tschakert a survey of urban weavers in the 1970s (1975).

Two other French anthropologists worked in the highland during the 1970s. Marc Abélès has published a description of warfare as perceived by the Ochollo people (1977), an ethnography of Ochollo (1978), and an essay on the introduction of the state to the Gamo Highland which "attempt[s] to demonstrate that in a society such as the Gamo, without classes, exploitation and inequality may still prevail" (1981, 36). Jacques Bureau, who did fieldwork in Bonke, discusses Gamo churches (1976), the political use of the titles of ka'o and balabat in the Gamo Highland (1978),* recent Gamo history (1979a), and the Gamo Highland political system (1979b; 1981). His most recent work focuses on local myths and stories (1988; 1994).

Life Histories of African Women

Several approaches are found in the published life histories of African women. The first, like this book, focuses on the life of one woman and explores in depth her place in her society. Two such full-length volumes have been published. The second approach brings together short life history narratives, often previously published as separate articles, spoken by women from different regions. A third and promising form gathers in one volume a group of life histories from the same geographic area and/or ethnic group. Although each life history is much shorter than a book-length narrative, the reader comes to see one cultural area from multiple points of view.

Published in 1954, *Baba of Karo: A Woman of the Muslim Hausa* shows the richness of life that one Nigerian woman achieved while living behind the veil. Baba had strong relationships with other women and held an important role within her household and kinship network. Although childless, she adopted children and created broad kinship ties through their marriages. Baba told her story to Mary F. Smith, the wife of an anthropologist whose project was to study the Hausa people but whose emphasis on Hausa men is revealed by the contradictions between his description of Hausa life and Baba's account.

In a second work that focuses on one woman, *Nisa: The Life and Words of a !Kung Woman* (1981), Nisa speaks with Marjorie Shostak about her life in the Kalahari Desert. Shostak's interweaving of her own thoughts about, reactions to, and obser-

---

*The ka'o lineage described for Dita in this article is missing one generation. The man shown as Chimate's son is actually her grandson. A second correction is that the current holder of the title of ka'o at the time of the article was the son of a second son, not a secondborn son.

vations of !Kung society with Nisa's story fosters an appreciation and understanding of Nisa's life history. In a 1989 essay, Shostak reflects on the process of writing a life history and the reasons for the choices she made.

Life Histories of African Women (1988), edited by Patricia W. Romero, includes seven women from six countries and a time span ranging from the early 1800s to the 1980s. Two are of particular relevance to readers of this book. Mercha was a central Ethiopian potter who told her story to Anne Cassiers, a French potter living in Addis Abeba between 1970 and 1976. For Mercha, life in Addis Abeba, so romanticized by many Dita people, was one of poverty, family difficulties, and hard work, albeit at a beloved craft. From European historical documents and Asante oral history, Ivor Wilks reconstructs the life of a nineteenth-century Ghanaian woman leader. Akyaawa Yikwan was an Asante woman from local royalty who was the chief negotiator of the 1831 Anglo-Asante peace treaty under which Asante remained politically independent until 1896.

A second West African female political leader is described in an article by Carol P. Hoffer (1974). At the time of her death in 1906, Madam Yoko had created the Kpa Mende Confederacy, an area so large that fourteen separate chiefdoms were eventually created from it. Like Akyaawa Yikwan, Madam Yoko played an important role in dealing with the British.

The third approach to life histories, with women from the same region or ethnic group included in one volume, is exemplified by the rest of the works reviewed in this section. Marcia Wright's *Strategies of Slaves and Women: Life-Stories from East/ Central Africa* (1993) spans the middle of the nineteenth century until the early twentieth century, when the region was an area of immense economic, political, and social change and conflict. Some women escaped slavery by taking refuge at Christian missions. Missionaries recorded selected women's life stories, in part to campaign against slavery, in part to obtain moral and financial support from their home congregations through graphic tales of enslavement, dislocation, courage, and initiative. The ex-slave narratives edited by Wright remain as riveting as they must have been to earlier readers. In Wright's words, these women were "demonstrably persons of ambition and courage" (1993, 174).

Women living in contemporary times of turmoil and change speak in two volumes that focus on women's experiences in wartime. In Irene Staunton's *Mothers of the Revolution: The War Experiences of Thirty Zimbabwean Women* (1991), women of Shona or Ndebele ethnicity describe how they were affected by, and at times engaged in, that country's revolution. Some express disappointment about the aftermath of war; others found it well worthwhile, ushering in important changes in their lives. Northern Ethiopian women were still in the midst of fighting for Tigrayan liberation when they were interviewed by Jenny Hammond in 1987 and 1989. Testimonies from fifty-two women are collected in *Sweeter than Honey: Ethiopian Women and Revolution* (1990). In poignant counterpoint, Hammond includes traditional Tigrayan poetry that laments the conditions of peasants' and women's lives.

In her introduction to *Voices from Mutira: Lives of Rural Gikuyu Women* (1989), Jean Davison discusses her concern with the representativeness of women's life histories. To address this concern, Davison began her work by surveying 101 women, using information from the survey to gain perspective on the lives of the seven women she chose to interview. An interesting theme is the women's differing perceptions of female circumcision—the older women accepted and even sought out circumcision to gain social adulthood, the younger women have rejected it.

The urban Muslim women who speak in *Three Swahili Women: Life Histories from Mombasa, Kenya* (Mirza and Strobel 1989) were chosen by Margaret Strobel in the 1970s both for their accessibility and because they represent some of the class and ethnic diversity of Swahili society. All three lived in a female-oriented social world with many festivals, ceremonies, and rituals. The oldest, a freeborn native of the area, was absorbed in domestic life; the second, a descendant of slaves, was a leader in female rituals; and the third, of Arab parents, obtained a Western education and was active in politics as a leader of women's associations and political groups.

A second book on urban Muslim women is based in Sennar, a Sudanese town on the Blue Nile close to Ethiopia. Susan M. Kenyon conducted interviews in 1980–81, choosing her *Five Women of Sennar* to represent the lives of women as she knew them during a six-year stay (1991). Kenyon used discussions of each woman's work as a nonthreatening initial topic for her interviews. Included are a hairdresser, market woman, midwife, renowned holy woman, and a spirit possession cult leader.

Mark Mathabane, a South African writer, combines the life histories of his sister Florah, mother Geli, and grandmother Ellen in *African Women: Three Generations* (1994). He was inspired to write the book because of the strong interest in his mother taken by readers of his autobiography, *Kaffir Boy*. The women speak in turn throughout the book, creating what Mathabane aptly calls a "harrowing, poignant, heroic, and inspiring saga of three women who, in their individual ways, refused to buckle under tradition, custom, and oppression" (1994, xiii).

On the general subject of women's life histories, see the excellent review article by Susan Geiger in *Signs* (1986), who cites the work of many authors who interviewed African women. Additional references not cited here can be gleaned from Geiger's work; in this essay I have emphasized work published since her review.

Readers who wish to explore broad questions about the ethics and epistemology of oral history can turn to two books: the Personal Narratives Group, *Interpreting Women's Lives: Feminist Theory and Personal Narratives* (1989), and Sherna Berger Gluck and Daphne Patai, *Women's Words: The Feminist Practice of Oral History* (1991). The journal *Signs* published an update on the issues raised by the Personal Narratives Group (1993, 389–425).

Spirit Possession

Spirit possession did not figure prominently in the lives of Chimate or most other Dita women, but an extensive anthropological literature is available to readers intrigued by the subject. *Women's Medicine: The Zar-Bori Cult in Africa and Beyond*

(Lewis, Al-Safi, and Hurreiz 1991) is a collection of essays relevant to the Ethiopian zar cult, which I briefly witnessed and which Chimate discussed with me. Janice Boddy's essay in the *Annual Review of Anthopology* (1994), which reviews over two hundred sources on spirit possession, is an excellent resource for finding information on particular geographic areas or topics. For a detailed case history of an Ethiopian man that gives a sense of the social dynamics of one zar group, see Alice Morton, *"Dawit"* (1977).

Politics

I will be discussing two types of literature here, each relevant to different aspects of Chimate's life. The first concerns the structure of imperial rule and the role of intermediary between an empire and a local political entity. The second focuses on the political roles women have played in African societies and emphasizes that the modern era has seen a general diminution rather than expansion of these roles.

John Gledhill's *Power and Its Disguises: Anthropological Perspectives on Politics* (1994) provides a thorough discussion of how empires differ from modern nation-states that is helpful in understanding Chimate's life within the Ethiopian Empire. Peter Skalník's edited volume, *Outwitting the State* (1989), has direct relevance to the Gamo Highlanders and Chimate Chumbalo's situation. Contributors document, in a variety of situations worldwide, how indigenous groups created "strategies of constructive coping with the imposition of state power" (1989, 3). The use of Chimate, a woman not recorded in official documents, as Dita's balabat is one example of how her people coped with Haile Selassie's government.

Chimate's role as political intermediary has many parallel examples in the anthropological literature. These may be traced among the varied themes included in Joan Vincent's *Anthropology and Politics* (1990). Vincent discusses the period 1860–1989, dividing the time into six different historical periods. Vincent, ever the self-reflective political scientist, places the anthropological work into its academic, national, and international political contexts. The first political intermediary she mentions is Kanosh, a Ute leader of the 1870s (Vincent 1990, 42–43). Toda politics of 1901–2 as described by Rivers "largely revolved around the respective struggles and alliances of the *monegar* (or government headman, appointed by the imperial power for the collection of taxes from the administered population) and the clan and lineage headmen" (109–12, 443n). The Wisers' work in an Indian village between 1925 and 1930 included a description of "a government-appointed village headman who did not exploit his office" (210). The various approaches taken by political anthropologists in later years to the role of political intermediary are discussed in a section on the Manchester School (280–81).

For a more recent article on these issues, see Philip A. Dennis, "The Oaxacan Village President as Political Middleman" (1991). In this Mexican case, balancing the roles of state representative and of local community member was so onerous that many men actively avoided recruitment into the presidency.

An important and growing literature describes African women's political roles both before and after European colonizaton and the eventual creation of independent African states. Jean O'Barr's 1984 finding remains the case today: "On the one hand, women's political roles in pre-colonial Africa provide stimulating examples of how social systems have been organized to include positions of power for women. On the other, a survey of contemporary Africa reveals few women in decision-making roles and an underlying tension in gender relationships which impedes the exercise of political power" (1984, 140). O'Barr includes in her article "African Women in Politics" a discussion of "three well documented cases of women's resistance to colonial imposition" (1984, 145). These included Igbo women in Nigeria in 1929–30, Pare women in Tanzania in the 1940s, and Kom women in the former British Cameroons in the 1950s (1984, 145–47).

Nina Emma Mba's *Nigerian Women Mobilized: Women's Political Activity in Southern Nigeria, 1900–1965* (1982) describes how in many southern Nigerian precolonial societies certain important political positions were reserved for women. After British colonization, women's solidarity and respect for their leaders was carried forward into a series of mass protest movements from 1925 to 1964. After Nigerian independence and despite their demonstrated capacity for political action, however, very few southern Nigerian women were active in political organizations or in electoral politics by 1979, the year Mba completed her study.

Several edited volumes touch on the diversity and complexity of African women's political status. In *Women and Class in Africa,* the editors Claire Robertson and Iris Berger provide a unifying concept, that of access to critical resources. This concept "reveal[s] more precisely the factors that shape women's class position, both independently and relative to that of men" (1986, 21). The varied theoretical debates and case studies contributed to *Women and the State in Africa* (Parpart and Staudt 1989) are summarized in contributor Naomi Chazan's article "Gender Perspectives on African States" (1989). Chazan's discussion applies as well to Chimate's situation:

> The image of the relationship between women and state institutions revealed in these studies is one of confrontation. States and social groups are portrayed in adversarial terms. Society is engaged in a continuous effort to avoid domination by ever-expanding state bodies. In this vision, few channels of linkage between formal institutions and informal networks mediate societal exposure to state impulses. Women demonstrate, perhaps more starkly than many other social groups, the broad strokes of sociopolitical conflict in contemporary Africa: formal versus informal, official versus off-the-books, manipulation versus agitation, repression versus avoidance, hegemony versus escape. (1989, 196)

African women scholars joined two scholars from the United States to produce a special issue of *Signs* focusing on "Women, Family, State, and Economy in Africa" (Awe, Geiger, Mba, Mbilinyi, Meena, and Strobel 1991). The contributors cover precolonial, colonial, and postcolonial conditions. "All of the articles . . . show women as active agents of history, engaged in various forms of accommodation and resistance" (1991, 647).

To pursue these issues through the worldwide reach of anthropological theory and ethnography, see two *Annual Review of Anthropology* articles published together in 1988: Irene Silverblatt, "Women in States," and Carol C. Mukhopadhyay and Patricia J. Higgins, "Anthropological Studies of Women's Status Revisited, 1977–1987." Published in the same year, Henrietta L. Moore's *Feminism and Anthropology* contains an explicitly feminist analysis of women and the state (1988, 128–85).

Glossary

The glossary contains words used several times in the text; those used just once or twice, with an accompanying gloss, are omitted. These words were in current use in the Gamo language, although some are of Amhara or Oromo origin. In general, spelling is phonetic; the diacriticals for glottalized consonants have been omitted.

ayana
: A spirit thought to possess a person, riding that person as a horseman rides a horse. See chapter 14 and the section on spirit possession in Appendix 3.

balabat
: A title and administrative position conferred by the Ethiopian Empire on the leader of a local community. The balabat supervised tax collection, organized corvée (unpaid labor), and mediated some disputes, referring others to the courts. In this system of rule, which has been used in many parts of the world, it is hoped that the legitimacy granted the local leader by the traditional political system will transfer in part to the new government.

buluko
: A long, heavy handwoven cloth made of handspun cotton, worn as a cape or used as a blanket.

chale
: Necklace; also, a spirit possession cult in which the unidentified spirits are propitiated by annual ceremonies during which special necklaces are worn.

chikashum
: An official of the Ethiopian Empire, appointed from a local community, who worked under a balabat. Usually each balabat supervised several chikashums.

chima
: Old; elder; by extension, mediator.

dejazmach
: High-ranking military title. See also *fitawari.*

fitawari
: High-ranking military title, ranking below dejazmach. See note in appendix 1.

gabbar
: The system through which southern Ethiopia was first governed by the Ethiopian Empire, in which individual families called "gabbar" were assigned to work for and provide tribute to individual soldiers and military leaders.

gabi	A long cotton cloth, lighter in weight than a buluko but also made of handspun cotton. Used as a cape or, belted around the body, as a dress.
gome	A taboo; central to Gamo Highland thought and social control. Chapters 9 and 10 contain extensive explanations of this topic.
gozda	Ceremonial necklace made primarily of translucent blue glass beads, probably imported from Italy in the nineteenth century or earlier.
halaka	Elected representative of the democratic assemby, who though high in prestige could be dismissed at any time by the assembly (for a detailed description, see Sperber 1975; Olmstead 1976).
hashu	An exclamation meaning "prosper!"
hilo	A person who is being ostracized. The local assembly "makes" a person hilo as they make someone a halaka.
ka'o	Senior sacrificer for a community. Depending on political circumstances, he could be a powerful local king or an unobtrusive ritual leader.
kenyazmach	Prestigous military title, ranking below dejazmach and fitawari. See note in appendix 1.
kosso	A purgative herb, consumed as a beverage.
injera	Flat, unleavened bread used in northern Ethiopia. Rarely eaten in Dita in the 1970s; its use was a sign of assimilation into the national culture.
teff	A grain indigenous to Ethiopia, used to make injera bread. It could not be grown in the high altitude of Dita and had to be imported.
tsilo	Right; in the right; upright. Said of a person in a dispute.
woga	Rules of taboo (gome); also, the man who understands taboos well and who is consulted by others for his interpretations of their circumstances.
wordo	Wrong; in the wrong. Said of a person in a dispute.

Bibliography

Abélès, Marc. 1977. "La Guerre Vue d'Ochollo." *Revue Canadienne des Études Africaines* 11(3):455–71.

———. 1978. "Pouvoir et Société Chez les Ochollo d'Éthiopie Méridionale." *Cahiers d'Études Africaines* 18:293–310.

———. 1981. "In Search of the Monarch: Introduction of the State among the Gamo of Ethiopia." In *Modes of Production in Africa: The Precolonial Era,* ed. Donald Crummey and C. C. Stewart. Beverly Hills, Calif.: Sage Publications. Pp. 35–67.

Andargachew Tiruneh. 1993. *The Ethiopian Revolution, 1974–1987: A Transformation from an Aristocratic to a Totalitarian Autocracy.* Cambridge: Cambridge University Press.

Awe, Bolanie, Susan Geiger, Nina Mba, Marjorie Mbilinyi, Ruth Meena, and Margaret Strobel, eds. 1991. *Signs* 16(4) special issue on "Women, Family, State, and Economy in Africa."

Bahru Zewde. 1991. *A History of Modern Ethiopia, 1855–1974.* London: James Currey; Athens: Ohio University Press; and Addis Abeba: Addis Abeba University Press.

Boddy, Janice. 1994. "Spirit Possession Revisited: Beyond Instrumentality." *Annual Review of Anthropology* 23:407–34.

Bureau, Jacques. 1976. "Note sur les Églises du Gamo." *Annales d'Éthiopie* 10:295–301.

———. 1978. "Étude Diachronique de Deux Titres Gamo." *Cahiers d'Études Africaines* 18:279–91.

———. 1979a. "Histoire Contemporaine des Gamo d'Éthiopie." *Abbay* 10:201–4.

———. 1979b. "Une Société sans Vengeance? Les Gamo d'Éthiopie." *Ethnographie* 79:93–104.

———. 1981. *Les Gamo d'Éthiopie: Étude du Système Politique.* Paris: Société d'Ethnographie.

———. 1988. "La Mort du Serpent: Une Nouvelle Version d'Éthiopie Méridionale." In *Proceedings of the Eighth International Conference of Ethiopian Studies,* ed. Taddese Beyene. Frankfurt and Addis Abeba: Institute of Ethiopian Studies. Pp. 779–84.

———. 1994. *Le Verdict du Serpent: Mythes, Contes et Récits des Gamo d'Éthiopie.* Paris: Centre de Recherche Africaine, Maison des Études Éthiopiennes.

Burley, Dexter. 1979. "The Despised Weavers of Addis Ababa." In *Proceedings of the Fifth International Conference on Ethiopian Studies, Session B,* ed. Robert L. Hess. Chicago: Office of Publications Services, University of Illinois, Chicago Circle Campus. Pp. 145–49.

Cassiers, Anne. 1988. "Mercha: An Ethiopian Woman Speaks of Her Life." In *Life Histories of African Women,* ed. Romero. Pp. 159–94.

Chazan, Naomi. 1989. "Gender Perspectives on African States." In *Women and the State in Africa,* ed. Parpart and Staudt. Pp. 185–202.

Clapham, Christopher. 1988. *Transformation and Continuity in Revolutionary Ethiopia.* Cambridge: Cambridge University Press.

Davison, Jean. 1989. *Voices from Mutira: Lives of Rural Gikuyu Women.* Boulder, Colo.: Lynne Rienner Publishers.

Dennis, Philip A. 1991. "The Oaxacan Village President as Political Middleman." In *Anthropological Approaches to Political Behavior,* ed. Frank McGlynn and Arthur Tuden. Pittsburgh, Pa.: University of Pittsburgh Press. Pp. 199–209.

Donham, Donald. 1986. "Old Abyssinia and the New Ethiopian Empire: Themes in Social History." In *The Southern Marches of Ethiopia: Essays in History and Social Anthropology,* ed. Donald Donham and Wendy James. Cambridge: Cambridge University Press. Pp. 3–48.

Fallers, Lloyd. 1955. "The Predicament of the Modern African Chief: An Instance from Uganda." *American Anthropologist* 57:290–305.

Forster, R. 1969. "Economy of the Gamu Highlands." *Geographical Magazine* 41:429–38.

Geiger, Susan. 1986. "Women's Life Histories: Method and Content." *Signs* 11:334–51.

Gledhill, John. 1994. *Power and Its Disguises: Anthropological Perspectives on Politics.* Boulder, Colo.: Pluto Press.

Gluck, Sherna Berger, and Daphne Patai. 1991. *Women's Words: The Feminist Practice of Oral History.* New York: Routledge.

Hammond, Jenny. 1990. *Sweeter than Honey: Ethiopian Women and Revolution.* Trenton, N.J.: Red Sea Press.

Hoben, Allan. 1973. *Land Tenure among the Amhara of Ethiopia: The Dynamics of Cognatic Descent.* Chicago: University of Chicago Press.

Hoffer, Carol P. 1974. "Madam Yoko: Ruler of the Kpa Mende Confederacy." In *Woman, Culture, and Society,* ed. Michelle Zimbalist Rosaldo and Louise Lamphere. Stanford, Calif.: Stanford University Press. Pp. 173–87.

Jackson, R. 1971. "Periodic Markets in Southern Ethiopia." *Transactions* 3:3–41.

Jackson, R., P. Mulvaney, T. Russell, and J. Forster. 1969. *Report of the Oxford University Expedition to the Gamu Highlands of Southern Ethiopia.* Oxford: Oxford University Press.

Kenyon, Susan M. 1991. *Five Women of Sennar: Culture and Change in Central Sudan.* Oxford: Clarendon Press.

Lewis, I. M., Ahmed Al-Safi, and Sayyid Hurreiz, eds. 1991. *Women's Medicine: The*

Zar-Bori Cult in Africa and Beyond. Edinburgh: Edinburgh University Press for the International Institute.

Lortat-Jacob, Bernard. 1975. "Notes sur la Musique Dorzé d'Éthiopie Méridionale." In *Éthiopie, la Terre et les Hommes.* Paris: Musée de l'Homme. Pp. 61–66.

———. 1977. *Éthiopie: Polyphonies des Dorzé* (recording). Paris: Collection C.N.R.S., Musée de L'Homme. Le Chant du Monde, LDX 74646.

Machiavelli, Niccolò. [1513] 1952. *The Prince.* Trans. Luigi Ricci. Ed. E. R. P. Vincent. New York: New American Library.

Marcus, Harold G. 1975. *The Life and Times of Menelik II: Ethiopia, 1844–1913.* Oxford: Clarendon Press.

———. 1987. *Haile Sellassie I: The Formative Years, 1892–1936.* Berkeley: University of California Press.

———. 1994. *A History of Ethiopia.* Berkeley: University of California Press.

Mathabane, Mark. 1994. *African Women: Three Generations.* New York: Harper-Collins.

Mba, Nina Emma. 1982. *Nigerian Women Mobilized: Women's Political Activity in Southern Nigeria, 1900–1965.* Berkeley: University of California, Institute of International Studies.

McClellan, Charles W. 1988. *State Transformation and National Integration: Gedeo and the Ethiopian Empire, 1895–1935.* East Lansing: African Studies Center, Michigan State University.

Mirza, Sarah, and Margaret Strobel, eds. and trans. 1989. *Three Swahili Women: Life Histories from Mombasa, Kenya.* Bloomington: Indiana University Press.

Moore, Henrietta L. 1988. *Feminism and Anthropology.* Minneapolis: University of Minnesota Press.

Morton, Alice. 1975. "Mystical Advocates: Explanation and Spirit-Sanctioned Adjudication in the Shoa Galla Ayana Cult." In *Proceedings of the First U.S. Conference on Ethiopian Studies, 1973,* ed. Harold G. Marcus. East Lansing: Michigan State University Press. Pp. 73–89.

———. 1977. "*Dawit:* Competition and Integration in an Ethiopian Wuqabi Cult Group." In *Case Studies in Spirit Possession,* ed. Vincent Crapanzano and Vivian Garrison. New York: John Wiley and Sons. Pp. 193–233.

Mukhopadhyay, Carol C., and Patricia J. Higgins. 1988. "Anthropological Studies of Women's Status Revisited, 1977–1987." *Annual Review of Anthropology* 17:461–95.

O'Barr, Jean. 1984. "African Women in Politics." In *African Women South of the Sahara,* ed. Margaret Jean Hay and Sharon Stichter. New York: Longman. Pp. 140–55.

Olmstead, Judith. 1972. "The Dorze House." *Journal of Ethiopian Studies* 10(2):27–36.

———. 1973. "Ethiopia's Artful Weavers." *National Geographic* 143:125–41.

———. 1974a. "Female Fertility, Social Structure, and the Economy: A Controlled Comparison of Two Southern Ethiopian Communities." Ph.D. diss., Columbia University.

————. 1974b. "The Versatile Ensete Plant." *Journal of Ethiopian Studies* 12(2):147–58.

————. 1975a. "Farmer's Wife, Weaver's Wife: Women and Work in Two Southern Ethiopian Communities." *African Studies Review* 18(3):85–98.

————. 1975b. "Land and Social Stratification in the Gamo Highlands of Southern Ethiopia." In *Proceedings of the First U.S. Conference on Ethiopian Studies, 1973*, ed. Harold G. Marcus. East Lansing: Michigan State University Press. Pp. 223–34.

————, with Rhoda Halperin. 1976. "To Catch a Feastgiver: Redistribution among the Dorze of Ethiopia." *Africa* 46:146–65.

Parpart, Jane L., and Kathleen A. Staudt, eds. 1989. *Women and the State in Africa.* Boulder, Colo.: Lynne Rienner Publishers.

"Personal Narratives: A Selection of Recent Works." Special issue of *Signs* 18:389–425.

Personal Narratives Group, ed. 1989. *Interpreting Women's Lives: Feminist Theory and Personal Narratives.* Bloomington: Indiana University Press.

Robertson, Claire, and Iris Berger, eds. 1986. *Women and Class in Africa.* New York: Africana Publishing.

Romero, Patricia W., ed. 1988. *Life Histories of African Women.* Atlantic Highland, N.J.: Ashfield Press.

Shostak, Marjorie. 1981. *Nisa: The Life and Words of a !Kung Woman.* Cambridge, Mass.: Harvard University Press.

————. 1989. "What the Wind Won't Take Away: The Genesis of *Nisa—The Life and Words of a !Kung Woman.*" In *Interpreting Women's Lives*, ed. Personal Narratives Group. Pp. 228–40.

Silverblatt, Irene. 1988. "Women in States." *Annual Review of Anthropology* 17:427–60.

Skalník, Peter, ed. 1989. *Outwitting the State.* New Brunswick, N.J.: Transaction Publishers.

Smith, Mary F. [1954] 1981. *Baba of Karo: A Woman of the Muslim Hausa.* New Haven, Conn.: Yale University Press.

Sperber, Dan. 1975. "Paradoxes of Seniority among the Dorze." In *Proceedings of the First U.S. Conference on Ethiopian Studies, 1973*, ed. Harold G. Marcus. East Lansing: Michigan State University Press. Pp. 209–22.

————. 1977. *Rethinking Symbolism.* New York: Cambridge University Press.

————. 1980. "The Management of Misfortune among the Dorze." In *Proceedings of the Fifth International Conference on Ethiopian Studies*, ed. Robert Hess. Chicago: Office of Publications Services, University of Illinois at Chicago Circle. Pp. 207–15.

Staunton, Irene. 1991. *Mothers of the Revolution: The War Experiences of Thirty Zimbabwean Women.* Bloomington: Indiana University Press.

Straube, Helmut. 1963. *Westkuschitische völker Süd-Äthiopiens.* Stuttgart: W. Kohlhammer Verlag.

Tschakert, Harald. 1975. "Traditionales weber hand werk und sozialer wandel." In *Äthiopien*. Saarbrücken: Verlag der SSIP-Schriften.

Vincent, Joan. 1990. *Anthropology and Politics: Visions, Traditions, and Trends*. Tucson: University of Arizona Press.

Wilks, Ivor. 1988. "She Who Blazed a Trail: Akyaawa Yikwan of Asante." In *Life Histories of African Women*, ed. Romero. Pp. 113–39.

Wright, Marcia. 1993. *Strategies of Slaves and Women: Life-Stories from East/Central Africa*. New York: Lilian Barber Press.

Index

Aba pond, 40

Abyssinia: expansionary dynamic, 28–29; history of Abyssinian empires, 26–28; military ethic underlying, 28–29; multiethnic, 29

Addis Abeba: after the revolution, 202–3; and chale sickness, 137, 144; Chimate in, 178–95; described, 180; fashions, 170; Masa in, 49, 50, 56; peoples' attraction to, 174–75; transportation links to highland, 86; weaving in, 14, 88, 89, 159

Administration of empire: women's role in local level. *See* Intermediary, political

Adultery. *See* Extramarital sex

Adwa, 27–28

Agriculture, system of, 88. *See also* Commercial farming; Crops

Airplanes, 50, 56

Akirso, 39, 40; genealogical chart, 217

Alimetu, 50, 71, 145, 157; conflict with Kebede, 152–53

Almaz, 59, 62, 71; hosts Chimate in Addis Abeba, 181–83

Amano: and ayana woman's prophecy, 141–42; birth, 36; Chimate raises his children, 79–80; curses Dita, 126; death of, 86, 102; during Italian occupation, 61; funeral and burial, 126, 127; genealogical chart, 217; given balabat title, 66, 67–68; and gome, 102; ostracized, 125, 127; Straube's photograph of, 16

Ambilineal descent. *See* Kinship

Amhara: expansion, 26–28; Gamo opinions of, 29; kinship system, 28; political institutions, 28–29; women during Italian occupation, 58

Amharic language, 27, 46, 90

Anchem, 48–49

Angel Gabriel: and church for, 10, 47, 90

Animal sacrifice. *See* Sacrifice, animal

Arbaminch: antimalarial medicine and, 88; court, 125; Dita laborer in, 114; as provincial capital, 86, 168

Arson, 133–34, 135

Artisans, 89. *See also* Potters; Tanners; Weavers

Assimilation: to Ethiopian identity, 87–88, 89; to husband's patrilineage, 72

—to Amhara culture: choices made by Chimate and her family, 35, 37, 39, 69–70, 89–90, 126, 144, 145–46; duro wat and, 70; within Gamo Highland, 14, 85; initial resistance, 20th century, 34; mechanisms of, 28–29, 69–70; medieval period, 27; military expeditions, and role in creating Gamo-Amhara bond, 46; as reason for disinheritance, 39; role of Christianity in, 69, 85, 90, 149; role of economic integration in, 87–88

Atumo: in Addis, 205; after Italian occupation, 66; becomes Dita's king, 212; blinds Zeto, 80–81; Chimate pregnant with, 38; genealogical chart, 217; as musician, 80

Awa Geloso, 57

Awash River, 137, 144

Ayana. *See* Spirit possession

Axumites, 26, 27

Balabat: after revolution, 197; bridge between Amhara and Gamo systems, 69; difficult role, xv, 69, 71; fees and privileges, 70, 82, 96; Gamo Highland kings appointed as, 34; responsibilities of, xiii, 69, 122; transfers of title, 38–40, 45, 62–64, 65, 67–68, 122; women as, 73, 219, 223. *See also* Intermediary, political; Succession

—of Dita: genealogical chart, 217. *See also* Amano; Chimate; Masa (king and fitawari); Mijola (king); Sono (fitawari); Wombara

Balaye's Mother: and author, 97; bakes injera, 97; and chale, 137, 144; Chimate jealous of gifts to, 157; described, 100–101; in Gulta, 165

JUDITH OLMSTEAD is an anthroplogist who works as a dispute mediator—a professional choice influenced by living in the Gamo Highland of Ethiopia with the local leader and mediator Chimate Chumbalo, whose people learn from early childhood to mediate disputes among themselves. After receiving her Ph.D. from Columbia University in 1974, Olmstead taught at the University of Massachusetts–Boston and was an applied anthropologist doing research in child welfare and long-term care for the State of Washington before becoming a full-time mediator in 1994. She lives in Olympia, Washington, with her family.